Power in Caring Professions

Richard Hugman

First published 1991 by
MACMILLAN PRESS LTD
Houndmills, Basingstoke, Hampshire RG21 6XS
and London
Companies and representatives
throughout the world

ISBN 0–333–49854–2
ISBN 0–333–49855–0

A catalogue record for this book is available
from the British Library.

This book is printed on paper suitable for recycling and
made from fully managed and sustained forest sources.

11   10   9   8   7   6   5
03   02   01   00   99   98

Printed in Hong Kong

For Alex

Contents

List of Figures

Acknowledgements

The origins of this book lie in my own experience of practice and research in a 'caring profession', an important feature of which has been learning that the theoretical is also personal, in particular through a developing awareness of my own position as white, as a man, and as able-bodied. This I have tried to communicate, and I am grateful to the many service users, students and colleagues who have taught me so much. I intend, too, that my commitment to these professions is clear, albeit critical. These occupations have a strong antipathy to the lofty academic pronouncements of those who do not have to accomplish 'caring professionalism' in the contradictions of the everyday world. Yet I am writing *for* and not *against* these professions, and I hope that my explorations of wider structural issues will be of interest as much as my comments on practices.

More specifically, this analysis has benefited from the advice and assistance of a number of people to whom it is a pleasure to be able to extend my thanks. I owe a special debt to the friendship and critical support of Janet Finch throughout the development of these ideas, from the beginning to the manuscript. Jo Campling has also provided advice and encouragement which has been central in enabling this book to see the light of day. Detailed criticism of various drafts has been given willingly by Roger Hadley, Dass Martin, Malcolm Payne, Graham Rodwell, Protasia Torkington and Anne Williams. Because of their help this book is much better than it would have been otherwise; any errors or omissions which remain are my own responsibility entirely. In addition, I am grateful to Mike Hutchinson, Lynne Lightbown, David Morgan, Eric Sainsbury, Paul Stubbs and Sue Wise for comments or assistance at various stages in thinking and writing about these issues.

I would like to thank the authors for their kind permission to use an amended version of Figure 9.1 from B. Glastonbury, D. Cooper and P. Hawkins (1982) *Social Work in Conflict*, 2nd edn (Birmingham: BASW), and also to acknowledge the kind permission of D. C. Heath & Co. to use an amended version of figure 7, 'functionally unrelated promotion units with racial segregation', from P. B. Doeringer and M. J. Piore (1985) *Internal Labor Markets and Manpower Analysis*, 2nd edn (New York: M. E. Sharpe).

Lastly, this book would not have been completed without a period of leave from other academic responsibilities and I would like to record my appreciation for the work which colleagues undertook to make that possible.

University of Lancaster   RICHARD HUGMAN

1

Professions, Caring and the State

Key questions

Social power is an integral aspect of the daily working lives of professionals. The centrality of power in professional work has been increasingly recognised (Wilding, 1982; Cousins, 1987), yet the interconnection of power and caring work in health and welfare provision has been relatively under-explored. For example, there have been debates, chiefly but not entirely within social work, about whether the relationship between care and control (as a form of power) is one of mutual opposition or interlocked contradiction (Satyamurti, 1979; Day, 1981). At the same time the extent to which professional caring might itself emerge from and be sustained within power relationships has often been neglected.

To what degree, and in what ways are caring professions produced through power relationships at both the interpersonal and structural levels? In what ways do issues of power relate to the historical development and contemporary structures of caring professions? In what ways are relationships between professionals and service users, and between different professional groups, created and maintained as forms of power? What possibilities are suggested for the future of caring professions by an analysis based on the idea of power? These are the key questions which are central to this book.

1

Professions and professionalism

In this introductory discussion I want to examine the importance of professionalism and professionalisation, and to consider the connections between these issues and the question of caring within particular occupations. How may nursing, remedial therapies and social work be understood in relation to the process of professionalisation, and what is the significance of the claim to the idea of caring which can be identified in each of these occupations?

The dominant perspective in early studies of professionalism, and one which reflected the views of established professions, was that of 'trait' theory, which relied heavily on the delineation of the characteristics which were held to constitute a profession. Each occupation to be considered as a candidate for the label 'professional' could be compared to the list of traits, and the degree to which it matched was then taken as an indication of the extent to which that occupation was professionalised. The trait approach was developed particularly in the work of Greenwood (1957) and Carr-Saunders and Wilson (1962).

Using the trait approach, the occupations of nursing, the remedial therapies and social work were subsequently analysed as being 'semi-professional' (Etzioni, 1969; Toren, 1972). They were seen to have developed some of the attributes of what was taken to be a 'full' profession, but not others. Exponents of the trait approach proceeded to discuss the functional implications this had for practitioners in the so-called semi-professions; in other words, to look at the role such occupations had in wider structures, and to explain their semi-professionalism in terms of the needs of the structures.

The traits which were said to define nursing, the remedial therapies and social work as semi-professional were: that they lacked clearly demarcated scientific knowledge bases; that they were based on skills rather than knowledge; and that they had not achieved independent occupational self-government (Etzioni, 1969). Such a view can be criticised in several ways. First, the model for what constitutes a profession is taken from some occupations (notably medicine and law) which should themselves have been part of a critical analysis. The argument is circular, as it is the characteristics of those occupations which have become established as professions which are taken to be the traits of a general model of professionalism (Glastonbury *et al.*, 1982, p. 120). Second, the model ignores the extent to which a trait that is assigned to an occupation is a claim which should be investigated rather than an unproblematic social fact. An example of this is the issue of service to the community, which is mentioned in relation to both 'full' and 'semi'-professions (Greenwood, 1957; Etzioni, 1969; also see Wilding, 1982, p. 108–12, for a critical discussion). Third, the trait approach ignores the problem of power in the success of an occupation in achieving professional status within a society. It takes issues such as the claim to a particular area of knowledge as the property of one occupation as given, rather than as a subject for enquiry and debate.

Friedson (1970) suggests that a 'profession' should be regarded as a description of a type of occupational control. Johnson's (1972) examination of professions as structures of power within occupations takes this argument further, providing the basis for the criticism of the trait approach. Rather than beginning with the question, 'what characteristics does a profession have?', he asks, 'what are the structures of occupations claiming to be professions, and how are they controlled?'. To answer these questions Johnson looks at those occupations which have been successful, at least in part, in making claims for professional status. This leads to the conclusion that what is important in understanding the professionalisation of occupations is the way in which the power structures of those occupations develop. Johnson advances three types of professional structure which can be observed.

The first type is the *collegiate* profession, in which power is exercised by members of the occupation itself, to define the processes and outcomes of work, as well as who shall be considered as members of the occupation and who shall receive its services. Johnson notes that not all the members may exercise power equally, as there may be a hierarchy operating. However, the occupation presents an image of internal unity to those outside. Examples of collegiate structures can be seen most clearly in the so-called 'full' professions of medicine and law, which have achieved a large measure of autonomy in the self-governing of their occupations.

Second, Johnson outlines the *patronage* profession type, in which power is exercised between the occupation and those who pay directly for its services. The boundaries of the occupation are defined in an interchange between the practitioners (who are not without some degree of power) and those who control the resources which its practices require (its patrons). The examples which Johnson gives are those of accountancy and architecture, whose practice is defined in contractual obligations between the professional and the recipient of the service.

Third, there is the *mediated* profession, in which power is exercised through a mediator between the occupation and the users of the services which it provides. The mediator may be another profession or it may be a patron but, as Johnson shows, in industrial society it has increasingly become an agency, which is often part of the state. The examples he gives are nursing and social work. Each of these provides a service to a recipient on behalf of an agency which exercises power over the occupation.

Clearly these are ideal types, in the sense that they are typifications in the realm of ideas rather than 'pure' examples. Attempts to construct such lists, which should be regarded as the basis for analysis and not as ends in themselves, can only succeed to the extent that they represent the multidimensional nature of the social world. (It is necessary also to acknowledge the extent to which ideal types may constrain possibilities for understanding the world as much as they provide a basis for doing so.)

Johnson recognises that the type of profession which he explores are not discrete and mutually exclusive elements. For example medicine and law may be employed by agencies, and (to a considerable extent) they have their boundaries protected by the state; accountancy and architecture have a good deal of collegiate control, especially in relation to entry to their ranks; nursing may be purchased privately by a patron, as may some social work services in some countries (for example, the USA). The application of these types may be seen, therefore, as a series of possibilities, rather than as mutually exclusive categories. They may also vary across national boundaries as well as within professions. Johnson's exploration of power as the key element of professionalism opens up the possibility of a more critical approach to the study of professions. However, it is successful only if it moves beyond a concern with the description of specific forms, and begins to analyse the processes through which the occupations under consideration emerge as professions.

From this model it becomes possible to ask if the doctor employed in a state hospital exercises power differently from the doctor in private practice, or whether nurses in the same situations would show the same power differences. Furthermore, as much as this model describes historically dominant power structures, it may also account for why two professions in the same context exercise power differently; for example, why the state hospital doctor exercises power differently to the nurse, the occupational therapist, the physiotherapist, the social worker and so on. This is a dimension which appears to be missing from Wilding's (1982) analysis, in which he was concerned to draw out the similarities between different types of profession in relation to the centrality of power. That some professions may experience themselves as less powerful than others, or that some members of a profession may see themselves as subject to the power of other members was not part of Wilding's concern.

Power is exercised in professions, then, in several ways. It may be exercised by members of the profession in relation to each other (for example, senior to junior); it may be exercised by those who control the resources on which its practice depends (those who pay for it); it may be exercised by those who use the services; it may be exercised by wider social institutions (often the state). As I have noted, in practice it is likely that all of these elements will be involved in most professional action, and in many cases there will be an overlap between the membership of the different groups exercising power. For example, I have suggested that the control of resources is directly related to the state agency basis of both nursing and social work. Considering the control of resources may also include the possibility that power is exercised within the professions themselves (do all nurses, therapists or social workers control resources equally?), and that power is exercised in relation to the users of services (how does the access of professionals to resources differ from that of service users?). Each aspect must be investigated, as must the relationships between these various questions.

The language of professionalism frequently serves to obscure the issue of power. Indeed, several of the criteria employed by the trait theorists appear to be candidates for enquiry on these grounds, a task which has been undertaken by Wilding (1982). For example, the concepts that professions are defined by an ethic of service to the wider society and by their inherent trustworthiness can be explained in terms of occupational bids for status and privilege (Berlant, 1975; Pearson, 1975). As Wilding argues (1982, p. 4), the extent of our knowledge about the service ethic even of widely researched professions remains sparse, and whether or not professionals do possess an ethic which is not evident amongst non-professionals is unclear. However, this does not prevent professions from using such a concept with a tone of conviction, and it is the conviction which is the important point when the observable extent of such an ethic in practice is so lacking in definition (Wilding, 1982, p. 77). The concepts of expertise, of colleague control and public accountability can be regarded similarly (Hughes, 1958; Friedson, 1970; Johnson, 1972; Wrong, 1979; Wilding, 1982). In this context the control of the language of professionalism, appealing to the sentiments which are encapsulated in the trait approach, becomes an important element of the power over an occupation which is at the centre of professionalisation.

Such claims can be seen in the public statements of those occupations which claim professional status. Jolley (1989) examines nursing from this perspective, summarising the literature of trait analysis. Although Jolley recognises the issue of gender in particular as a problematic aspect of nursing development, nevertheless her underlying purpose remains the reconciliation of contemporary nursing with the orthodox traits in order to construct a political stance which incorporates trait analysis on its own terms. Wallis (1987a) undertakes an analogous exercise in relation to occupational therapy, and Atkinson (1988) similarly emphasises the importance of an empirical body of knowledge as a trait defining the professional status of physiotherapy. Wallis and Atkinson, like Jolley, are aware that power is used by a profession corporately, and are especially conscious of the power of medicine in relation to the remedial professions. Like Jolley, their ultimate concern is 'total professional autonomy' (Wallis, 1987a, p. 265).

Whereas social work has successfully established its own structural independence from other professions, Glastonbury *et al.* (1982) argue that it has done so at the price of professional autonomy. Although they develop a more lengthy and sophisticated historical and organisational analysis, they share with Jolley and Wallis the goal of enhanced professionalism based around the trait of autonomy which they argue could be realised through occupational self-management. In each case the concern for the fate of a specific occupation leads to a challenge and redefinition of the traits which are claimed as the deciding factors (Johnson, 1972, p. 25).

In contrast to the delineation of traits in the orthodox concern of studies in professionalism, the work of Johnson (1972) and Wilding (1982) amongst others develops a position where the critical analysis of professionalism is the central question. That is, the ground has shifted from the questions of whether nursing, occupational therapy, physiotherapy or social work are professions, to the analysis of how they have attempted to professionalise and with what outcomes. Nevertheless, some important questions have remained largely unexplored. In particular, questions of how the organisational structures of such occupations and the power relationships between occupations relate to their patterns of development must be asked. These in turn interconnect with issues of how power is exercised between members of these occupations and the users of their services. From this point, wider questions are opened up, concerning gender and racism as arenas of power within which all the caring professions are located.

Becker (1970) has noted that the idea of 'profession' is used also as a 'folk concept' in everyday speech. It forms part of the language structure of society in which it is used as a collective symbol to convey a high value. By this I take Becker to mean that in their claims to professionalism members of occupations are making statements about the nature of the work they undertake, the value which it holds or which they think it should hold and the status which follows from these phenomena. The use of 'profession' as a folk concept presents an analytical problem. It has a taken-for-granted place in the everyday world of members of the occupations in question. Consequently meanings and emphases of meanings shift in relation to the context in which the concept is invoked to communicate ideas about these occupations. So the attempts to use traits as defining features could be said to represent something of an advance on this because they are seen as having objectivity. Yet the concern about traits, which I have noted in the work of Glastonbury *et al.* (1982), Wallis (1987a), Atkinson (1988) and Jolley (1989), indicates that even though there may be a taken-for-grantedness at a surface level there still is an underlying contention. In other words, the appeal to the idea of professionalism is itself part of a bid for autonomy and social value expressed in status, and the search for objective criteria part of that bid. As Titmuss observed, professionals are pre-eminently people with status problems (1968, p. 72).

So in order to progress beyond the trait approach and to examine nursing, the remedial therapies and social work in relation to their structures and practices it may be sufficient to accept that they claim the status of profession, but vital to ask what this has meant for their historical development, their contemporary forms, the relationship between members of these occupations and those who use their services, and the connections with wider social issues such as racism and gender. So having rejected the concept of 'semi-professions' as reliant on the trait approach I will refer to these occupations simply as professions and focus on the meaning of such a claim in these specific instances. Also I wish to avoid the pitfall of sliding back into a debate about whether they are 'real' professions. Instead I will take the description which also is used often to demarcate occupations, and which itself may be regarded as a folk concept, namely that of 'caring profession'. Yet even this cannot be taken at surface value, but must be examined, and it is to that task which I turn now.

Professions and caring

The idea of caring carries a multidimensional and even ambiguous set of meanings (Mayeroff, 1972; Graham, 1983; Dalley, 1988). For Mayeroff there is an important distinction to be made between caring for a person and caring for an idea (Mayeroff, 1972, p. 2). However, the common links between the two, which enable both to be understood in the same terms, as 'caring', are to be found in the *commitment* of the person who cares towards the other person or the idea. This commitment is expressed through the enabling of the other person or the idea to grow, develop and achieve the maximum possible of her, his or its potential (Mayeroff, 1972, pp. 10–12). Caring is to be found also in the *intellectual and emotional characteristics* of the person who cares, in the possession and use of knowledge, in moral values (for example, honesty) and in personal traits (for example in patience and humility, in constancy and guilt) (Mayeroff, 1972, pp. 13ff., pp. 28ff.).

Using these criteria it would be possible to create a wide, possibly all-embracing understanding of caring professions: on these grounds are not all professions caring? The doctor is committed to her or his patients, to the use of knowledge, to honesty and so on; similarly the lawyer, the architect, the professor, in relation to clients, patrons and students. Further, all may be said to be caring for the ideas which are the foundation of their respective occupations (Greenwood, 1957; see also Wilding, 1982). So on what grounds may the epithet 'caring professions' be applied selectively?

A parallel but somewhat different distinction has emerged from more recent work, especially that which is grounded in feminist concerns with social welfare (Graham, 1983; Ungerson, 1983, 1987, 1990; Dalley, 1988). Where Mayeroff subsumes the idea of caring as a task *within* his overarching ideas of commitment and human relations, feminist scholarship suggests that the issues of commitment (intellectual and emotional) should be separated from questions of the performance of given tasks. In relation to the former we should speak of caring *about*, while in relation to the latter caring *for* is a more appropriate term (Ungerson, 1983). Graham makes a similar distinction when she refers to caring as 'feeling concern' and as 'taking charge', as 'love' and as 'labour' (Graham, 1983, p. 13). The latter is seen in the accomplishment of daily living: feeding, dressing, ordering the domestic environment, managing personal budgets and so on; it may be referred to also as tending.

In this approach questions of *who* it is who performs caring tasks as well as feeling concern, and questions of *where* caring takes place are made explicit. This can be seen in a rereading of an example given by Mayeroff: 'The father who goes for the doctor in the middle of the night for his sick child does not experience this as a burden; he is simply caring for the child' (1972, p. 9). Now while I may suggest that this is a tautology (the father who *does* experience this as a burden will no doubt be seen as uncaring), the concepts advanced by Graham, Ungerson and others prompt us to ask who will administer any medicines prescribed, mop up vomit, faeces and urine, and launder soiled clothes and bed-clothes. They suggest it is unlikely to be doctors, or even fathers, for the most part. Further, where is the child likely to be when it is cared for? The most plausible answers are that it will be in its own home, a children's home or a hospital, and these are places where caring as a task (caring 'for') is usually performed by women, either in the general roles of mother, wife, daughter, daughter-in-law, or in the professional roles of residential social worker, nurse and so on (Graham, 1983; Davis and Brook, 1985; Ungerson, 1987).

Distinguishing between caring as commitment and caring as a task in this way therefore begins to identify 'caring' as an issue in the claim to professionalism of particular occupations. While occupations such as medicine, law or architecture (all predominantly masculine historically) may be said to care 'about', it is occupations such as nursing, the remedial therapies and social work (all predominantly feminine historically) which care 'for' to differing degrees as well as care 'about', often acting on the pronouncements of the 'masculine' professions. (See Hearn, 1982, for a discussion of masculine and feminine in this context.) The interconnections between caring, gender and professions form a major thread in the discussion following in this and subsequent chapters, and issues raised here will be explored in more depth below.

Caring, as a combination of intellectual and emotional expression with the performance of tasks, is not the sole province of professionals; in both senses caring is undertaken by relatives, friends, neighbours and volunteers. I distinguish volunteers from family, friends and neighbours because the basis for their commitment is more likely to be found in a sense of community, citizenship or humanity (Bulmer, 1987; Qureshi, 1990). The social obligations associated with caring are ambiguous, and for family in particular assume that people will demonstrate emotional ties in action even at the point when the emotional ties are no longer experienced as real (irrespective of whether they once were) (Ungerson, 1987). For many 'informal' carers the reality is one of a relentless 'daily grind' which offers little in the way of emotional recompense or reciprocity (Bayley, 1973; Hicks, 1988). Indeed, the division between informality and professionalism can become increasingly tenuous for many family carers as the burden of caring for takes over from the experience of caring about (Oliver, 1983). This view has been echoed repeatedly in research findings; many carers come to talk of themselves in professionalistic language (for example, borrowing idioms of nursing) and at the same time to resent the professionals' use of the epithet 'caring' (Ungerson, 1987). In such situations caring becomes an aspect of power in which other people (professionals, the cared-for, wider society, the state) define the lives of those who are doing caring work informally. This occurs through the design and implementation of policies and practices which are overtly designed to care, expressing concern and at the same time taking charge through the control of social structures within which daily life takes place. Caring is 'taking over', but it may be the carer who is taken over as much as the person who is cared for.

Yet identification with the idea of caring has been sought by health and welfare occupations with only slightly less enthusiasm than the idea of professionalism itself. The reason why this has been so can be seen in the relationship between the two senses of caring and moral claims to the status of professionalism. As I have noted, occupations which are regarded as professions are those which can be seen as caring about, expressing commitment and so on. It is part of the professional enterprise that occupations show they are caring through their application of knowledge with honesty and trust (Mayeroff, 1972, pp. 18–22). However, those occupations which appear to combine *both* senses of caring have been less successful in claiming the status of professional. It is despite, even because of, their caring 'for' as well as caring 'about', that these occupations have come to be regarded as not 'fully' professional. Caring for is seen as less expert, it is women's work, it is work done by black people, it is work which 'anybody could do' (but which not everybody does or wants to), it can be done by volunteers as well as by people who are paid, by people who are less highly trained or even untrained. So the circularity of low status is reinforced: the task is low-status, so the people who perform it are low-status, so the task is low-status, *ad infinitum*. Nursing, the remedial therapies and social work are caring professions because they are caring in both senses of the term, and the ambiguous social value of these concepts can be seen in the historical origins of these occupations. The claim of other occupations to be *caring* professions is based, therefore, on grounds which demarcate a separate though related range of issues in the analysis of occupational structures and practices. For these reasons this study will concentrate on those occupations which are based in some degree on caring 'for' as well as on caring 'about'.

The origins of the modern occupations of nursing, occupational therapy, physiotherapy and social work can be seen in the social, political and economic changes of the nineteenth century (Corrigan and Corrigan, 1979). These occupations provided, in various ways, an opening-up of professional life for women, although they were and continue to be shaped by the patriarchal structures in which they emerged (Walton, 1975; Hearn, 1982). All of these occupations arose in areas of life such as the tending of the sick, the care of small children, the day-to-day management of the household and the tending of dependent adults, which were seen as the responsibility (primarily if not entirely) of women in Western European, North American and Australian society. That these are still seen as women's work has been shown in a range of empirical and theoretical studies in all three continents (Finch and Groves, 1982; Wærness, 1984; Day, 1985; Estes, 1986). Different aspects of the histories of these occupations will be examined in more detail in Chapters 3 and 4.

So from the beginning, nursing, the remedial therapies and social work were women's occupations. This is not to say that men were uninvolved; rather that they were either located at the margins or else they dominated through relationships with other professions. In broad terms, where women did the work men managed and controlled it. (I will return to these issues in more detail in Chapter 7.) The professionalisation of women's work occurred in social spaces that were defined in terms of men's work, sometimes in overt struggle between the two spheres (Hearn, 1982). Lawyers, doctors and the clergy, prototypically (white) male professions, exerted definitional power over the boundaries of the emerging professions through access to resources and legitimacy, controlling them in both the material and ideal spheres. Just as contemporary carers have found their position to be ambiguous in relation to power, giving others power over the carer as much as or more than giving the carer power, so the occupations of nursing, the remedial therapies and social work have been under the power of the more established professions and the state from their beginnings.

Caring as an expression of feeling also has a role in the development of these occupations in the nineteenth century. This was a period in the history of the industrialising nations in which a geographically mobile workforce was essential, but at the same time posed a serious threat to the stability of society (Corrigan and Corrigan, 1979). One aspect of the social responses to this contradiction was the growth of interventions in the lives of the working classes, which sought to provide ameliorative help for those whose health or well-being were threatened to the extent that they would not be able to provide an active contribution to the economy. This was tied to the more punitive responses directed at those who were seen to be willingly taking themselves out of the labour market, through the concern to distinguish between the 'deserving' and the 'undeserving' poor (Donzelot, 1979). Care thus became inextricably linked to control (Satyamurti, 1979), and, as I will examine further in Chapter 3, this had implications for the internal organisation of the caring professions as well as for their relationship with the wider society.

So both nursing and social work can be seen as the feminisation of social responses to ill-health and poverty. Both were constructed around a distinction between the 'deserving' and the 'undeserving', although they developed along different lines in respect of the class locations of the recipients of their care. Where early social work provided care for the respectable working classes, the recipients of nursing were to be found in both the working and the propertied classes. (The latter also can be seen as 'deserving' in this context.) Yet within these different class locations nursing as much as social work can be seen as the taking-over of the tasks of living (caring as taking charge), while social work as much as nursing was the expression of commitment (caring as concern).

The idea of concern expressed for others has an importance, then as now, which is central to the understanding of occupations as caring professions. As I have noted above, this importance is of a moral order. It derives not only from the supposed inherent social value of concern for other people (as in Mayeroff, 1972), but also from the content of the work involved: caring about and caring for. However, while the opposite of 'caring' might be 'callous', the opposite of 'caring work' is less clear. It is not 'controlling work', as both nursing and social work contain clear social control elements which it may be argued are not only compatible with but essential to the caring role (see, for example, Day, 1981). What it includes is a sense of impersonality, instrumentality, and a concern for ideas or values above that expressed for people (Philp, 1979). So it is not a matter of the difference between constraint and tending, but is about the distinction between work based on personal relationships and social skills on the one hand and an instrumental approach to the world on the other (in which the 'objective' features of the world are the overwhelming focus of professional interest). In this sense the doctor may care about the well-being of the patient, through skills and knowledge devoted to the diagnosis and treatment of disease and illness, whereas the nurse both cares about and cares for the patient in skills and knowledge devoted to the tending of the person (often including the administration of the doctor's prescriptions).

This is not to say that technical or controlling work is generally seen as morally unacceptable; indeed, the opposite usually is the case, as both law and order and economic and technical development (especially in health) may be regarded widely as aspects of a stable, developing society. What is different is that caring work involves a degree of intimacy, of closeness socially (emotionally and/or physically) between the carer and the cared-for. Moreover, it requires the professional to recognise, even to make central in theory and practice, the individuality of the person receiving the service (Philp, 1979). As Philp has demonstrated, the underlying logic of the established professions has been to see the individual as an example, an instance of general cases and categories. For the caring professions the focus is reversed, and the caseness or categorical features of an individual are regarded as facets, aspects of the wider person. For example, for the legal profession the focus of concern may be burglars (amongst other types of criminal), of which Mr A. happens to be one; for the social worker the focus of concern will be Mr A., who happens to have been convicted of burglary (but is also a husband, father, tenant of the local authority and so on) (see Philp, 1979). Such an understanding places caring work clearly in the realm of the interpersonal rather than the instrumental, but is not a matter of moral choice on the part of individual professionals: it is the underlying structure of their occupation. Where such occupations as nursing and social work lacked the basis of technical or abstract knowledge, they were based in a claim to harness interpersonal and domestic skills for professional service. As I will discuss in Chapter 7, it is the social status of these skills as 'women's work' which is used to devalue such work in debates about professionalism, and which underpins the '*semi*-professional' concept (Phillips and Taylor, 1980).

This brings us back to gender divisions in the origins of caring professions. The separation of the interpersonal and instrumental may be understood as gender-based in so far as general social ideas as well as scientific thought in psychology and psychiatry tend to associate the former with women and the latter with men. Graham (1983) is critical of approaches to understanding caring which take this at face value, and which do not explore the implications this division has for power exerted over women by men through the association of the former with the caring role. There is nothing about either women or the caring role which is inherent in this connection: it is a social and historical construct. Moreover, the centrality of power as the basis for this construct suggests that other social divisions, in particular racism, should also be analysed.

In individual contexts, it may be argued, women exercise

power over men and black people exercise power over white people, as nurses or remedial therapists over patients, as social workers over clients. However, as I will explore in more detail in subsequent chapters, such individual power is exercised within wider social structures and relationships, including the standing of nursing, the remedial therapies and social work *vis-à-vis* other professions, their internal pattern of management and control, and the wider social contexts of racism and sexism. In other words, it will be seen that individual women (as professionals) exercise power over individual men (as service users) within roles and structures which have developed from and are sanctioned by patriarchy through the greater power and authority of 'masculine' occupations. Similarly, where black caring professionals exercise power over white service users they do so in the context of racism in wider social structures and relationships.

Through a recognition of the problematic place of 'caring for' in industrialised society we can begin to see the importance of power as an issue in those occupations which are based on both senses of caring. It may be apparent also why other occupations, most notably medicine, are not central to this discussion. Medicine often lays claim to the notion that it is a 'caring profession' (Watkins, 1987). Within such claims it is caring 'about' which is the central concept, although this carries with it the implication that doctors' relationships with their patients are interpersonal as well as instrumental. This idea appears especially in general practice and in psychiatry, although even in these branches interpersonality has been increasingly questioned in recent years (Brewer and Lait, 1980; Diasio-Serrett, 1985). Yet medicine's status as a profession is based predominantly on its claims to be regarded as a set of practices derived from rigorously tested knowledge about and skills in treating disease and illness. In other words, of having defined itself over more than two centuries as an instrumental practice *par excellence* (Watkins, 1987). In this regard it has influenced the strategies for professionalisation of other occupations which I will examine in more detail in Chapter 4. (See, for example, Sim's discussion of research in physiotherapy (1989).) Furthermore, it derives from the historical action of men in the emerging middle classes, who were able in the early stages of medical development to achieve a considerable degree of self-control (Friedson, 1970). Its claims to the epithet 'caring' therefore have to be seen as having a different significance to those of nursing, the remedial professions or social work, and one which will largely remain outside this discussion (although which will provide occasional points of comparison).

The inclusion of particular occupations within the boundaries of 'caring profession' is therefore not related to any intrinsic characteristics which any occupation may be held to display, but based on the criteria which its members invoke to communicate their perception of its nature. Nursing, the remedial therapies and social work, in different ways and to differing degrees, make claims both to care about and to care for the people who use their services. Even the idea of 'love', which is central to the social construction of caring (Graham, 1983) may be seen as an element in some professional statements, collective or individual (for example: British Association of Social Workers (BASW), 1977, p. 35; Robinson, 1989, p. 159; Mackay, 1989, p. 133).

Professions and the state

The ways in which caring has been incorporated into the practices of nursing, the remedial therapies or social work has not occurred simply as a consequence of the nature of these occupations. The growth of the caring professions has taken place within the context of the development of the welfare state. As Johnson noted (1972, p. 77) the state has two roles in relation to caring professions. First it acts as a mediator between professions and their clientele, to the extent of defining who the clientele should be and the manner in which they should be helped. This does not mean that the professions lack a voice in the processes of definition. However, the mediative role enables the state to exert control over a profession through legal and financial constraints and through political influence. The power of the professions to define their own clientele lies only within the areas of agreement which they have been able to negotiate with the state. Here the state is mediating not only between professions and their clientele (as collective entities) but also between various professional interests. This can be seen in the various legal frameworks in the UK, the USA and other countries which restrict the right of nurses and remedial therapists to diagnose and prescribe in favour of the right of doctors to do so. In this example the state mediates between medicine and other professions in a way which reveals an aspect of the power of the former over the latter (it has greater influence in the state) and which at the same time serves to ensure the continuation of the power of the former (it is the institutionalised basis for medical control over nursing and the remedial therapies).

Second, the state acts as a 'corporate patron' in the form of public agencies which provide services on behalf of the state (Johnson, 1972, p. 77). Agencies exist to provide services which are deemed to be 'in the public good' (p. 78) and in which the needs of the state are the primary consideration. In this sense it is the state itself which can be seen as the 'client' and not the group of direct services users. The state, as a set of institutions in which social groups act and interact, can be said to have needs to the extent that goals are given to these institutions by those whose interests they express. (In other words, the needs of the state are the needs of the dominant groups within the state.) This position gives state-employed professionals a great deal of power over individual service users (Wilding, 1982, p. 68). Although the ideology of professionalism serves to disguise the relationship, the power of professionals over their clientele in such circumstances derives from the professionals' role as agents of the state.

This theme has been echoed within the critical histories of nursing and social work (Parry *et al.*, 1979; Davies, 1980; Jordan, 1984; Dingwall *et al.*, 1988; Maggs, 1989). In these analyses of the development of nursing and social work, the role of the state is seen to be one of considerable control and influence over the structure, form and content of the caring professions. The origins of the caring professions are placed in the context of capitalist and middle-class concerns about the productive labour of the working classes. A division between the goals of enabling 'respectable' workers to return to the productive labour market and discouraging the avoidance of work by the 'disorderly poor' marked out the contradictory strands of caring and controlling which are a feature of nursing and social work into the late twentieth century (Jones, 1983; Hawker, 1989). This is not to suggest that the motivations of individual reformers were necessarily cynical. Humanitarian concerns, although often couched in terms which are alien to a later age, did inform the actions of some early activists (see, for example, comments on the settlement movement in Parry and Parry, 1979, pp. 24–6). Yet the extent to which they were able to achieve the ends which they thought necessary was bounded by the power of other interests, especially those of industrial capitalism in having a healthy and hard-working labour force. This converged more with the views of other professionalising reformers who placed considerable moral value on productive labour.

The views of the state on which these analyses are constructed derive from neo-Marxist and neo-Weberian concepts of the economic and political structures of society. Briefly, these views share a perception of the institutions through which society is ordered, ruled and reproduced as reflecting and at the same time serving the interests of certain classes and social groups (that is those which dominate or rule). These institutions include the government, the administration, the military, the police, and the judiciary. Taylor-Gooby and Dale summarise the debate within Marxism concerning the inclusion of schools, churches, and the family as elements of the state, and they reject the wider use of the concept (1981, p. 177). I think that they are correct in their conclusion that a more limited definition produces greater clarity. For example, it enables distinctions between different forms of state structure and action is to be made. It allows also for a considerations of the way in which the state may use, even penetrate the family while at the same time allowing that the family, such as black families in white society to which Bryan *et al.* (1985) refer, may also be a site of mutual and supportive relationships. Yet institutions such as the health services, social services and education have an ambiguous, even contradictory relationship to the more overtly coercive parts of the state. Such institutions serve the interests of both dominant and dominated classes in that they provide tangible goods and services which benefit members of all classes (in different ways) while at the same time these services reinforce the legitimacy of the social structure (O'Connor, 1973; Gough, 1979). As Taylor-Gooby and Dale themselves argue (1981, p. 191) health, welfare and education serve to produce a healthy and skilful workforce while at the same time often arising from concessions in response to the demands of the labour movement. For this reason the idea of the *welfare* state is both a useful and a necessary distinction which acknowledges the contradictory nature (simultaneously controlling and caring) of welfare institutions as part of the state.

The contradictions of the roles which such institutions play in the maintenance of late capitalism and the relationships they have to different social classes have created a situation in which the welfare state has come to be in a long-term crisis (Offe, 1984). This crisis can be seen in the growing conflict over the economic structures of the welfare state and over the ideological legitimacy of state welfare (O'Connor, 1973; Habermas, 1976). The growth of the welfare state has exacerbated the contradictions between the economic and ideological aspects of society, so that to resolve the ensuing crisis the long-term interests of capital are placed before those of welfare (Gough, 1979). In order to achieve this end while maintaining social stability it is necessary for those groups exercising power within the state (the dominant classes) to challenge the legitimacy of state welfare services, and consequently that of the professionals whose interests also are served by the development of the welfare state. The outcome is that the interests of professionals as state employees are threatened. In this analysis Gough emphasises the interests shared between professionals and their clients against the state, and stresses the commonality of their class position (as employed workers).

In contrast, Taylor-Gooby and Dale (1981) seek to extend the notion of class to include groups defined other than as workers. In this they appear to move away from the economic system as the paramount feature for understanding the welfare state and look instead at several forms of 'capitalist oppression', including sexual, national and racial groups, as the basis for the exercise of power. This view assumes a more complex division of classes, not only separating them on economic grounds, but also subdividing the broader economic classes along lines of race, gender and other factors. Such an understanding suggests that the position and actions of professionals as groups must therefore be considered in relation to each subdivision. Not only is the class position which caring professionals share with other employed workers raised as a question, but also the connections which this has with issues of the relative power and interests of men and women, white and black, and so on, as these are institutionalised in the welfare state. For example, although a nurse may share with patients the experience of being an employed worker, whether or not either is male or female, black or white will also affect their social relationship, including the extent to which one exercises control over the other.

Mishra (1984) is critical of Gough's position to the extent that it does not allow for the power which professionals exercise over their clients by virtue of the position professionals hold within the state (although Mishra (1984, p. 95) does recognise Gough's view (1979, p. 143) that professionalism is a 'two-edged sword' in this respect). At the same time Mishra questions the primacy allocated by Taylor-Gooby and Dale to the concepts of capitalism and class, arguing that for women patriarchy and gender may be structures of oppression which cut across class lines (Mishra, 1984, p. 93). To see professionals only as workers ignores the bases of their power deriving from their sponsorship by the state, and it is necessary to incorporate both aspects (worker and state agent) in order to understand the location of professionals within social classes. Furthermore, professional relationships with clients are structured around patriarchy and racism (not specifically discussed by Mishra) as well as capitalism. Patriarchy and racism are not confined by economic class relations although they may take specific forms in relation to capitalism. In the example of the nurse given above, patients may well not see her/him as 'like us', but as different because of the agency basis of her/his work. This applies equally to remedial therapists and social workers. The significance for understanding the location of professionals within the welfare state is that they must be seen as multidimensional. Yet in this aspect of his discussion Mishra does not proceed further than to note the impossibility of examining welfare state organisations and the professions in isolation from each other (1984, p. 177).

For Hadley and Hatch (1981) the major theme in the control of welfare by the state in the UK is that of centralism, under governments of both Right and Left. In the provision of welfare the professions and the organisations within which they are employed follow the forms of representative democracy, in which the participation of citizens is restricted to the periodic choosing of those who make policy decisions (in effect parties rather than individuals), representatives who are themselves removed from the day-to-day management and practice of welfare services. This, Hadley and Hatch argue, has led to the growth of both professions and bureaucracies as relatively freestanding, and power is exercised through an interplay between professionalism and bureaucracy. The crisis in the welfare state is, therefore, a crisis of legitimacy for professionals, for the service organisations within which they are employed, and for the state itself because of the exclusion of citizens within the political process. Indeed, in their analysis, state services have come to have a dynamic independent of the state as such.

In contrast, the concept of corporatism suggested by Cawson (1982) is based on a concept of the state as a strong collective actor. The relationship between the state

and professions is discussed in terms of a corporate negotiation, in which professions exchange their expertise and
cooperation for favourable policies and resources. The
state needs the professions to supply health and welfare
services, and to legitimise state intervention in terms of
expertise. In return the state grants privileges to the professions which vary in degree between different occupations
(also see Wilding, 1982). Cawson (1982) suggests that the
position of medicine represents the most fully developed
corporate position through the monopoly controls which
are exercised by the profession over itself. Indeed, the
strength of Cawson's argument lies in the extent to which
the state does not intervene directly in medicine in the way
that it does in nursing or social work, for example, where
in the UK education and training are controlled by governmental bodies and recruitment is controlled by local state
agencies.

Where Hadley and Hatch (1981) conceptualise the state
in terms of the system of administration, so underemphasis-
ing the extent to which there is a corporate exercise of
power in the interests of dominant classes, Cawson (1982)
appears to overlook the extent to which the relationship
between the state and the professions is one of struggle
and conflict rather than cooperation and accommodation.
The consequence for Hadley and Hatch is that organisational forms are given greater prominence than other
forms of power in professional action, and for Cawson that
professional power is uncontentious.

By the late 1980s a different pattern can be seen to have
emerged which suggests that relationships between the
state and professions are being disputed and renegotiated,
with the state taking the leading and dominant role. The
outcomes are the increase of centralising financial controls
through the establishment of new managerial and administrative structures in tandem with the increased use of
market rationality in planning and policy (Cousins, 1987).
It is difficult to determine whether these changes represent
an end either to existing administrative structures or to
any form of corporate relationship, or whether they are a
reformation of structures and relationships in new alliances

and divisions. One possibility is the development of new divisions within the professions, which I will discuss further in Chapter 4.

'Crisis of the welfare state' theories suggest that substantial and rapid changes in professional services which seek to reduce their costs to the state have been possible only because the legitimacy of the professions has become less secure. The 'New Right', especially in the UK, has not attacked professionalism as such, but rather the exercise of power by professionals in state services over economic and ideological aspects of those services, as well as using the notion that they are *state* services as part of the undermining process (which curiously echoes social democratic and socialist criticisms). The critique of professions as self-interest groups has been strengthened by associating them with 'the state' as administrative bureaucracies rather than as the institutionalised interests of the dominant classes.

The importance of the *idea* of semi-professions is that it has legitimated a different status and corporate relationship with the state for nursing, remedial therapies and social work in comparison to medicine or law. This has made it easier for the 'New Right' to attack aspects of nursing or social work (although there are differences between the two), but at the same time may have placed them in more advantageous positions to adapt to some of the implications of change. For example, nursing and social work had already developed managerial structures and were struggling with the integration of professionalism and managerial organisation. I am not suggesting that members of any of these professions have been unequivocally accepting of the managerialist changes or that such changes are uniform or monolithic (and in Chapter 3 I will examine aspects of managerialism in more detail) but that the position of the less well-established professions such as nursing, the remedial therapies and social work must be seen as different to that of the more established professions, especially medicine.

Models of mediation

The concept of mediation outlined by Johnson (1972), in which the state stands between professions and their clientele to define ends and control means provides a linear picture of the relationship between the three groups. This can be portrayed diagrammatically, as in Figure 1.1.

the professions ◄————————► the state ◄————————► the clientele

Figure 1.1 *The state as mediator*

Orthodox professional criticisms of the state have tended to use this linear model implicitly, which can be seen in relation to nursing (for example Jolley, 1989) occupational therapy (for example Wallis, 1987a) and social work (for example Glastonbury *et al.*, 1982). The common feature of these arguments is that caring professions should be strengthened (along lines comparable to medicine and law), weakening the role of the state between the professionals and the clientele so that more responsive and service user-centred practices can develop.

In contrast, the role of professions as the agents of the state suggests a somewhat different picture in which it is the professions which stand between the state and the clientele (Figure 1.2).

the state ◄————————► the professions ◄————————► the clientele

Figure 1.2 *The professions as mediator*

The implication is that professionalism is either a delusion which obscures the common class interests of state health and welfare workers and their clientele (as in Simpkin, 1983) or else the claims of professionalism are to be seen as locating professionals with the dominant classes (as in Illich, 1976).

Each of these models assumes that professions derive their power from their relationship with the state, but whereas the former places the state between some professions and their clientele (acting to limit the power of those professions) the latter constructs professions as the agents of the state (with the state creating professional power). We have seen that each of these linear models communicates something of the reality of the caring professions which can be grasped theoretically. However, neither conveys the sense that the relationships operate simultaneously. Overall this requires a model which acknowledges the triangularity of the relationship, that the state both creates and seeks to constrain professions (see Figure 1.3). Although the state exercises power over caring professions and those citizens who use professional services, there is a qualitative distinction in the relationship between the state and the professions on the one hand, and the relationship of either with the clientele (actual or potential) on the other, recognising that not all professions have the same relationship with the state. So although the concept of mediation is useful it is incomplete if it does not enable the connections between both sets of relationships to be seen. Such a model suggests that analyses of professions which either stress their independence from the state (actual or potential) or emphasise their role as agents of the state to the exclusion of the other possibilities are only partial.

Wilding (1982) implicitly adopts such a triangular approach in the conclusions of his study, in which he argues that both the state (in the institution of government) and the professions have a responsibility to exert influence against each other in the interests of those who use public services. A mediative pluralism is proposed, in which each

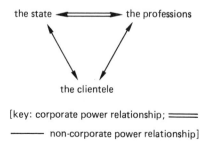

[key: corporate power relationship; ══════
──────── non-corporate power relationship]

Figure 1.3 *The triangular model of mediation*

group would be obliged to accept the influence of others in return for the right to influence those others. Wilding's argument assumes the legitimacy of both state and professions which, as I have noted, in the 1980s have come to be very uncertain (especially the legitimacy of the latter). It also assumes the possibility of socialist or social democratic political structures which the ascendency of the 'New Right' has apparently forced off the short-term historical agenda. Nevertheless, within Wilding's conclusions there are elements which provide the basis for reconsidering professionalism in caring services and I will return to these in the final chapter.

Caring professions and power

I have rejected the trait approach to the analysis of professionalism and argued for an examination of the historical, structural and ideological elements of those occupations which claim professionalism. This argument has accepted the use of the term 'professional' as empirical, and sought to replace the question 'are these claims valid in terms of key traits?' with the question 'what are the features of these occupations which make such claims problematic?' In doing so it has drawn on the issues of caring and the location of professions within the welfare state to chart the important dimensions of the occupations under consideration. This has identified nursing, the remedial therapies and social work as 'caring professions', and also placed these occupations within the mediated context of state welfare. Caring is both a central feature of the claims to professionalism and a key element in the legitimation of the welfare state.

Yet at the same time the concept of caring stands as a critique of the way in which nursing, remedial therapies and social work have developed not only to provide tending services but also as part of the regulatory institutions of society, in which the interests of the state are those of the dominant classes. So the caring professions can be seen to exercise power not only through skilled practices which meet the needs of their clientele but also through state sponsorship (with its attendant constraints) that provides the institutional basis for those practices.

This approach makes repeated reference to social power, and to certain dimensions of power, notably class, race and gender. The issue of power has been placed at the centre of understanding professionalism, caring and the state. So in the next chapter I will examine further the concept of power as it may be applied to an analysis of nursing, the remedial therapies and social work.

2

Dimensions of Power

Theories of power

In the preceding discussion of professionalism, caring and
the state, the concept of social power has been a core
element. Using this concept to understand caring professions is somewhat problematic because of the necessary
and constant theoretical debate about its meaning (Lukes,
1974, 1987; Clegg, 1979). So, there is no one underlying
concept which informs all work in this area. Nevertheless,
it is possible, within contemporary discussions of power,
to identify two broad approaches. The first of these can
be summarised as 'power as an element of social action',
and the second as 'power as an aspect of social relationships'. I will consider each in turn. It will then be possible
to outline specific contexts in which power is a significant
issue for caring professions.

The central debates about the social action approach to
power are summarised by Lukes (1974). There are, he
suggests, three dimensions to action perspectives on power.
These dimensions are:

(1) situations of observable decision-making, focused on
    key issues over which there is overt conflict concern-
    ing the subjective interests of the individuals or groups
    involved;
(2) situations of 'non-decision-making' in which only
    some potential issues become explicit, where there is

covert as well as overt conflict concerning the subjective interests of individuals or groups;

(3) situations in which the social agenda is established (that is, potential and explicit issues are created), in which there is actual (overt and covert) and also latent conflict over both objective and subjective interests of individuals or groups. (See, especially, Lukes, 1974, p. 25.)

It is the third dimension which Lukes argues is the most useful as a conceptual tool, because it encapsulates and extends the earlier approaches to the issue of power that are expressed in the first and second dimensions (see Dahl, 1957; French and Raven, 1959; Bachrach and Baratz, 1962). It encapsulates them because it continues to allow the questions they would raise to be asked; it extends them because it enables more subtle and pertinent questions to be framed, and it provides for a clearer distinction between coercion, influence and authority as forms of power. In Luke's terms it emphasises the *social* nature of action on which it is focused, recognising that there is 'power over' others as well as 'power to' (act) (Lukes, 1974, p. 38, p. 31).

The difference between the three dimensions can be illustrated with an example from nursing practice, in which a nurse administers a drug to a patient. The one-dimensional approach would only permit the application of the concept of power to an analysis of the nurse's actions in situations where the patient refused to take the drug. An objection by the nurse to the doctor's prescription would also constitute an observable instance of conflict which could be understood in these terms. In contrast, the two-dimensional view would also allow for consideration of situations in which the patient covertly conflicted with the nurse over the administration of the drug, but in which power was evident through the nurse's actions in avoiding the possibility of an overt refusal. (The same point applies to the doctor's control of the interaction with the nurse on the issue.) The three-dimensional view moves beyond this in so far as it allows for consideration of situations in which the patient is in agreement, but where such agreement conflicts with the patient's objective interests (for example, in understanding the treatment so that 'informed consent' can be exercised). The power of nursing can be seen in the general acceptance by patients of treatments administered by nurses, or, indeed, acceptance by patients and nurses of doctors' prescriptions. Comparable examples in remedial therapy and social work would differ in the detail of the actors involved and the nature of the professional intervention; the issue of power is the same.

Emphasising the social nature of the phenomena to be explained is necessary, according to Lukes, because the first and second dimensional approaches are essentially *behavioural* in their focus (1974, p. 15, p. 20): both are concerned with concrete instances in which action-making and non-action take place. For Lukes the three-dimensional view has two important elements representing a more social understanding of action, the first of which is that 'the bias of the system is not sustained simply by a series of individually chosen acts, but also, more importantly, by the socially structured and culturally patterned behaviour of groups, and practices of institutions, which may indeed be manifested by individuals' inaction' (pp. 21–2). Power, Lukes is saying, is socially structured in that it does not depend on the capacities of individuals, although historically it may be seen in the actions of individuals. In the example of the nurse, the patient and the drug the individually of patients and nurses who might be observed is not at issue. Second, questions are raised about the resistance or compliance of the powerless: '*A* may exercise power over *B* by getting him to do what he does not want to do, but he also exercises power over him by influencing, shaping or determining his very wants. Indeed, is it not the supreme exercise of power to get another or others to have the desires you want them to have?' (p. 23). So, not only is power socially structured, but because it is socially and culturally located it may have the appearance of consensus. That patients may be in full agreement with nurses' administration of drugs may in itself be considered as part of the exercise of power by nurses collectively, for example; it may be a 'normal' part of everyday life.

There are two implications of the three-dimensional view which are important for an understanding of caring professions. First, individuals or groups who exercise power may be unaware of doing so, and nurses, remedial therapists and social workers may even reject the idea that they exercise power. The lack of apparent conflict in the perceptions of either the powerful or the powerless may be a distortion of the power which provides the basis for their interaction. Therefore, any apparent consensus within a profession, between professions or between professionals and the users of their services must be taken as the object of enquiry as much as any observed conflict.

Second, the three-dimensional view raises the question of the links between the activity and inactivity of social groups and the institutional structures within which they act. So what professionals do and do not do, what they see as properly their concern and not their concern must be examined in relation to the structural positions of those professionals. This necessitates considering the connections between areas of professional life (including the organisations within which professionals work, their relationships with service users, and so on) and the wider social structures and cultural patterns of the society of which the professions are a part.

In summary, Lukes' three-dimensional model distinguishes force and coercion as examples of power relating to observable conflict of interests, and manipulation of bias as the form of power relating to latent conflict of interests (1974, p. 32). In his use of these ideas, Lukes may appear to be reintroducing a 'one-dimensional' typological approach of the kind developed by French and Raven (1959) (in which they distinguished between coercion, reward, legitimacy, reference and expertise). However, Lukes avoids the problem of ideal types (which I discussed in Chapter 1) by recognising that these ideas are themselves contestable in that they are open to dispute about their meaning through their use to analyse concrete situations. Therefore they cannot stand as classificatory labels, but have utility as starting-points for analysing empirical or theoretical examples.

This view appears to be contradicted by Arendt's 'communications' theory that power is exercised most clearly in situations where there is no conflict (Arendt, 1970). Indeed, for Arendt, to speak of force or coercion is not to speak of power, but to speak of violence. When violence appears, then power disappears. Yet this does not allow for those situations in which the imposition of one group's interests over another's can depend on different forms of compliance in different circumstances. In other words, legitimate power may be supported by latent coercive power despite the continuing absence of overt coercion, and without the potential for coercion being made explicit in any observable instance. An example of this in the caring professions would be the use of compulsion in mental health work in the UK. The actions of both nurses and social workers in the UK may, under certain conditions, compel a person to enter a mental hospital or remain there. The legitimacy of this power is established under specific legislation. However, the power includes recourse to the use of force (through a third party, the police), even if neither the person compelling nor the person being compelled make it explicit at a given time. When force is used in these conditions, I would argue, it remains an aspect of the power of the professional.

Arendt has, I think, confused power with authority. It is the latter which has crumbled when force is exercised. In this sense authority can be said to be the exercise of legitimate command based on social status. It includes legitimate power, but may also be seen where there is a genuine (that is, objective) consensus of interests. In Lukes' terms authority is a form of influence which can be exercised outside power relationships (whether observable or latent) as well as within them (1974, p. 32). This is an important distinction because Arendt bases her theory on the concept of collective consent, power as the consequence of the collectivity, a society, consenting to its exercise and it is this idea of consensus which Lukes questions.

Although they are in contradiction over the relationship

of force and authority, Lukes and Arendt share a concern to relate action to an understanding of social structures, that the exercise of power takes place in the context of relationships between social groups and classes. Yet both Lukes' and Arendt's concepts rest, ultimately, on the possibility of actors (whether individual or collective) exercising power. While any understanding of power must be able to account for action, both Lukes and Arendt remain confined by their reliance on action as their frame of reference, and their analyses do not succeed in making clear the social basis of power.

An alternative approach, grounded in an analysis of social relationships, is proposed by Habermas (1977) in his critique of Arendt. Habermas argues that Ardent's concept of communications assumes two phenomena which, historically, cannot be assumed. The first is that everyone in the society is equally able to voice or withhold their consent; the second is that communication is directed to reaching agreement rather than achieving ends. In this critique, Habermas advances the opposite view, that power is often exercised through the manipulation and/or distortion of communication, in which different groups have a different say in the construction of what passes for consensus and in which communication is directed towards the achievement of ends and not towards reaching agreement. This could be seen, for example, where a caring professional 'asks' a service user to comply with an intervention (to take the medicine, do the exercises, take part in family therapy), but the request is directed to accomplishing the professional goals and not to reaching an agreement with the service user which gives the service user's goals an equal status in the relationship.

In this way communication is directed towards the achievement of the ends of those whose interests it expresses, becoming the dominant way of thinking and talking about issues. This structuring of social relationships through dominant communication may be summarised as discourse. So power, in this view, is exercised in the structuring of the social framework within which interests, ideas and issues are formed and known. Professional knowledge, skills and ways of talking may form a discourse in this sense, expressing the interests of a profession.

The relationship between power, discourse and knowledge has also been developed in French structuralist thinking, associated with the work of Foucault (Gordon, 1980), from which it has been used to analyse the development of health and welfare policies for families (Donzelot, 1979). Expressed somewhat simply, discourse analysis demonstrates that through knowledge and language caring professions not only provide help, but also, and more importantly, they define the object of their work in the form of a general concept of the client/patient (Rojek *et al.*, 1988). This is because their theories and practices together create an idealised general concept of the service user which stands between actual professionals and actual service users. The power of the professional is based in the control of language and knowledge which rests with that professional (Philp, 1979).

At the individual level, in those contexts usually termed 'practice' by professionals, the power of professionals over service users is expressed in discourse (Fairclough, 1989). There are three aspects to this: the content of a meeting, the relations between the participants and the roles which they are occupying. Usually the content is controlled by the professional, and even when the client is able to introduce topics for discussion the professional can avoid these either by ignoring them or by introducing those which she or he considers important. As Fairclough shows (for example, 1989, pp. 43–9) this has a surface appearance, such as in the use of particular words, tone of voice, and non-verbal expression, and also a structure in which the expectation of social roles (professional, client) serve to create 'scripts' which, while not totally constraining, establish the dimensions of normal communications. Fairclough also discusses an example of a conflict in which the wider rules of normal communication are used to control the specific infringements by an individual (1989, pp. 68–70). The 'uncooperative' client (that is, one who does not follow the rules of professional/client discourse) may be kept within the discourse through the use of more general conversational rules. 'Cooperation' in this sense is when the service users' actions are in agreement with the expectations of the professional. The structural capacity of the professional to have 'the final word' on what constitutes cooperation is a central element of the social relationship between professional and service user.

Discourse is about more than language. Discourse is about the interplay between language and social relationships, in which some groups are able to achieve dominance for their interests in the way in which the world is defined and acted upon. Such groups include not only dominant economic classes, but also men within patriarchy, and white people within the racism of colonial and post-colonial societies (Fanon, 1967; Spender 1980), as well as professionals in relation to service users. Language is a central aspect of discourse through which power is reproduced and communicated.

To return to the earlier example of the nurse, the patient and the drug, attempting to understand power in this situation would suggest that the social relationship of nurses and patients is the nub of the investigation. The nurse may 'ask' the patient to take the drug, but what if the patient refuses? Can the patient comprehend refusing? If so, under what circumstances? The same questions may be asked of an instruction from the nursing sister to a staff nurse to administer the drug, or the prescription from the doctor. What is the context of the relationships between patients, nurses and doctors which provides the basis for power in these situations? These are discrete instances of more general questions about the structural power which is exercised between caring professionals, and between professionals and service users.

It is in relation to these questions that detailed distinction such as those outlined by French and Raven (1959) can be reconsidered, although the meanings of reward, coercion, legitimacy, reference and expertise now take on a different significance. Each of these concepts may be useful in considering caring professions, but they must be examined in terms of the social relationships between caring professions and those who are involved in providing or receiving their services. Even the notions of caring and professional are an element in the enquiry, as they form part of the cultural forms in which such occupations have developed.

A strong distinction has been drawn between action and structural relationships as a basis for understanding power. This replicates an ancient polarity of doing and being (and the associated dichotomy of freedom and constraint). However, there are theoretical and empirical difficulties in operating with so rigid a distinction. Doing nursing, remedial therapy or social work is not that easily separable from being a nurse, a remedial therapist or a social worker. In this respect I would agree with Lukes that the extremes of voluntarism or determinism (freedom or constraint) are equally overstated (1974, p. 54). Yet Lukes makes a choice in that, in the end, he maintains a view of power which depends on the *capacity* of individuals or groups to act (1974, p. 55), and in so doing does not address the basis on which they act. The result is that action appears to be internally generated. In contrast, the consideration of social relationships provides the basis for a discussion of social action which does not explain social action in terms of itself. This is not simply to propose a 'fourth dimension' to Lukes typology, but to suggest a broadening of the debate to the point at which it is possible to recognise the interplay between action and structure through a consideration of aspects of power in the development and operation of the caring professions.

Aspects of power

If power is not an isolated element of social life, but one which interweaves occupational and organisational structures with the actions of professionals, individually and collectively, then it must be examined in terms of the contexts within which the caring professions are structured and operate. In the remainder of this chapter I will outline the aspects of power in caring professions which are central to the analysis, and this outline will provide the basis for the subsequent discussion.

Hierarchy

In Chapter 1 it was noted that even in the collegiate type of profession there can be found differences of power between members of the same occupational group (Johnson, 1972). These may be a consequence of the use of qualifications as a device to construct levels within the occupation, so that even the person who can be regarded as qualified by the non-member may have fewer or lower qualifications than another, and so be seen as less qualified. Alternatively there may be differences of power between branches of the occupation, constructed around the types of problems with which those members work or the way in which they work.

The occupational structures of professions tend to be hierarchical, based on these ideas about how senior and junior positions are to be defined in relation to each other; seniority is power and authority over a junior person by virtue of the occupational relationship. This can be seen in the distinctions between staff nurses and sister, or basic grade and senior social worker, for example. The concept of a career takes on a specific significance as the moves from junior to senior are stages not only of increased status, but also of developing power in the form of control over one's own work, over the necessary input of others to the work process, over the conditions of that work and so on. To the extent that seniority confers power in this way is taken for granted, not only by the senior but also by the junior professional, then the occupational hierarchy is a secure power structure.

Professions are, almost invariably, not free-standing but are located in organisational structures. In historical terms this appears to have been a process which has been followed by all professions, including those which have their practice defined by a free contract between the professional and the service user. Mills (1956) noted what he called the 'managerial demiurge', the tendency for medical and law firms to expand through the creation of levels of professionals as well as through distinctions between professionals and administrative staff. (He refers to the growth of 'law factories', p. 24.) For the developing professional groups which do not spring from this type of individualised practice historically, some form of organisational hierarchy has been evident from the early days. This can be seen in nursing and in social work (Parry and Parry, 1979; Cousins, 1987). The more recent issue of managerialism also may be considered in relation to this process, and poses further questions about professionals as employed workers and the control of their labour (Braverman, 1974; Larson, 1980; Derber, 1982, 1983). To what extent do the hierarchical structures of the caring professions and the growth of managerialism represent forms of 'proletarianisation'? This question raises issues about the relationship between hierarchy and professionialism which will be discussed in more detail in Chapter 3.

Types of hierarchical structures have varied within and between different professional groups over time and in different nation states. Where, for example, a phenomenon such as the 'managerial demiurge' can be seen in North America and in Western Europe, the detail of the form which it takes differs between countries in relation to legal structures, local cultural patterns, and so on. Differences are even more apparent if consideration is given to the extent of professional employment in state agencies. In broad terms Western Europe has seen the widespread development of professional employment directly by the state in comparison to North America, but even so there are major differences also between the United States and Canada on the one hand, and between France, Sweden and the United Kingdom on the other.

That hierarchy should be analysed in terms of power may appear to be a tautology: hierarchy is power and authority in an organisation, embedded in organisational language (job descriptions, forms of address, and so on). However, for the purposes of this discussion it is necessary to be aware that the overt exercise of power is only one of its forms in hierarchical organisations, and that the structure may operate through the mobilisation of bias, for example, in the day-to-day work of caring professions. Thus the types of organisation within which such occupations are conducted will be important, because their hierarchical nature may be 'invisible', or if not that then at least 'normal'. It is necessary in this discussion to render them visible in order to question the taken-for-grantedness of hierarchy, and these issues will be discussed in more detail in Chapter 3.

Occupation

There are three dimensions in which occupation may be considered as an aspect of power. The first of these relates to hierarchy, namely the way in which occupations are power structures *within themselves*. It is this dimension which is at issue when the question of professionalism is raised. As I noted above, professions are structures of power over an occupation. Nursing sisters, senior therapists and senior social workers exercise both organisational and occupational power simultaneously.

Second, there may be power relationships between occupations. In the context of the caring professions the clearest examples may be seen in the extent to which the medical profession exercises power over nursing and the remedial therapies. Yet this power relationship is not one which can be conceived of as operating in a single direction. Parkin (1979) and Salaman (1979) have suggested, variously, that power can be exercised 'both ways' (as it were) in a relationship. Parkin (1979), examining the way in which occupations achieve closure (the definition and maintenance of the boundaries of the occupation) argues that some exercise power in *excluding* others while those who are excluded may exercise power in *usurping* (challenging) the position of the former. This is seen for example in the way in which medicine, having defined its occupational boundaries to exclude nursing in such a way that nursing is separate but controlled, faces the efforts of nursing to achieve its own autonomy through closure as a distinct occupational group. The concept of closure will be explored further in Chapter 4.

Salaman introduces the connection between occupation and hierarchy, in so far as his concepts of power as *control* and *resistance* imply their relation to superordinate and subordinate groups respectively. These concepts enable the reintroduction of the hierarchical element into the consideration of the occupational relationship between medicine and nursing. Where the power of doctors is seen in medical control of nursing, the power of nursing is seen in its resistance (which in turn is part of a struggle towards self-control). These forms are occupational because they are based on concepts of the nature and scope of the work undertaken by the different groups, and not (at face value) on other social factors. (However, as I will argue below, there are other aspects to be considered, notably gender and race, and occupational power cannot be explained without reference to these.)

Third the power of occupations may be considered in the context of the relationship between the members of an occupation and those who use or receive the sevices which it provides. (This question forms the subject of Chapter 5.) Patients and/or clients are created by caring professions but stand outside as distinct social groups. Here again we can see a pattern of exclusion, and the beginnings of usurpation. The extent to which this relationship is also one of control and resistance is less clear, although Wilding (1982) argues that control is present, derived from the support by the state (even where the state is not the direct employer) which gives professions a central role in defining needs and problems and in allocating resources. Resistance is more fragmented, and may be seen in the range of criticisms and attacks which are levied against professions by groups of service users, by politicians, by journalists, by academics and so on. Examples of this range from the growth of autonomous service user groups, through criticism of social work in the UK over the issue of child sexual abuse throughout the 1970s and 1980s, to the more general challenges to legitimacy by the state as a basis for greater control (as discussed in Chapter 1).

So, it can be seen that there are occupational aspects of power, which are not discrete, but which overlap with the hierarchical aspects. Indeed, the argument which will be developed in subsequent chapters of this book will be that hierarchy and occupation as aspects of power in the caring professions interweave with each other.

Clients

I have referred already to the power of professionals in relation to their clientele, both in the context of individual meetings and also more generally through professional discourses in which 'clients' are socially constructed as objects of an occupation. However, for the most part any implicit 'theory of the client', the conception of the object of professional service with which a caring professional operates, remains locked within the self-definition of the professions. 'The patient' or 'the client' are defined in relation to nursing, remedial therapies or social work, and although an implicit 'theory of the client' may be a central feature of those professions the client is constructed by inference through the professional definition of needs and in general and shifting images (Pithouse, 1987; Gilmore, 1988). Hadley and Hatch note one possible outcome as the treatment of service users in some situations as if they were 'lower level employees' (1981, p. 21), although there are ambiguities about this position to which I will return in Chapter 5.

Beresford and Croft (1986) argue that as a consequence of the primacy of the professions in concepts of 'the client' the users of services are marginalised within the organisation and practice of caring professions. They are marginalised organisationally through their location in the production of health and welfare, and this sets the scene for their subordination within the context of individualised practice. In both instances the client is an object rather than a subject. They may be researched, but they are not consulted or involved in the definition of the needs which caring professionals address, either generally or specifically.

The client is contrasted with the concept of the citizen by Jordan (1987), Croft and Beresford (1989) and Taylor (1989). This concept of the citizen is of someone who is not only the actual or potential user of professional services, but who is also involved democratically in the control of those services. Professionalism within the welfare state is marked by a lack of participation on the part of actual or potential service users (Hadley and Hatch, 1981; Taylor, 1989) and a failure to be relevant to the commitments and interests of actual or potential service users (Jordan, 1987; Croft and Beresford, 1989). Hadley and Hatch (1981) explain this as the consequence of the faith in the central state on the part of the advocates of welfare, and suggest localised, participatory forms of organisation as the way forward. In contrast, Croft and Beresford (1989) and Taylor (1989) place emphasis on the class basis of the state services which have been the main context in which caring professions have developed. The majority of the clients of public services are from the working classes while the services are controlled by the state which represents the interest of the dominant social classes. So for Croft and Beresford, and for Taylor, the developments suggested by Hadley and Hatch will not be possible while a strong central state is controlled by the 'New Right' and is concerned to create privatised markets in welfare in which the client is cast in the role of consumer, emphasising their separation from the production of health and welfare, and reshaping rather than challenging the overall power of professionals.

'Race'

'Race' is a social construct. That is, it does not refer to any essential features of distinction between human beings but rather reflects a series of historical constructions of social, political and cultural differences. Racism can be seen as the combination of prejudice (based on physical and culture differences) with the exercise of power (Manning and Ohri, 1982; Brittan and Maynard, 1984). The development of white racism is bound up with the history of imperialism and colonisation but although it is a long history it is one which has a continued immediacy (Kovel, 1970). White societies are the product of their colonialist past. Either they are colonising societies which have drawn in people from their colonies (as in Western Europe), or else they are colonial societies which have drawn in people from other societies as well as colonising an indigenous population (as in North America or Australia). In each case, the society has developed around white racism, in which conflicts of interest implicit biases and the language with which they are structured create and sustain distinctions of supposed racial superiority and inferiority between white and black. Here I am following the convention of generic terms, that the use of the concept 'black' in this way covers a diversity which includes people of African, Afro-Caribbean, Arab, Asian, Chinese, native American and native Australian origin. In the USA the term 'people of colour' is used in the same way.

Racism, as oppression in structure and practice, is interwoven with capitalism and patriarchy and is embedded in structural and cultural processes (Benedict, 1942; Fanon, 1967; Kovel, 1970; Brittan and Maynard, 1984; Gilroy, 1987). Indeed, because colonialism is so closely bound up with the historical growth of capitalism it is more difficult to disentangle racism from capitalism as a relatively autonomous structure in a way which is relevant to understanding patriarchy (Walby, 1986) (I will return below to this point). For example, Phizacklea and Miles (1980) argue that the class location of many black people in the UK is directly related to the recruitment of manual workers from former colonies in the 1950s and 1960s. Similarly the location of black people in US society is directly related to the history of slavery in that country, and to its subsequent economic development. Nevertheless, as Phizacklea and Miles themselves point out, it is inadequate to reduce issues of racism to those of class or to see racism only as a reflection of the class structure. What it is important to recognise is that the structure are essentially intertwined (Brittan and Maynard, 1984; Gilroy, 1987).

The echoes of colonialism are reproduced in contemporary health and welfare work in the relationship between white and black, both professionals and non-professionals. The first area of this reproduction is the internal structures of the caring professions. Who does what is a question not only of hierarchy and occupation but is also a matter of the ways in which white people benefit at the expense of

black people. The patterns of entry into different professional groups and the types of jobs to which people are
recruited when they are admitted are organised around
race. The opportunities for black people to enter the ranks
of qualified nursing or social work are considerably fewer
than those for a white person. In the USA, for example,
the role of licensed practical nurse is the part of the profession which black nurses are most likely to occupy, and
this compares equally with the UK, where black nurses are
most frequently represented amongst state enrolled nurses
(the lower qualified grade) and nursing auxiliaries (Brown,
1975; Doyal *et al.*, 1981). In social work the situation is
similar in many respects. There are relatively few black
social workers in the UK, for example, and they are
located mostly in the less prestigious areas, such as residential work (see, for example, Rooney, 1987).

   The second area in which racism is reproduced within
the caring professions is in the relationships between members of these occupations and the people who use their
services (whether such usage is voluntary or involuntary).
This can be characterised as a situation in which white
professionalism meets the black citizen. Such meetings take
place in the context of societies which structure the
relationships between white and black people, and so set
the boundaries within which caring professions provide
their services. The consequences of this have been either
that black service users have become constructed as patho-
logical or else their needs have been marginalised (Bhalla
and Blakemore, 1981; Bryan *et al.*, 1985; Stubbs, 1987;
Rooney, 1987; Williams, 1987). Racist power is expressed
through the construction of black people as 'other', which
in turn is based on a construction of white people as the
'standard'. This permeates the ideas and practices of the
caring professions in ways which are often not clearly
articulated, but which create services that continually
reproduce the dominance of white over black personally,
culturally and structively. It is more than an issue of inap-
propriateness in service delivery, although that is a crucial
element; it is about the exercise of racially ordered power
in every aspect of professional structure and action.

Racism should not be seen as a uniform, monolithic aspect of power. The connections with other issues, such as class and gender, are complex. The experience and structural realities of black people differ between classes and between women and men, so that an analysis of racism is necessary but not sufficient to grasp the whole picture. The position of a black woman enrolled or licensed nurse, for example, can only be understood in relation to racism, gender and class. Nevertheless, discussions about professions and professionalism frequently fail to make these connections because they fail to take racism into account. While there are exceptions, such as Brown's (1975) exploration of nursing in the USA, or recent analysis of social work in the UK (Cheetham, 1982; Stubbs, 1985; Rooney, 1987), much of the literature has portrayed the caring professions in a 'colour blind' fashion. Racism in caring professions is examined further in Chapter 6.

Gender

As with racism, patriarchal power in caring professions is a part of the wider social structures of Western European and North American societies, although they are not simply parallel but simultaneous (Carby, 1982; Brittan and Maynard, 1984; Bryan *et al.*, 1985). Patriarchy must be understood as a structure of power in that through these social relationships men dominate women in the resolution of conflict, the definition of publicly disputed issues and the formation of the language through which actions and institutions are structured (Spender, 1980). The most extreme examples of the former are rapes and physical assaults (Brownmiller, 1976; Hanmer and Saunders, 1984), although much feminist analysis (and that of men sympathetic to feminism: Morgan, 1987; Hearn, 1987) argues that *all* men benefit from the social processes in which violence is an end of the continuum and not a separate phenomenon. The continuum moves across sexual harassment through instances where men routinely dominate women, such as in the family and the workplace, in ways which are perceived as natural and even benign by some women as well as by most men (Hearn and Parkin, 1987).

Analysis which is informed by feminist or pro-feminist ideas tends to be associated with two main approaches: socialist feminism and radical feminism (Walby, 1986; Wise, 1985; Rojek *et al.*, 1988). In addition, Rojek *et al.* (1988) also identify liberal feminism as an approach in analysing the development of caring professions (particularly social work). Liberal feminism is characterised by a concern with 'equal rights', rather than with patriarchy. Expressed briefly, socialist feminism and radical feminism differ in respect of their understanding of the connections between patriarchy and capitalism. Socialist feminism regards patriarchy as contingent on capitalism, while radical feminism sees patriarchy and capitalism as autonomous structures whose interconnections are more diverse. Yet this debate often fails to recognise subtle variations in aspects of the relationship between patriarchy and capitalism (Walby, 1986, p. 7). In contrast Walby proposes the concept of 'relative autonomy' as necessary to enable varying relationships between production (capitalism) and reproduction (patriarchy) to be considered and for the significance of racism to be grasped. Indeed there are parallels here with concepts of racism as relatively autonomous (Brittan and Maynard, 1984). Women in different class positions, and black and white women, share oppression under patriarchy while at the same time being separated by class and racism.

Patriarchy is not monolithic. Not only does it take different forms in different contexts, operate on different levels and articulate with other structural aspects such as class and race, but also it must not be seen as impervious to criticism. Nevertheless, there is a relative absence of gender and patriarchy as issues in organisational studies, in particular the classic theoretical texts, which can be seen as a lacuna created by the male dominance of research and other academic work (Hearn and Parkin, 1987). Recently the issues of gender and patriarchy have become somewhat more evident in studies of professions and occupations, although in this area also the critique has been small, if sharply focused (Davis and Brook, 1985).

As with racism, there are two elements which tie gender into the issues of hierarchy and occupation in the caring professions. First, the extent to which the internal structures of the caring professions are gendered is an issue which has become increasingly apparent. Not only are the numbers of men in senior positions within nursing and social work, in absolute terms as well as in proportion to their numbers in these professions as a whole, closely allied to wider social conceptions of management as a masculine activity (Brown, 1975; Popplestone, 1980; Hearn, 1982; Davis and Brook, 1985; Keddy *et al.*, 1986: Hearn and Parkin, 1987), but gender divisions may also be seen in the ways the practices of the caring professions are constructed (Carpenter, 1977; Dale and Foster, 1986; Howe, 1986b). Both these aspects are related to the stereotypical understanding of caring as a feminine aspect of social life. The consequence is that caring professions become bifurcated between 'men's work' (controlling) and 'women's work' (caring). This division may be internal, as in nursing and social work, or external (the male/masculine control is exercised by another occupation) as in the relationship between medicine and nursing, occupational therapy or physiotherapy (Wallis, 1987a; Schutzenhofer, 1988). As I will argue in Chapter 7, the issue is often that of the presence or absence of men at all as much as it is that of their numerical dominance.

There is a gender distinction also in the way in which the users of services are constructed by caring professions, and this is the second element of gender as a form of power. Again, research evidence shows that the way in which health and social services are provided is related to the sex of the service user and her or his immediate family members (Finch and Groves, 1980; Davis and Brook, 1985; Gelsthorpe, 1987; Robinson, 1989). For example, women service users tend to be treated less favourably than men in the degree of support they may be given, and women's behaviour is often viewed differently to that of men within professional theories. This differential treatment combines with the gendered nature of the professions themselves, so that the power exercised by a nurse, a remedial therapist or a social worker will be related to whether or not the nurse, the therapist or the social worker is a man or a woman, and whether or not the service user also is a man or a woman.

In these ways gender opeates as an aspect of power, explicitly and implicitly. Gender is interwoven with issues of hierarchy, occupation and racism in the structures and practices, the theories and the language of the caring professions, forming both the taken-for-granted biases within and between occupations, and between them and service users, as well as the socially constructed grounds of open conflicts of interest.

The relationship between aspects of power.   In the preceding discussion I have made repeated reference to the interconnections of the different aspects of power with which this discussion is concerned. The caring professions cannot be understood without reference to issues of hierarchy, occupation, the clientele, race, and gender, which are not isolated from each other in the lived historical world.

To return to the earlier instance of the nurse, the patient and the drug treatment, it may now be seen that power in such a situation may only be understood if actions (of the nurse, of the patient, and of other possible actors such as a doctor) are placed in context. The context is the social structure, the set of relationships of which hierarchy, occupation, the construction of clients, race and gender are part. So how power is exercised in the hypothetical situation will be related to factors such as the hierarchical and occupational position of the nurse, the class of the patient, whether the nurse and the patient are male or female, whether the nurse and the patient are black or white, and so on. It may be anticipated that a white male senior nurse exercises power very differently from a black female nursing assistant, and that both will have a different basis for their actions towards a middle-class white male patient and towards a working-class black female patient. This supposition may be tested against empirical evidence, and

I will discuss various issues arising from this understanding of power in the following chapters.

Two problems emerge for this study from the interconnectedness of aspects of power. First, there is an analytical dilemma involved in the separate discussion of each aspect of power. So that each may be considered fully this book focuses on each in turn. However, this approach brings with it the risk that each form could take the appearance of total autonomy, distinct and self-contained. So it is necessary to comment briefly here that while useful as a device for sharpening attention to a particular set of issues the ordering of subsequent chapters does not imply a prioritising of questions. The thread of my argument is that the problems of hierarchy and professionalism are not only to be understood internally or in relation to each other but also in relation to the position of service users and problems of racism and gender.

This approach also will address the second question, namely the explanatory role which any one aspect may have in relation to the other aspects. The concept of relative autonomy suggests that there are degrees of causal effect between aspects of power, but that each should also be seen as having an independence of formation and development. So, while none of the aspects identified here can be said to cause the other, in the caring professions or the wider social structure, each has an effect on and is affected by the other. For example, while patriarchy alone does not create occupational divisions, nevertheless occupational development may be based on varying degrees of gender segregation in types of employment and between paid and unpaid work (Barron and Norris, 1976; Hakim, 1979; Dex, 1985; Walby, 1986; Hearn and Parkin, 1987), so that we can say that gender is a significant issue in the way caring professions like nursing, the remedial therapies and social work have developed. In turn, gender segregation is given concrete form in divisions within and between occupations.

The aspects of power with which this study is concerned do not interconnect in a vacuum, but in the context of the historical development of caring professions. Indeed, power can be seen as an integral part of their professionalisation, and it is to the histories of the caring professions that I will turn in the next chapter.

3

Professions and Hierarchy

Historical developments

The organisational structures of the agencies within which caring professions are employed have grown and increased in complexity as their relationship to the welfare state has developed historically. From small numbers of nurses in hospitals, or the voluntary societies of the nineteenth century which were the beginnings of social work, the processes of change have led to vast health and welfare bureaucracies employing many thousands of people, and touching the lives of large numbers of citizens.

In this chapter I want to examine one particular aspect of the organisational developments of the caring professions: hierarchy. The reason why this aspect is identified for detailed scrutiny is that it forms a central aspect of power in the organisation of nursing, remedial therapies and social work, and an aspect which, as I will discuss, contributes to the forms taken by specific professions in the course of their development. As a consequence of this central place in understanding such professions, the concept of hierarchy has become one of the key issues in debates about their nature and structure. To paraphrase Howe (1986a, p 97), we have to ask what it is about the development of such professions that they find themselves organised in particular ways, which are based on managerial hierarchies.

There has been a hierarchical element in nursing from the earliest days, in the role of the hospital matron. If the origins of nursing as a trained profession are dated from

53

the reforming work of the nursing schools which were founded in various parts of Europe in the mid-nineteenth century, then it may be seen that a nascent hierarchy was developing from the beginning (Abel-Smith, 1960). This is evident in the way in which nurses took over the role of matron and brought it within the profession, where previously matrons had been effectively the senior administrators of hospitals, overseeing cleaning, cooking, the purchase of stores and so on as well as nursing (often with less priority given to nursing) (Williams, 1980; Dingwall *et al.*, 1988, pp. 15–16). The hierarchy was based on class and gender assumptions. Specific recruits for special training were sought on the grounds of their capacity to be prepared for supervisory roles early in their careers and on their ability to pay for their training (the two factors seemingly intertwined), while men were recruited into mental hospitals but not general nursing (Bellaby and Oribabor, 1980; Baly, 1987; Dingwall *et al.*, 1988). The trained professional nurses became integrated into the structures of the hospitals as they were then organised, including a hierarchical distribution of power and authority within nursing and between nursing and other occupational groups.

The prototypes of early social work are diverse, including the workhouses, the settlements, the police court missions, housing schemes and the Charity Organisation Society (COS) (Young and Ashton, 1956; Parry and Parry, 1979). Here also hierarchies are evident from the beginning. The early social workers were supervised and directed, in workhouse visiting, in the police court missions, in the settlements and in casework. As with nursing, recruitment was divided on class and gender lines, with 'respectable' working-class men and women being employed in some areas (workhouses, police court missions, some casework) while middle-class recruitment was largely of women into casework and the developing supervisory positions (Young and Ashton, 1956; Walton, 1975; Parry and Parry, 1979; Hearn, 1982). Throughout the subsequent century it has been casework which has continued to dominate social work hierarchies in the UK. The position of middle-class men was more ambiguous, as social work was seen as part of general pre-professional experience for men intending to go into law or the church. Indeed, these men often continued their association with social work in the power exerted over social work by such professions.

The histories of the remedial therapies follow closely those of nursing and social work. For example, in the UK, nurses and midwives were active in the origins of physiotherapy in the late nineteenth and early twentieth centuries (Chartered Society of Physiotherapy (CSP), 1980). Occupational therapy also emerged from the actions of sections within nursing, social work and medicine (Diasio-Serrett, 1985; Levine, 1987; Wallis, 1987b). As a consequence, they too began in organisational contexts already defined hierarchically, including the dominance of doctors and matrons within hospitals (Lankin, 1983; Diasio-Serrett, 1985). With nursing and social work, occupational therapy and physiotherapy share origins as occupations overwhelmingly for women, from the working classes as well as the middle classes but dominated by the latter. So their formation, as with nursing and social work, must be understood in the context of the organisational and gender hierarchies of the society which produced them.

Late nineteenth and early twentieth century Western European and North American societies were epitomised by the German sociologist Weber as hierarchical (Gerth and Mills, 1948). Weber traced the development of hierarchy as a diffuse social form to the influence on industrial society of the military as a model for the organisation of large social groups. For example, this can be seen in the growth of the civil service and local government in the UK, within which, to varying degrees, nursing, the remedial therapies and social work have come to be located. So the origins of hierarchies are not to be found in some intrinsic aspect of the caring professions under discussion, but in the wider social structures and processes of which their development was a part. Hierarchy was becoming endemic in the organisation of every area of public life.

These caring professions can be said to have originated from the work of women (for the most part) who in other respects had limited opportunities for professional or public life, and even amongst the middle and upper classes had limited access to independent action relative to men (Hearn, 1982). These occupations developed under the close control either of men in the established professions, or of middle-class women who were themselves acting under hierarchical gender relations. More recently studies of caring professions have identified racial divisions (although these were present also from the beginning stages of such occupations) which are grounded in the racisms of Western European and North American societies, and which at times have been expressed in deliberate recruitment policies (Carpenter, 1977; Torkington, 1983; Stubbs, 1985; Rooney, 1987).

A debate has emerged in writing about caring professions, especially social work, between the view of hierarchy as a recent phenomenon which has become an issue only in the latter period of occupational development and the view that hierarchies have been an integral part of these occupations from their origins (Leonard, 1973; Carpenter, 1977; Cohen and Wagner, 1982). This debate about the phenomenon of hierarchy requires explanation. It is associated with the issue of autonomy as a key aspect of professionalism, and so draws our attention to the importance of the theory of professional proletarianisation which has emerged in the same period in which managerialism has become the dominant ideology of the organisations employing caring professionals (Derber, 1982).

The issue of hierarchy relates to our understanding of the histories of caring professions and also to our understanding of their contemporary forms and structures. The substantial changes in the structures and organisation of caring professions over the last century have been shaped within the expanding scale of the services provided by these professions, and the degree of direct state sponsorship and control. The size and institutional location of the caring professions, in turn, have been related in particular to the growth of managerialism, and to recurrent debates about the relationship of hierarchy and professionalism. These issues provide the background to the analysis of the modern organisation of caring professions.

Management and managerialism

The development of work organisation in industrial society has been described by Braverman (1974) as 'deskilling', a process in which the conceptualisation of work and its execution are separated. Deskilling is the separation of work and the knowledge required to produce that work, locating each aspect of production with different groups of people, so that production can be standardised and can be controlled by managers rather than by expert craftspeople. The expertise of management takes precedence over the technical competence necessary to produce goods or services and so managers dominate the workforce, which, because tasks are standardised and easily learned, is readily replaceable. Braverman argues that this description applies to approximately 70 per cent of the working population (1974, p. 35).

Although Braverman does not deal at any length with caring professions, they are located clearly within his formulation that middle layers of employment have characteristics of work rationalisation and systematisation while at the same time having areas of work discretion and to various degrees controlling the work of other people. That caring professions show elements of work rationalisation and discretion places them in an ambiguous conceptual position, which may serve as a vehicle to explain the debates around managerialism and hierarchies in those professions. This is particularly so as Braverman envisaged an increased proletarianisation of such work, and refers to health and welfare services as having been turned into commodities where previously they were produced informally within the family and the community (Cousins, 1987, p. 37).

The concept of deskilling managerialism has been applied to social work in the UK by Simpkin (1983), who argues that after the 1971 creation of local government social services and social work departments, consolidated by the 1974 local government reorganisation, social work has become subject to increased separation of control and practice through a burgeoning of management posts and functions. Simpkin describes the large local government social services and social work departments as 'Seebohm factories', producing welfare (1983, pp. 17–19). A similar portrayal of social work in the USA is produced by Cohen and Wagner (1982), who list salary levels, forms of bargaining power, physical working conditions, workloads, supervision, the divorce of policy and practice and low opportunities for advancement as factors demonstrating the industrial nature of social work employment. They draw a parallel with nursing also (1982, pp. 159–60) that proletarianisation equates with a failure of professionalism.

The concept of proletarianisation may be traced to the work of Mills (1956) in his analysis of what he called the 'managerial demiurge'. This phenomenon is the tendency, as Mills saw it, of all occupations to segment, with power located in a managerial segment. The image is freely adapted to caring professions, in that Mills was referring to the separation of professionals as the managers and a newly created group of administrators as the office proletariat. That practitioners in caring professions, occupying relatively low hierarchical positions, should see themselves in this way may be taken as a reflection of the increased visibility of hierarchy in the managerial revolutions and the clash between that and the dominant occupational cultures of professionalism.

Nursing in the UK went through organisational changes similar to those experienced by social work, following the implementation of the Salmon Report (1966). There was an increase in the number of management levels, but also, perhaps more significantly, there was a change in the language of management, with the introduction of 'nursing officers', which formed a series of management grades up to 'chief nursing officer', at the same time as the 'matron' disappeared from the scene (Ralph, 1989). These titles changed again in the NHS reorganisation of 1974, with its concentration on geographical structures forming levels at region, area, district and division (further refined in 1982) (Carpenter, 1977). These changes brought nursing into the management groups of hospitals and health authorities in a pattern which had some similarities with USA structures (Mauksch, 1966), but which established nurses in the UK on an organisational level with doctors and administrators. This period of incorporation into management was superceded by the later introduction of the principle of general management in which the separation of management from all professional aspects of work has reduced the power of nursing in the decision-making process (Cousins, 1987, p. 167).

For Bellaby and Oribabor (1980) the contradictions expressed in the idea of 'nursing management' can be traced to the foundations of the profession. The struggles to professionalise, they argue, were based on the capture of an autonomous space in which nurses could control their own occupation. This was achieved through compromises with the medical profession and the management of hospitals. The proletarianised strand was in-built, and is brought to the fore in the efforts of the modern state, discussed in Chapter 1, to control the growth of health costs and to limit professional power in order to accomplish that end. Bellaby and Oribabor suggest that the increased separation of clinical and managerial levels can be seen as a more constant development, and can be related to the increases in trade union membership amongst nurses (1980, p. 172).

The organisation of the remedial therapies has developed in a manner similar to that of nursing, although this has depended on the type of employing organisation. For example, in the UK occupational therapists have been employed increasingly in social services and social work departments, in which they have occupied positions similar to those of basic grade social work practitioners (Stewart, 1988). Sometimes this has meant accountability to a manager who has a social work background (a point which will be pursued in the next chapter), although in all instances it has been within the hierarchical management structure. Occupational therapists and physiotherapists who are employed in the (UK) NHS have developed separate hierarchies, which are shorter (in terms of the number of levels between the basic grade practitioner and the most senior manager) at the cost of semi-marginalisation from the main locations of power (Robbins, 1972; Tolliday, 1972). For example, there has not been an equivalent position to the director of nursing with a specific place in the highest levels of agency management for each remedial therapy; although there are separate managers at district level (CSP, 1984), there is subsuming of remedial therapies within the broader grouping of 'professions ancillary to medicine' in the management committees. This situation has parallels, also, with the older pattern of management in US hospitals (Mauksch, 1966, p. 119). It appears probable that the structural location of the remedial therapies is reflected in the inattention to organisational and structural issues in the writings of remedial therapists, and the relative ignoring of remedial therapists in academic studies of organisation, in comparison either to nursing or to social work.

In both nursing and social work these developments may represent quite rapid periods of change, in which processes become clearer and sharper; but there are two questions which must be asked of the proletarianisation argument. First, can these developments be said to be radical new departures for these professions in which previously unknown organisational structures and processes of power were introduced? Second, what were the aspects of the changes which encouraged some parts of the caring professions to accept or even seek the changes?

The reorganisations in the UK of health and social services took place within a climate of much wider change in the management of the welfare state. Throughout the 1960s there was a concern with the relationship between the size and scope of local government services and the National Health Service and the organisational forms within which they were provided. This period saw the growth of enthusiasm for the principles of corporate management, culminating in the Maud Report (1967) in which the organisation of local government was to be based on that common in large-scale corporate businesses (Cockburn, 1977), and in the reorganisation of the NHS which was driven by the objective of controlling costs (Bellaby and Oribabor, 1980, p. 172). The impact on nursing in the UK was focused on the recommendations of the Salmon Report (1966), on social work in the Kilbrandon (1966) and Seebohm (1968) Reports. Contained within these developments was a shift of thinking about the principal aim in state services from one of 'adequate administration' to one of 'effective management' (Cockburn, 1977, p. 15). As Cockburn notes, it was not only the services, and the people working within them which were to be managed, but the whole of society at the local level. The idea that the purpose of local government was more explicitly the management of society rather than the administration of services on its behalf produced the formulation of the 'local state' (pp. 41ff.) which has passed into common analytical usage.

The effect of corporate management principles was to reduce the number of separate departments in UK local government, and to increase the size of each department. Its explicit purpose was to enable a single general manager (the Chief Executive) to have a sufficiently small span of control. The impact on the constituent departments was to increase the hierarchy by creating the need for more managerial levels so that the process could be repeated at lower levels. Within the UK health service the impact of corporate management was even more complex, because of the bringing together of separate professions, between which there were relationships of supervision and direction which were separated from line management, and which continued to be seen in sub-hierarchies (Hickson and McCullough, 1980, p. 30).

The principles of general management can be regarded as a further development from corporate management. Where the corporate model makes a comparison between departmental heads (for example Director of Social Services, or Director of Nursing) and industrial directors (sales, production, and so on) and places the chief executive in a Managing Director role, general management creates a cleavage between the top manager with an overall view and the sectional managers whose junior position is much clearer. In summary the senior role has developed from first amongst equals, through leader of a team, to a qualitatively distinct senior management role. In the UK this has been more pronounced in the NHS than in local government, and the impact has therefore been more noticeable in nursing and the remedial professions than in social work, with the exception of Northern Ireland where there is a common organisational structure between health and social services.

The connections between caring professions and the state are to be found not only in the combination of caring and controlling tasks which they undertake but also in the organisational structures within which they are employed. Through these structures the caring professions are accountable to the local state, whether this is the elected local council or the appointed health authority. Accountability in this sense should be understood as a social relationship in which one party has the capacity to require of the other an account for the other's actions. Hierarchies, therefore, are the means by which power is exercised over these professions by the state and which in turn provide the basis for the exercise of power by the professionals.

Hierarchies as control and resistance

The preceding discussion began with a consideration of Braverman's theory of the labour process. However, it is necessary to note that this theory has been subject to a number of criticisms, the areas of which Cousins (1987, pp. 39ff.) identifies as:

- the concept of control – empirical studies have shown that there are wide variations in the capacity of organised labour to exert resistance to managerial control (Cousins cites Littler, 1982; Gospel and Littler, 1983);
- the frontier of control – in day-to-day work the process of control is made explicit at its boundaries, the points at which there is struggle between workers and management;
- forms of control – there have been a variety of ways

of organising work control, and Cousins cites Edwards' (1983) distinctions between direct, technical and bureaucratic forms of control;

- the problem of control – in practice, to ensure cooperation from the workforce, management must allow some degree of autonomy so that the creative potential of that workforce can be utilised in production, and;
- management – management itself is not a monolithic entity, but made up of groups which may have competing interests, and at the same time has the problem of working through other groups which may misunderstand or subvert its intentions.

In each of these areas, Cousins argues, Braverman is limited by two factors (1987, p. 38). First, he does not permit himself to take into account the subjectivity of social action. Both managers and workers are seen to be determined by the structures of advanced capitalism. Second, Braverman combines the determinacy of Marx with the pessimism of Weber, and sees the development of managerialism and deskilling as inevitable.

A different approach to the interplay between Marxist and Weberian ideas is to be found in the work of Salaman (1979). Salaman argues that in understanding organisational structures it is important to look beyond the detail of empirical observation and description to the underlying processes of an organisation. Hierarchy is frequently portrayed as a technical solution to the separation of design and execution of work tasks (from empirical observation), an understanding which masks the connections between hierarchies at the general level (theoretical analysis), where they can be seen as ways in which some human groups control other human groups. Ideas of efficiency or rationality (for example, in coordination) can then be seen as ideological, obscuring the political nature of organisations, that hierarchies are power structures (Salaman, 1979, pp. 21–2). The hierarchy appears natural, also, because it is a reproduction of social relationships throughout society. As Salaman notes, 'power within organisations is related to *the distribution of power outside the organisation*' (1979, p. 112, emphasis original).

Furthermore, just as the structures of organisations must be examined in the context of the wider society of which they are part, so the actions of both workers and management are affected also by the roles and statuses they occupy outside as well as inside the organisation, and these are influenced by other institutional forces such as education, religion, race, gender and the family (Silverman, 1970). These may reinforce ideologies of hierarchy, that the unequal distribution of power is natural or necessary, or they may serve to undermine such ideologies in some way, by making possible questions about the naturalness or desirability of hierarchical structures.

In addition to the outside influences which may make hierarchy a disputed form of organisation, there are also the effects of the division of labour already noted, that subordinates may gain knowledge and skills beyond those of the superordinate, and so have to be allowed a degree of freedom to undertake their work. This is of particular importance in considering caring professions, where the personalisation of work is especially evident. As a consequence, Hickson and McCullogh argue: 'Subordinates are aware of the counterpower they possess which limits the power of the boss. They come to know their own jobs better than their superiors know these jobs, and so . . . superiors then have to depend on their subordinates' expertise and the latter gain power as a result' (1980, p. 44). The consequences are that while the superordinate may have more power than individual or groups of subordinates, such power is not absolute: it is not greater than the total power of all subordinates (1980, p. 30). Salaman has defined the collective power of subordinates as the power of resistance, most usually expressed in trade union activity (1979, p. 151), although this may not always be the case. It may take the form of a professional association, or it may be a more informal action on the part of a group whose knowledge and skills are crucial in relation to a certain task. In each case the hierarchy provides a framework within which the superordinate is able to exert some leverage, through control over other parts of the organisation, whose cooperation may at some stage be necessary for the group exercising the power of resistance. So, control constantly has to be reasserted in response to resistance, organised or otherwise, leading to the conclusion that neither control nor resistance are foregone conclusions, but are reproduced in the social relationships of the workplace.

The implications of these critiques for the caring professions are that while the growth of hierarchies has followed the pattern already outlined, this should not be seen in a determinist way. An example of theories used deterministically has been the work strata concept, which has been applied to both health and social services (Rowbottom *et al.*, 1973; Rowbottom *et al.*, 1974; Billis *et al.*, 1980). The work strata concept argues that hierarchies have developed as a technical solution to the variation in work capacity of individuals. This has been grasped with enthusiasm by senior managers (for example Harbert, 1988), but has been critically analysed by Whittington and Bellaby (1979) who argue that symptoms have been mistaken for causes. Rather than seeing hierarchies as the product of varying capacity, they show that heirarchies shape capacity through constraints placed on action and individual development. Furthermore, hierarchy has grown as a means of controlling professional workers in periods of expanding demand and rising costs. Hierarchies are not the inevitable consequence of the type of occupations which comprise the caring professions, nor of their individual members, but have been produced and are sustained and change in context. So to understand the contemporary organisation of the caring professions and the significance of hierarchies for these occupations, three further questions must be asked. First, what are the important aspects of hierarchical organisation in everyday practice for caring professionals? Second, under what circumstances are hierarchies resisted by lower-level professionals and other workers? Third, to what extent are caring professions themselves organised around the hierarchies with which they have developed?

Hierarchies in everyday practice

The hierarchies of the organisations employing caring professions may be seen as the organisational means whereby the day-to-day actions of the members of these occupations are controlled. To this end they legitimise and make possible the control of some professionals (the subordinate) by others (the superordinate). For much of the time these hierarchies have a matter-of-fact place in the perceptions of the people working within them. Hierarchical power is exercised through routinised sets of expectations about work, about objectives, methods, scope, and so on, in a context in which some professionals are defined as having the right and the capacity to influence and at times direct how that work should be undertaken. It is important to emphasise that these rights and capacities are structural rather than the properties of individuals. For example, a person may be seen as having the capacity to exert influence because of a degree of professional knowledge or skill which is recognised by colleagues, but to lack the power to exert influence because of the organisational position held. In contrast, someone who is not regarded as having such an outstanding level of professional competence may, nevertheless, have the capacity to exert influence because of the organisational position he or she holds. This has been noted in an empirical study by Satyamurti (1981), and also in my own study of UK social services departments in which one social worker summed up the point: 'Some [team leaders] I've felt more equal with . . . equal in terms of experience, intellectual capacity, (and there are some I've felt superior to, but that's an aside, in brackets). Professionally equal to, I think. Whilst accepting that because they're a [team leader] and I'm not, they have certain areas of experience and abilities I don't have' (Hugman, 1984, p. 435). This view of immediate managers is shared also with staff nurses, who may see their sister/charge nurse in a similar vein: 'with increasing specialism and advances in medical knowledge nursing administrators are sometimes embarrassingly ignorant of the complexities of the ward situation and tends to lead ward level staff to resent what appears to them to be a power structure which does not accord with this situation' (Carpenter, 1977, p. 185). Remedial therapists may regard the power of a manager in the same way, seeing the 'administrative' role as detached from the values and purposes of professional practice (Mercer, 1980; Bailey, 1988; Munroe, 1988).

An example of the way in which this power is routinised can be seen in the way in which hierarchies in caring professions regularly involve the separation of decision-making from contact with individual clients/patients. This might be in the context of a social worker making an assessment with a service user of the latter's needs, for example, which then has to be discussed with a manager in the social services department before a decision is made about the allocation of resources (where they are controlled by the manager); or it might be in the context of the ward sister/charge nurse making decisions about the allocation of work to nurses on the ward. In each of these instances we see the same phenomenon, namely the routine patterning of work so that the subordinate is brought directly under the control of the superordinate.

Such a way of conceptualising the roles of the people involved in hierarchical relationships emphasises particular differences, those of organisational position, while at the same time obscuring any similarities, such as those of professional background. In the instances given above the manager exercises power because of seniority, and that position carries an element of authority with it, legitimating the control over the subordinate. This stems from the ambiguous way in which organisational and professional hierarchies are interwoven. The manager is appointed on the basis of performance in a subordinate role, that of a practitioner in the case of appointments to first-level management, junior management to middle management, and so on. In this sense the organisational position, which is the source of power for that role, is gained as a consequence of professional criteria. Therefore, the manager is senior both in organisational and professional terms. So there is a situational logic, for the social worker quoted above and other professionals in similar contexts, that, even where the personal competence of an individual may not be accepted, expertise and capacity attach to the post which is occupied.

I have made passing reference to two ways in which hierarchies operate in caring professions: the separation of contact with the service user from decision-making; and in the way they may depend on and sustain particular forms and usages of knowledge. I want now to look at each of these in more detail.

The separation of decision-making from contact with service users. This is a phenomenon which can be seen in the caring professions in different forms and to varying degrees. In social work, for example, there is substantial evidence that this separation is routinised in most UK social work or social services departments (Smith, 1980; Satyamurti, 1981; Hugman, 1984; Pithouse, 1987). A similar pattern can be seen in the USA, whether in public or in independent agencies (Cohen and Wagner, 1982). The division of labour is such that the practitioner grade professional has the responsibility for forming an assessment with the service user about the latter's needs, which is then presented to a relevant manager for a decision. This is based on two assumptions: that the sphere of competence of the practitioner is in the interpersonal area (assessment of need, and interpersonal intervention such as counselling); and that the allocation of scarce resources is more appropriately made by someone with an overview of the range of service users for whom the assessment of need has been made. This may even extend to decisions about whether or not the service of the practitioner's time will be provided. The superior is able to enforce this through the organisational arrangements of agencies, in which resources are processes clerically, and the clerical staff are sanctioned to act only on the authorisation of the relevant manager (Hugman, 1984).

A parallel exists in nursing, where both registered and enrolled (UK) or licensed (USA) nurses administer treatments and undertake other direct work with patients, but where their sphere of competence is limited within the supervisory agreement of their superiors. For example, although a nurse may think that a particular treatment should be given in a certain way, if directed otherwise by the sister or charge nurse the nurse will be constrained to follow that instruction. The sanctions open to the sister or charge nurse to enforce an instruction are more rigid than those in social work, as they are based in concepts of hospital discipline. They relate, also, to the prescription of treatment by a third party (a doctor) (Mauksch, 1966). At the same time room for discretion on the part of the nurse may exist, as the work might be supervised only through a record written by the nurse rather than by direct observation on the part of the sister/charge nurse or the prescribing doctor, although the increased technicality of medicine reduces the scope for individual discretion in nursing. This analysis applies also to community nursing, although the balance between direction and the freedom of not being directly observed will vary according to the situation in which the nurse is working.

Hierarchy and the use of knowledge.   Forms of knowledge are related to the practices of different hierarchical levels. Indeed, as I have noted, a superordinate colleague is regarded as possessing such knowledge by virtue of occupying a senior position. There is a connection between the application of knowledge, such as the applied human sciences on which the caring professions' claims to knowledge bases rest, and the validation of this knowledge in the way it is used in power relationships (Gordon, 1980, p. 239). This is not to say that an idea is 'true' simply because it is promoted by the powerful (or that it is 'false' because it is promoted by the powerless). (There are instances when this becomes the case, such as in the public discrediting of midwives' independent knowledge by the medical profession, especially in parts of the USA (Versluysen, 1980; Friedman, 1987), although this involves a conflict between rather than within professional groups.) Even where there is no explicit conflict of interest in the knowledge of different subgroups, the dominant forms of knowledge with professions will be interrelated with the forms of knowledge expressed by the hierarchically senior members of a profession.

The hierarchical control of knowledge can be seen in the way in which professionals at the practitioner level rehearse or construct explanations of their work for a supervisor (Pithouse, 1987). Although nursing and the remedial therapies have an element of the relationship between practitioner and junior manager which combines inspection and advice, this has been developed in social work into a highly complex aspect of the managerial – professional practice (Satyamurti, 1981; Hugman, 1984; Pithouse, 1987). While the word supervision conveys a literal sense of looking at from above, and certainly expresses an explicit managerial function in social work, at the same time it has come to mean also a meeting in which a senior colleague helps a junior colleague to look at the professional aspects of the latter's work. In his study of a Welsh social services office Pithouse (1987) observed how this provided a context in which the hidden world of social work was made visible through written and spoken language. For the supervisors it was seen as a context in which they attempted to exert influence through promoting (teaching) ideas about what they thought constituted good practice (1987, pp. 73–4). Practitioners on the other hand described these encounters as exercises in self-presentation which stressed those aspects which they 'knew' to be congruent with the dominant forms of social work knowledge and not disclosing those aspects of their work which they 'knew' were incongruent (1987, pp. 76–8).

As Pithouse notes (1987, p. 73) this has parallels with Dingwall's (1976) observations about health visitor training, in which the assessment of task accomplishment is interwoven with judgements about the personal skills of the student. It is, as Dingwall says, the 'running together of doing and being' (1976, p. 338). As a branch of nursing, at the post-qualifying level, health visitors have differences from and similarities with the mainstream of hospital-based nursing in relation to this issue. They are different because, like social workers, their work is a hidden practice which has to be made visible through organisational means.

Usually it is undertaken in the patient's own home, without other professionals being present. The similarities are that as well as being supervised (in both senses of the word) through the nursing hierarchy there is also a consultative relationship with the medical profession, who, in addition, have the legally enshrined right to prescribe the treatments administered by nurses. The importance of being, as well as doing, in nursing appropriately seems to have been early feature as recent developments in nursing history indicate (Baly, 1987). In this context, the connection between being and doing is to be found in the realm of ideas, in both the formal theories and the informal everyday wisdom of the occupation.

The integration of an advisory and consultative role with that of inspection and control is evident also in the remedial therapies (Munroe, 1988). Here too the nature of supervision is ambiguous, reflecting both the professional and organisational aspects of the seniority on the part of the supervisor. Munroe breaks the supervisory role into constituent parts which not only include management, direction and organisation but also education and guidance. Each of these roles, it is suggested, are appropriately enacted on the basis of hierarchical seniority, and the problem which is identified is that of pursuading managers to encompass all aspects rather than dividing the roles into a dichotomy in which either organisation (management, direction) or professionalism (education, guidance) predominates.

The explicit uses of hierarchy. I have identified the control of the use of resources and the structuring of knowledge to define what is and is not appropriate within the caring professions. The common feature of these processes can be summarised as three elements: control; consultation; and communication.

• Control. The hierarchies of caring professions, through the interlocking of organisational and occupational seniority provide the framework within which control can be exerted over the junior members of the pro-

fessions, whose work can be routinely scrutinised and called to account.
- Consultation. The same framework also provides the basis for junior professionals to discuss their work with a senior, both to look at specific problems relating to individual cases and to look at the general formation and development of professional knowledge.
- Communication. Organisations operate on the basis of the flow of information, and in uncertain environments this will be more important. (Weeks, 1980, p. 203). Hierarchies provide the basis for the flow of information, about individual service users and about organisational policies, procedures and resources. However, this is not simply a value neutral, technical aspect of the organisation, but forms, as we have seen, the basis for the other features of the hierarchy.

These common features of the purposes of hierarchies in caring professions represents the interests of the powerful. That is, these uses of hierarchy as an organising principle enable the management of caring professions by superordinate members to be sustained. This is not to say that subordinates' interests are not also met to some extent in these processes, but rather that the interests of subordinates stand in a more ambiguous relationship to control, consultation and communication. Such ambiguity can be seen most clearly in situations of resistance, in which junior members of an organisation attempt, in different ways, to work against the hierarchy.

Resistance to hierarchy

There are three types of action on the part of practitioners which can be seen as resistance to hierarchical structures. The first of these, and that which is most widely evident, is in the maintenance of autonomous space in which the professional can exercise self-control over the work. The second and third types of action are less widely observed, as they involve, respectively, bending and breaking the rules of the organisation.

Brief reference has already been made to the maintenance of autonomous space by individual practitioners. It could be seen in the statements about the use of supervision to present a 'good' view of the practitioner to her or his senior and to obscure those aspects which would not be regarded as appropriate. The understandings which practitioners express about why autonomous space is important frequently make reference to the idea of the competent professional, and resistance to the intrusion of management levels into this work (Mercer, 1980; How, 1986a, p. 97; Mackay, 1989). This could be described as a 'professionalistic' understanding of one's occupation. Intellectually it draws on the trait approach to professions, in which individual autonomy of action is seen as a key characteristic, but in day-to-day work it can be seen as an attempt by professionals to maintain sufficient space to manage the demands of their job. For the practitioner in a managed profession this can present problems of self-image and of presentation of self in meetings with service users or other professionals. These problems have to be managed situationally (Pithouse, 1987). In my own study of social services departments, social work practitioners commented on this problem of image management in relation to the separation of contact with service users and decision-making about resources:

There is a feeling that something is 'wrong' in visiting a client and then being seen to go away, as it is distressing for the client where no assurances of what will happen can be given, and any detailed explanation of the procedure undermines the social worker's position; . . . it is sometimes the case that clients will look at me and think 'well, we're talking to the monkey rather than the organ grinder'. (Hugman, 1984, p. 224)

The same phenomenon was observed by Wasserman in a United States study, where such limitations extended to 'judgements about a client's need for an extra grocery order' (1971, p. 93). It would be possible to explain to the service user why the practitioner could not make a decision on the spot, but this would be experienced by the practitioner as undermining. Strategies which I observed included the worker saying that she or he would 'need to think about the situation', or would 'need to see what is available at the moment', which obscured the relatively powerless position of the practitioner to make such decisions. (This also indicates aspects of power exerted over service users, a theme which will be further developed in Chapter 5.)

The maintenance of autonomous space is, as I have already stated, ambiguous. The limits to the strategies I have just described are to be found in the way practitioners themselves make use of the separation of decision-making and contact with service users to avoid the problems of disagreement or antagonism from a service user. The dilemma here is to portray oneself as constrained in one's scope of action while at the same time maintaining the image of a competent professional. This is achieved through reference to legal requirements, agency policies or to ideas about the necessity of an action on professional grounds. Social workers see themselves as differing from nurses and remedial therapists in relation to the latter category, as the status of social work knowledge is often claimed to be less secure (Howe, 1986a, p. 96). Nevertheless, the common element is an attempt to obscure the relative powerlessness of the hierarchical position within a generalised idea of what any competent professional would do.

This differs from those situations in which practitioners define their own actions as the bending or breaking of the rules which are the basis of hierarchical control. Where previously I have been referring to the situations in which practitioners attempt to create space for autonomous actions within hierarchical power, the bending or breaking of rules involves much more direct forms of resistance. Yet they are not simply different degrees of the same-type actions but represent qualitatively different phenomena.

Bending rules can be defined as actions which make use of the knowledge practitioners have about service users, that much direct contact with service users is not directly supervised, and that the agency rules themselves may be ambiguous. For example, Smith (1980) has described how the concept of need is used variably to manage requests for help in social work, to accommodate other factors, such as the personal views of the practitioner, the strength of demand by the prospective service user, and so on. Indeed, the same practitioner might use such concepts differently in relation to different managers. The deliberate presentation of aspects of oneself in supervision discussed above is also an aspect of rule-bending. Studies of practice (Satyamurti, 1981; Keddy *et al.*, 1986; Pithouse, 1987) have concluded that practitioners engage in rule-bending simply to survive within what are experienced as contradictions in their work.

Breaking rules, in contrast, is when practitioners deliberately engage in actions which are contrary to the rules and procedures of the agency. Pearson argues that this is a form of political action, which he calls 'social banditry' (1975, pp. 136–7). By their very nature such actions are more likely to attract an explicitly controlling response from managers, and are therefore obscured from them (although they may be visible to colleagues of the same grade: Hugman, 1984, p. 450). An example of rule-breaking can be seen in this account of a discharge from a psychiatric hospital, given by another former patient:

> I remember a friend telling me how she was in a classic 'Catch–22' situation: a voluntary patient who would be made a compulsory patient if she tried to leave the hospital. A senior nurse helped her to escape by arranging for her husband to wait outside in a car and smuggling her out during a change of shift. (Read, 1989).

The key feature which makes this an example of rule-breaking is the expectation that had the action been visible hierarchically superordinate colleagues would have had the power to prevent it from taking place. The covert nature of rule-breaking is also continuous: it is not disclosed after the event. It remains possible for superiors to define it as illegitimate, professionally and organisationally, and to invoke sanctions which at the extreme would include disciplining the practitioner.

Resistance to hierarchies, therefore, can take one of three forms (maintaining autonomous space, bending rules, breaking rules). Each depends on the exercise of the power by practitioners based on the knowledge they have about service users, the invisibility of their practice, and their use of professional ideas.

Mediating control and resistance: the ambiguous role of the supervisor

In each of the caring professions the development of hierarchies which are based around the separation of practice and management has seen a role develop which is centred on the bringing together of practice and management, and that role is the first-line supervisor. In nursing this is the ward sister or charge nurse, while in social work it is the senior social worker or team leader. In the remedial therapies this has been less marked, partly as a consequence of the smaller numbers and the wider spread of work and partly as a result of the greater emphasis on working with other teams rather than being based within one's own professional team. Senior therapists also have striven harder than senior social workers or sisters and charge nurses to maintain a primary role in working directly with service users and not assuming responsibilities for supervision of junior colleagues (Hawker and Stewart, 1978, p. 87), although there is evidence that this has become a more contentious issue as a necessity for reinforcing professionalism through closure has re-emerged through the 1980s (CSP, 1989). Nevertheless, the role of the superintendent therapist (of either a speciality or a department) continues to be more distinctly managerial, and to take in less professional supervision than would be the case in nursing or social work (Mercer, 1980).

While the supervisory role marks the first line of management, these positions are contradictory in so far as they combine apparently exclusive elements. Galper (1975, p. 58) argued that the supervisory relationship is the source of a never-ending subordination of the practitioner. While the underlying relationship is one of superordinate and subordinate, as Pithouse notes, good supervisors are those who 'demonstrate to their teams their independence from higher management, and their disinclination to intrude *overly* in the workers' day to day practices' (1987, p. 64; my emphasis). 'Overly' is a crucial concept here, because it indicates a shifting boundary that is constantly renegotiated between managerial and professional definitions of workers' actions. What is 'overly' for one may not be for the other, and working agreement has to be reached, in the context of unequal and differing access to power. It is the point at which these competing sets of perceptions and practices articulate. As a consequence the team leaders are regarded by more senior managers as well as by the practitioners as occupying the borders between the two worlds, a position imbued with ambiguities (Hugman, 1984).

Payne (1982, pp. 16–17), borrowing from Likert (1961), uses the concept of the link-pin to describe this contradictory role. The link-pin is a person who has dual membership of work groups, where each group is itself a small hierarchy. The link-pin is the channel of control, consultation and communication down the organisation, but at the same time may be the means through which practitioners exert resistance and use consultation and communication for their own purposes. This role appears, therefore, to combine control and resistance in a way which separates practice and management while at the same time holding them together.

The position of supervisors encapsulates the way in which managed professions can be seen as contradictory in their subjection to scrutiny an control by hierarchical superiors while simultaneously the organisation of work enables, and even necessitates, the development of autonomous space. It is this contradiction which has led to much debate about the nature of professionalism in the caring professions, in particular around the mutual exclusivity or otherwise of professionalism and bureaucracy (Glastonbury *et al.*, 1982; Wilding, 1982; Howe, 1986a).

Professionalism in hierarchies

As Wilding notes (1982, p. 67), much has been written about how the location in bureaucratic structures is inimical to the development of professionalism, and much less about the way in which a bureaucracy may enable a profession to develop. Klein (1973) argues that it is through integration with an administrative structure, whether a private firm, a charitable body or a state agency, that sufficient resources can be available to enable the profession to consolidate its control over an area of work. Clearly, this only applies in such an open-handed way when the profession concerned has full autonomy for its actions within its area of defined competence. The argument of the trait theorists (Greenwood, 1957; Etzioni, 1969; Toren, 1972) is that this is a crucial trait missing from those occupations which are here referred to as caring professions. However, this is to miss the point that such a definition takes the historical development of occupations as the consequence of identifiable traits, rather than seeing such developments as the origins of those characteristics. This results, as Glastonbury *et al.* (1982) have shown, in a circularity of thinking. Such an approach to managed professions, they argue, can be represented by Figure 3.1.

This circularity, according to Glastonbury *et al.*, limits thinking not only about the current nature of the caring professions, but also about the possibilities for their growth and development. As we have seen, there have been hierarchical aspects of these professions from their beginnings. Moreover, if they are compared with the more successfully established professions such as law and medicine, it can be seen that the latter are also organised hierarchically (Johnson, 1972) in the modern industrial state. Where it could be said that the more established professions have been successful in gaining public acceptance in the extent of their autonomy has been in their colonisation of particular positions within developing organisations (Larson, 1977). This view would be supported by the assertion that the oldest of these occupations, law, has been the most successful in these terms (Johnson, 1972, p. 46).

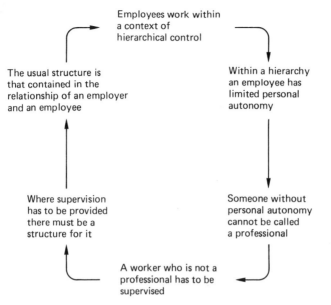

Figure 3.1 *The circularity of the semi-profession concept*
Source: adapted from Glastonbury *et al.*, 1982, p. 120.

From Johnson's analysis it can be seen also that the concern over professional status is about who controls which occupation (1972, p. 45). It is in the interests of a group to assert its professionalism as a means of exerting self-control, and it is in the interests of other groups to deny professionalism to the extent that they wish to exert control themselves over the occupation, either in whole or in part. The strategy of accepting supervision where the supervisor is a senior member of the same occupation both legitimates the relationship for the occupational members and provides a stronger basis for deflecting the claims of other groups to control the occupation. The circle is broken.

Where I have stressed the similarities between nursing, remedial therapies and social work in the foregoing discussion of hierarchy, at this point their divergences must be noted. Each had undergone a distinct development in diverse historical circumstances. This has produced different forms of integration between professionalism and hierarchy, and different approaches to the issue of autonomy.

Nursing and social work may be said to have colonised hierarchies and brought them into the respective professions. However, the Griffiths reorganisation of management in the NHS (UK) has been a major redirection to this development, as it has seen the demotion of some senior nurse managers, and the removal of automatic inclusion of the most senior nurse on the management boards (Cousins, 1987). This may create pressure for a re-professionalisation, as nurses look for more valued areas of work. There are signs of this in the moves for seniority to be available for clinical specialities as well as management (Carpenter, 1977). In the USA arguments have been proposed for a strategy of reincorporating first-line management with clinical expertise (Wallace and Corey, 1983). Similarly, social workers in the UK, following the creation of the single departments in local authorities, occupied the hierarchy from basic grade to director. In some sense, as I have already noted, it may be said that this too is being eroded, with an increased emphasis on managerial qualifications, and may come to resemble more the situation in the USA or some other European countries. However, these are most frequently seen as a post-qualifying addition, rather than a removal of the profession from the most senior positions. At the same time there are arguments from diverse quarters that seniority should be available for practitioners (Bromley, 1978; Glastonbury *et al.*, 1982).

The remedial therapies differ from nursing and social work in that they have never been in the position of dominating an organisation through colonisation, but throughout the twentieth century have been employed in contexts defined by other professions, notably hospitals and, more recently in the UK, social services or social work departments of local authorities. So, although clear hierarchies have developed in these contexts the degree of managerial change experienced by the other caring professions has not been of the same form or intensity in their own hierarchical organisation (compare Tolliday, 1972, with CSP, 1984, for example).

These developments and possibilities can be understood in terms of Derber's (1982) concept that the proletarianisation of professional work is to be understood as the separation of ideological and technical control in each occupation. In the growth of hierarchies the caring professions have maintained their technical autonomy at the expense of ideological control through the objectives of the employing agency. Technical control becomes unnecessary because in this process the goals of the professionals become subordinated to those of the organisation (Derber, 1983). In this context the idea of seniority for clinical practitioners would be contested by both managers and policy-makers to the extent that it was part of a struggle to gain ideological autonomy.

So, the more the ideologies of agencies and the ideologies of senior professionals are identified with each other, the more the professional colonisation of the organisation is likely to be sustained. This is the process which underlies the subjection, in the USA as well as in the UK and other parts of Western Europe, not only of managed professions such as nursing but also of the most established professions such as medicine in the economic controls established in health care services (Cousins, 1987, pp. 153ff.) Where the ideological basis of health and welfare becomes contested, then the organisational contexts of health and welfare provision also became areas of increased conflict involving the position of the professionals employed within them, and this can be seen in the developments through the 1980s in North America and Western Europe.

The outcome for the caring professions is unlikely to be a straightforward resolution to the circularity of argument noted by Glastonbury *et al.*, that nursing, social work and other caring professions can become more autonomous because they are already, effectively, self-managed. Rather, the future will be one of continued struggles around the relationship between professionalism and hierarchical, managed employment.

4

The Struggle for Professionalism

The concept of closure

It has been argued that the segmentation of the caring professions, their division into hierarchical levels, has occurred over a period of time through a process of increasingly specialised divisions between practice and management. This has taken place within the wider context of these occupations themselves becoming defined and established. To the extent that defining who is a nurse, an occupational therapist, a physiotherapist or a social worker also defines who is not, the development of each of these professions represents an example of what Weber called 'social closure'. That is a 'process by which social collectivities seek to maximise rewards by restricting access to resources and opportunities to a limited circle of eligibles' (Parkin, 1979, p. 44). As we have already noted, professions are not types of occupations but historical forms of controlling occupations. The concept of social closure enables the processes of professionalisation to be grasped, and the attempts by occupations to extend their power over their work to be examined.

Parkin develops Weber's concept further, through his distinctions between two types of closure: exclusion and usurpation (1979, p. 45; p. 86). Exclusionary closure occurs when a group is successful in restricting access to resources for the achievement of social objectives, based on that group's ownership of property or control over credentials (pp. 49ff.). Usurpation occurs when a group forms in relation to exclusion, in an attempt to resist or undermine that exclusion (pp. 75ff.). For Parkin, professionalisation is the principal example of exclusionary closure based on credentials. The more successful an occupation is in gaining control over the establishment and award of qualifications the greater the degree of closure it will have achieved.

Exclusionary closure not only affects the choice of who will enter, and be allowed to practice a profession. It serves also as a basis for defining the boundaries of the profession with other professions, and it provides the foundations for power exercised by the professionals in relation to the users of their services. Some relationships with other professions may also be characterised by usurpationary closure, in those cases where the developing profession encounters alternative claims by one which is more established. Professionalisation as a form of closure has many dimensions. This discussion, focusing particularly on developments in the UK, will examine in turn: closure based around knowledge and skills, credentialism; closure between caring professions and other occupations; and closure in relation to the maintenance of public images.

Qualifications and credentials

Within the trait approach to professions the issue of theory and knowledge is given a prominent position. Greenwood (1957) placed 'systematic theory' first in his list of the core traits of professions, and most attempts to produce such lists have incorporated either a discrete area of knowledge or a systematic body of theory as a key trait (Jolley, 1989, p. 5). However, as the critics of the trait approach have argued, the issue of training can also be seen to serve the interests of the professionalising occupation (Wilding, 1982), providing a weapon in the struggles for closure. The significance of knowledge as an important part of the aspiring profession's armoury lies in the connections between the development of specific forms of scientific knowledge and the division of labour in industrial capitalism (Jones, 1979). Indeed, the critique of knowledge as a base for professional claims was stated succinctly at the beginning of the twentieth century by Weber: 'when we hear from all sides the demand for the introduction of regular curricula and special examinations, the reason behind it is, of course, not a suddenly awakened thirst for education but the desire for restricting the supply for these positions and their monopolisation by the owners of educational certificates' (in Gerth and Mills, 1948, p. 241). This more critical understanding of the role of knowledge in emergent professionalism provides a basis for examining the patterns of development followed by the different caring professions.

The practice of nursing, known by that name, long predates the organisation of the practice into an occupation, which in turn predates the creation of systematic training for that practice. As Davies (1980) notes, the attempts to develop this type of training in the UK and the USA through the nineteenth century were diverse. However, Davies argues, the most well known and most influential of these developments, the Nightingale Fund, was not based around a 'school' and did not have a pre-existing body of specialised knowledge on which to base its work (1980, p. 104). The result was a compromise between theoretical teaching (of the type found in medical schools) and an apprenticeship model through which nurse training was located in practical work. It was an unequal compromise, however, because the social forces which led to it were centred on a reform of the practice, and because knowledge about health and the human body were already being claimed by medicine. So, nursing knowledge was constructed around concrete skills rather than abstract theories. This model was influential not only in the UK, but also in various parts of North America, where the first nursing schools were established in the USA in 1873 based on work as the medium of training (Davies, 1980; Reverby, 1987). In Australia, also, nurse training has been founded on an apprenticeship model, which continues to have wide implications in employment factors such as salary levels (Castle, 1987).

The establishment of schools of nursing, with an increasingly distinct knowledge base, was one means through which nursing could achieve independence of control. Yet while it was necessary it was not sufficient (Woods, 1987, p. 155). The consolidation of nursing professionalisation is seen by Woods in the drive for licensure or registration which occurred in the USA and the UK between 1900 and 1920. In the USA each state enacted its own legislation to license nurses, a process which took a number of years (Reverby, 1987), while in the UK state registration was introduced centrally in 1919 (Abel-Smith, 1960). Although varying in detail, such legislation was uniformly based on the same historical process: the state creation of an occupational monopoly grounded on a regulated form of training. Abel-Smith (1960) draws attention to the significance of the date of the UK legislation, and the large numbers of Voluntary Aid Detachments (a type of untrained or partially trained nurse) returning to civilian life following the 1914–18 war. The legislative closure of nursing followed campaigning by qualified nurses, and other interested professionals such as doctors, as well as politicians who were concerned to reduce opportunities for the unqualified nurses as a means of controlling women's employment in the immediate post-war period. So, the interests of the qualified nurses for employment opportunities coincided with more powerful concerns to regulate the supply of nurses. Although at the outset there was an inclusion of experienced unqualified nurses (p. 97), future registration was to be based on the possession of a recognised qualification. A similar criterion, the control of unqualified nurses as a threat to employment opportunities, was foundational in the USA (Reverby, 1987; Woods, 1987) and Australia (Castle, 1987). The control of knowledge was, therefore, a key component in early nursing professionalism.

By the late twentieth century nursing knowledge, and nurse education, has become much more theoretical and at the same time has achieved the status associated with higher education. While nurse training continues to be located predominantly in schools of nursing attached to hospitals, and consequently to have a high level of practical work, not only has the content become more theoretical with more time spent in academic settings, but also many schools of nursing have become associated with higher education institutions. Although this latter trend is most marked in North America, undergraduate and postgraduate level qualifications have gained acceptance also in the UK (Woods, 1987). *Project 2000* (UKCC, 1986), a review of nurse education and training which is concerned with the structure and content of nursing education, stresses the theoretical dimensions of nursing and the importance of graduate-level training.

However, because of the wide variation in the type of education provided between non-graduate and graduate nursing courses, and the considerably larger proportion of the former within the occupation, not every analyst agrees that this has been favourable for nursing professionalisation. Etzioni (1969) suggested that nurses would have been better served by stressing the practical skills and knowledge which are part of their tradition. Friedson (1970) argued that the largely transient nature of nursing employment compared to the stability of the small number of managers, educators and policy-makers, meant that nursing was weakened in relation to other professions, notably medicine, with which it is in competition for professional space. Yet neither Etzioni or Friedson develop the obvious gender bias in their analysis, that the practical skills and knowledge of tradition were women's skills, or that transience and other fragmentations of employment derive from the position of women, black people and other powerless groups in the labour market (Barron and Norris, 1976; Doeringer and Piore, 1985). (These themes will be expanded in subsequent chapters.) Furthermore, Etzioni's critique is framed within the trait approach, with its implicit assumptions about the essential nature of types of knowledge, and its lack of an understanding about the social construction of knowledge over time.

The history of social work knowledge has points both of similarity with and of divergence from that of nursing. In the UK the first formally identified training for social workers was the School of Sociology established by the Charity Organisation Society (COS) and the Settlement

Movement in 1903 (Jones, 1979). Thus from its beginnings social work education was established within higher education. There are three factors which can be identified which account for this: the growth of social work as a distinct occupation; the class and gender of early social workers; and the areas of knowledge to which claims were and continue to be made by social work.

Social work, unlike nursing, did not have a discrete identity before the mid-nineteenth century. Although in the UK some strands of the profession may be traced to the work of the relieving officers under the British Poor Law and the moral welfare work of the Church of England, other important elements, especially casework and community action, did not emerge until more recently – the COS was established in 1869 and the first university settlement, Toynbee Hall, in 1884 (Parry and Parry, 1979). Where nursing professionalism grew out of a reform of an older occupation, social work professionalism developed as part of the action of early social workers in creating the occupation from several strands.

The composition of nineteenth-century social work was, like nursing, dominated numerically by women (Walton, 1975). However, the class origins of the women were quite different. Early social work provided employment opportunities for middle-class women, as well as for some middle-class men. For the men social work was a precursor to another profession, usually either law or the church (which were closed to women), and both Attlee and Beveridge (later to have an impact on UK social policy in the creation of the welfare state) worked in settlements as part of their university education (Parry and Parry, 1979). For the middle-class women it was an occupational end in itself. There was enormous pressure from such women for a recognised training which would provide a similar professional opportunity as that which existed for men of their class. This class position gave greater influence to such demands.

Higher education as the location of social work training in the UK is also related to the class origins of nineteenth-century social work. The settlements were university foundations, designed to give men in training for the (Church of England) priesthood, or to a lesser extent law, experience of working in poor city areas. Fuelled by a radical form of Christianity, this work was also intended to empower working-class people through the sharing of knowledge. As women's settlements were created and links were forged with the COS at a time when the universities were being opened to women, the university appeared to be the 'natural' institution to which the aspirant profession looked for its educational base. Moreover, the forms of knowledge to which social workers made claims, social sciences and administration, were themselves becoming established in this period. Unlike nursing, which could be said to have been in competition with medicine for the biological sciences, social work was part of the same social movements from which the social sciences also were emerging.

Social work in the UK, in contrast to many other countries, did not follow nursing down the path of a national register. In part this may be understood in the context of the class origins of the drive for social work qualifications: the influence of the middle-class social workers could be exerted in other ways, through other social relationships. At the same time, social work was an emerging profession bringing together strands from other practices which made no claims to professionalism. The task of defining the profession by excluding 'quacks and charlatans' was of little importance, and, in any case, those aspects of social work which recruited from the working classes were not trained in the same way or in the same institutions. (The first professional training for caseworkers was at university level (Jones, 1979).) Furthermore, there was little attempt made as there had been with nursing (Abel-Smith, 1960) to campaign for a unified professional body. There were separate associations for caseworkers, almoners and probation officers in the early period, and a multiplicity of professional bodies existed in the UK until 1970.

The close connections with religious and legal professions could also be said to have had an impact. Possession of the right qualifications, recognised by a social institution, was in itself certification in these professions. The church recognised its priests, and the courts recognised those with legal qualifications. A similar pattern developed for social work, and despite the subsequent formation of professional associations, the role of employing agencies in the recognition of qualifications was established through their control over those whom they employed, which (unlike medicine, for example) preceded the establishment of the distinct occupational group.

The history of social work knowledge and qualifications in the twentieth century has paralleled that of both higher education and the social sciences. All three have expanded. There are those who would see this as inflation rather than expansion (Lait, 1980), but the case against social work knowledge rests entirely on an attack on the acceptability of social science as opposed to natural science as the basis of professional practice (see, for example, Brewer and Lait, 1980). In some respects the UK has not seen the same consolidation of the process which is evident in North America, where undergraduate (bachelors') and postgraduate (masters' or doctoral) work is much more common although not universal (Briggs, 1980), or even the rest of Western Europe (Barr, 1989) where a minimum of three years' higher education is required. What is more widespread throughout these countries is that in social work, as in nursing, the control of curricula has become dominated by the profession, but in social work this has been through the colonisation of academic posts by members of the profession rather than through determination of curricula by professional associations. In Larson's terms (1980) there has been a unification of the production of knowledge and the production of the professionals.

By the end of the 1980s the UK was also one of the few countries in Europe not to have introduced registration for social workers. Where nursing had been able to use a surplus of unqualified labour as a weapon in fighting for registration, contemporary pressure for registration of social workers in the UK (largely, but not entirely, from the British Association of Social Workers) has failed because of a shortage of qualified labour, and the needs of state agencies to employ unqualified staff to undertake work which is claimed by social workers. A struggle over class distinctions in levels of social work training, between higher education and in-service forms of training, is still evident in the USA and other European countries but appears to be most active in the UK. (It remains to be seen if the merger in the UK of the Certificate of Qualification in Social Work, higher education, and the Certificate in Social Service, in-service, to be introduced in the early 1990s, will resolve this or shift the struggle into other areas.)

Occupational therapy and physiotherapy emerged as distinct professional groups towards the end of the nineteenth century, and began to be consolidated in the early twentieth century. They have many features in common with nursing and social work, and are products of the same social processes. In some senses they are the outcome of professionalisation in nursing and social work, as members of these occupations took further specific aspects of their work, and made connections with other social movements.

A history of the Chartered Society of Physiotherapy in the UK identifies a group of 'nine nurses and midwives' as the earliest element in the development of physiotherapy (CSP, 1980, p. 164). This group, in 1894, created a council of trained masseuses, which formed the basis for a society in the following year that set examinations and established rules for professional conduct. In the early part of the twentieth century this society was influenced by Swedish remedial exercise concepts, and both massage and remedial exercise were found to be useful in the Great War in Europe. The war appears to have had a similar impact on the professionalisation process of physiotherapy as the Crimean War had on nursing, providing the basis for the occupation to influence opinion in powerful sections of society through its contribution to war work. Shortly after the war, in 1920, the society was granted a royal charter following petitioning by its members (Lankin, 1983). The significance of the charter lies not only in the recognition by the state, but also in the fact that such recognition confers monopoly rights in a field, and several competing groups amalgamated with the society to form the major professional body at this time. (There are other groups which have amalgamated as recently as 1970.) It was in 1920 that men were admitted to membership, although they had been admitted to training since 1905, and the first medical chair of the council was elected, an event which was followed by 52 years of medical dominance at this most senior level in the professional association (Lankin, 1983). Organisational unity brought with it other aspects of incorporation into the hierarchy of professions, with its associated gender and class implications. Medicine, over-whelmingly dominated by men, sought to control physio-therapy, and the struggle within physiotherapy to oppose medical control came largely from middle-class women (Lankin, 1983, p. 114).

The origins of occupational therapy are somewhat more diffuse. Reese gives 1917 as the date of its origins in the USA (1987, p. 393), and it was not until the late 1920s and early 1930s that it was introduced to the UK (Wallis, 1987b; Grove 1988). The influence of the arts-and-crafts movement, a derivative of the utopianism of Ruskin and Morris, encouraged some doctors and social workers to use activity rather than rest to promote physical and mental health (Levine, 1987). The holistic and even romantic con-cepts behind the arts-and-crafts movement did not blend easily with the scientism of medicine, and occupational therapy relied heavily on the patronage of sympathetic doctors, as council members and even presidents of the early occupational therapy associations (Levine, 1987; Wallis, 1987b; Grove, 1988). Indeed, it was the strong influence of doctors which generated initial debates about a more 'scientific' approach, in which activity became the means to an end rather than of value in itself. These debates mirror a distinction between the middle-class pos-ition of those who had pioneered arts-and-crafts, for whom creative activity as an end in itself was a possibility, and the working-class patients of large hospitals for whom such activity was a means to the end of leaving hospital and returning to the everyday world of industrial work which the arts-and-crafts movement regarded as unhealthy and dehumanising. In this sense occupational therapy formed around a contradiction between different class interests.

Professionalisation for both occupations was achieved through the claims to scientific bases which were established around the same class and gender factors which are evident in the histories of nursing and social work. Both physiotherapy and occupational therapy provided respectable employment for middle-class women (although eventually both contained small numbers of men), under the control of middle-class men in medicine either directly or through nursing and social work (Reese, 1987, p. 393). Furthermore both were able to play a role in the reproduction of a healthy industrial labour force, and in times of war to contribute to the physical and mental care of the military labour force.

The knowledge bases to which physiotherapy and occupational therapy have made claims have tended to converge over the century in which they have developed. Throughout the history of physiotherapy there has been a concentration on physical treatments, with massage and exercise being supplemented in a later period by the use of electricity in various ways, including most recently heat and ultrasound (van Doorslaer and Guerts, 1987). In this sense physiotherapy has had very strong claims to a 'scientific' basis, and was able to use this to gain the support of doctors and matrons in the achievement of professional unity and in control over the content and examination of qualifying courses (see, for example, Sim, 1989). Occupational therapy, on the other hand, appears to have begun from an anti-scientific critique inside medicine and related areas of social work which only later was confronted by the dominance of empiricist science and which continues to be valued within occupational therapy (Williams *et al.*, 1987). This is a key factor which is thought to account for the slower professional development of occupational therapy and the more recent emphasis on scientific and theoretical approaches (Levine, 1987; Wallis, 1987b; Atkinson, 1988).

More recently there has been a convergence of physiotherapy and occupational therapy in terms of areas of knowledge and expertise, and this has been accompanied in the UK by arguments about the possibility of a merger into a unified 'remedial therapy profession' (CSP, 1988), as the distinction can now be seen as one between specific areas of the body and types of movement in a way which emphasises commonalities and minimises differences. Both now place a high priority on areas of knowledge including anatomy and physiology, such that Reese, in the context of a critique of gender bias in the production of occupational therapy knowledge, can describe occupational therapists as 'scientists' (1987, p. 396). Increased claims to a scientific knowledge base have related to a move towards higher education as the location of training which parallels that of nursing. In the UK this is concentrated at first degree level (Atkinson, 1988), while in comparison graduate-level training is well established in the USA (Wallis, 1987b; Wyrick and Stern, 1987).

In the UK both physiotherapy and occupational therapy are regulated through the terms of the Professions Supplementary to Medicine Act (1960), which not only enshrined their subordinate status to the medical profession, but also made state registration compulsory. It is at this point that a trade-off between the state, the more powerful profession of medicine and the professionalisation of the remedial therapies can be identified. The relationship between the state and professionalisation has been discussed in Chapter 1, and this form of compulsory registration represents the consolidation of professional status for these occupations in exchange for a limitation of autonomy. The limit is defined through those areas of knowledge and practice over which the remedial therapies have succeeded in gaining control. However, as Wilding makes clear, such a position is not to be seen as a smooth functional balance within the system, but is it to be understood as 'a truce rather than an inevitable identity of interest' (1982, p. 61).

In the professionalisation of each of these occupations it can be seen that knowledge, institutionalised and controlled through education and training, has played a central role in the process. Although the detailed forms of professionalisation which have been achieved by each occupation differ, the general features are that each occupation has struggled historically to gain control in the establishment of knowledge-based credentials.

Closure through territorial claims on knowledge is not the only form which is evident in the caring professions. Internal divisions, which are themselves the product of professionalisation, and divisions between occupations can also be understood as closures which have helped to create these professions. The first, internal closure, is to be seen in the development of subgroups, often called 'assistants' or 'aides', and the development of specialists in contrast to generalists. The second, lateral closure, is evident in struggles between professions, and between professionals and other groups of workers on whom their work depends, including support and administrative staff.

Internal closure: creating subgroups

Each of the caring professions has generated associated areas of work which, over time, have been defined as appropriate for groups of workers with 'lower' levels of qualification, including those with a minimal form of training undertaken in the course of doing the work. These groups of workers form ambiguous satellites to the caring professions, being neither entirely distinct, nor entirely integrated. This ambiguity is often captured in the titles given to such workers: nursing auxiliary or nursing aide; social work assistant; occupational therapy aide or assistant; physiotherapy aide or assistant. They are categorised as being within and outside the professions at one and the same time. Their nature is given by the profession with which they are associated, but it is given by their exclusion. An auxiliary nurses but is not a nurse; an assistant does social work but is not a social worker; an aide provides therapy but is not a therapist.

The process through which these ancillary groups of sub-professionals are created has been described by Howe (1986a) in a study of social work as 'ditching the dirty work'. Howe argues that ancillary subgroupings have formed part of the professionalising process because they allow the (would-be) profession to lay increasing claim to higher-status activities, often those based on theoretical forms of knowledge. As Hughes (1958) noted in a classic sociology of work, an occupation which is concerned to enhance its status should chose its work carefully; and as Howe expresses it, choosing work is like choosing friends in that you will be judged by the company you keep (1986a). Work may be seen as dirty in two ways; either what is being done, or with whom it is being done. The dirt of dirty work may be literal (for example involving physical contact with human faeces) or it may be metaphorical (involving social contact with low-status groups). These pairs of criteria often combine, in a perception of low-status service user groups as 'polluting'. To counter this, professions concerned to maintain or increase their status tend to stress the glamorous side of their work and to minimise the routine or dirty side.

> Nurses are the technicians of the ward, skilled in reading medical instruments and administering drugs. Little is said about the making of beds or following a doctor's instructions. Difficult casework and delicate decision making in risky cases of child abuse are likely to be emphasised by social workers and not the half hour spent listening to an upset old lady explain that she has lost her pension book and there is nothing in the house to eat. (Howe, 1986a, p. 30)

In other words there is a claim to levels of skills which match the forms of knowledge.

The consequence of such claims is that the caring professions have aspired to what Davies (1985), following Nokes (1967), has called the virtuoso roles. Such roles:

> have glamour; they enable the practitioner to demonstrate skills and to reveal distinctive know-how; they carry effective autonomy; they produce observable and measurable outcomes; they are characterised by being concerned with limited objectives, clearly specified; and they usually involve a degree of

social distance which is institutionalised by occupational structures. (Davies, 1985, p. 33)

Such appeals to skills have a compelling logic for the caring professions. In hierarchies which have an agency base they provide a professionalistic rationale for the pursuit of careers and the attribution of seniority. This is of particular importance where the knowledge base is disputed or not fully regulated as virtuoso skills provide additional weight to claims that there are a specific set of social problems for which the profession has the solutions. Virtuoso skills provide the mediation between circumstantial practice and theoretical knowledge.

Davies (1985) distinguishes virtuoso roles from those he calls general caring roles. The former are about curing, the latter are concerned with tending. Gender is a crucial dimension to these categories (Howe, 1986b) and racial biases are evident in the composition of the ancillary groups (Torkington, 1983; Wyrick and Stern, 1987). I will discuss these issues in detail in later chapters. Because tending roles do not have the social status of those which are concerned with curing, they have been the roles which have been discarded by nursing, social work and the remedial therapies as they have sought professional status. The idea of tending has to be enlarged somewhat to encompass all the work which has been delegated to auxiliaries, aides and assistants. They are the necessary tasks which the aspiring professions have regarded as menial, such as counting linen and cleaning apparatus or sluices, removing vomit or faeces and domestic cleaning (Hawker and Stewart, 1978, p. 87; Johnson, 1978, p. 112; Reverby, 1987, pp. 63–4). As Johnson adds, these tasks often arrive at the ancillary level having previously been the responsibilities of students and trainees, and may continue to be used as punishments for students who commit breaches of discipline.

Two ironies are noticeable in this process. First the dirty work which is ditched may be an important element of the origins of the profession. For example, the reforms of nursing were based in part on cleanliness and order in hospitals (Baly, 1986). Second, it is precisely those areas of work which are concerned with caring which appear to be ditched in the struggle for professionalisation. These ironies are not lost on the ancillary-level staff, who respond by demonstrating frustration or anger (Johnson, 1978, p. 113; Hugman, 1984, p. 264), complaining that they do not assist anyone but undertake work in their own right (Parsloe and Stevenson, 1978). This is noticeable particularly in UK social work, where the assistant grade became interchangeable with unqualified staff who were used to make up the shortfalls in the numbers of qualified social workers following the creation of the local authority social work and social services departments. This in turn has led to arguments that a separate new profession could be said to be emerging, based on the welfare (that is, essentially, the caring) tasks for which social workers have come to be regarded as 'too highly qualified' (see, for example, Hey, 1980b).

The issue of specialism against generalism has also divided those who form the main bodies of the caring professions. Such divisions are based either around types of skills and knowledge, or they are based around ways of classifying the service users with whom a part of a profession works.

In the same way in which the caring professions have developed through claims to skills and knowledge, so groups within the professions have attempted to demarcate specific aspects of the skills and knowledge which are regarded as prestigious. One way of understanding this process is to see these specialisms as 'branches' of a profession, which benefit the practitioner by offering a choice of career according to interests and aptitudes. However, these specialisms also represent the successes of subgroups in marking out an area of practice which attracts enhanced status because additional training is required, and to which access by other members of the wider professional group can be restricted. At its broadest, this is evident in nursing in the divisions between hospital- and community-based practice. The distinctions in the UK between nurse, midwife and health visitor represent another pattern of specialism which, in part, cuts across the hospital–community divide. Within a setting, too, there may be specialism by type of practice, such as nursing in operating theatres or in intensive care. I would not wish to dispute that these are skilful and complex areas of work, but rather to suggest that it is because they are that they provide opportunities for closure *within* nursing.

Similarly, within social work there has been some development of the idea of specialism by type of practice, in the distinction made between casework, groupwork and community work (Stevenson, 1981). Residential work could be added to this list, and the fact that Stevenson's research only looked at fieldwork is an indication of an even greater division by practice type. However, Stevenson argues, the idea of specialisation defined by method of intervention in social work has remained relatively underdeveloped in the UK, except in the broadest terms, in comparison to the USA (1981, p. 17). This is because, despite sustained critical assault (for example, Bailey and Brake, 1975; Pearson, 1975; Simpkin, 1983), the greatest prestige continues to be ascribed to the main form of practice, namely casework (Satyamurti, 1981; Howe, 1986a; Pithouse, 1987). Casework has a long history as the method of practice in which social workers were trained, and this is allied to the individual organisation of practice in personal caseloads. Attempts to introduce a unified model of practice have tended to subsume other methods within the dominant model which defines the existing practice culture and which is interwoven with forms of organisation (Pincus and Minahan, 1973; Specht and Vickery, 1977).

The pattern evident in the creation of subprofessional groups, a skill/knowledge hierarchy in which virtuoso curing roles are dominant and general caring roles are subordinate can be seen in specialism by practice type. In nursing the more prestigious forms of practice are those which require post-qualifying training, and they are either highly technically-based (theatre, intensive care) or have a good deal of autonomy and a status separate from the main body of nursing (midwives, health visitors) (Johnson, 1978; Bellaby and Oribabor, 1980). Within social work, in contrast, the development of such specialism has been limited, but for a similar reason. Virtuosity has been based around skilled practice, but this practice is the core of the profession.

The caring professions are divided also in terms of the service users with whom they work. Two divisions are identifiable: age; and characteristics of the service user. The age dimension is the distinction of service users in age groups; children, adolescents, younger adults, older adults. Professional divisions have formed around these distinctions; paediatric nursing, child protection social work, geriatric nursing, social work with elderly people. The other dimension makes reference to the professional ascription of health and social problems (Whittington, 1977); paediatrics/child care, psychiatry/mental health, learning difficulties, physical disability, geriatrics/old age. The repetition of some of these labels is an indication that, in practice, the dimensions are not mutually exclusive but are closely interwoven, with each contributing to the overall structure.

There are hierarchies of practice constructed around these divisions of service users, and there is considerable evidence that the caring professions follow similar patterns (Bellaby and Oribabor, 1980; Mercer, 1980; Howe, 1986a; Pithouse, 1987). In broad terms, work with children has occupied a particularly high place in all the caring professions, while in contrast work with elderly people has occupied a relatively low place (for example, Howe, 1986b). However, if sharper distinctions are used, it can be seen that these groups themselves are divided, and that work with children who have profound learning difficulties or physical disabilities is less highly valued than work with other children, or that work with elderly people who have acute problems is more highly valued than work with those whose problems are regarded as chronic. In other words, these distinctions should be understood in terms of the dichotomy between curing and caring which has already been identified. The prestigious work, that which it is claimed requires highly trained and skilful practitioners, is the work which is directed towards curing and problem-solving; low-status work, in which there are fewer claims about credentials, is that which is directed towards caring and long-term support. Yet these distinctions are not eternally fixed, but are in a state of continuing change. I will return below to indications of the ways in which such changes are occurring.

The role of caring professions in social control does not negate the importance of knowledge and skill as the basis for closure precisely because there was a dynamic relationship between the ends claimed by the growing professions (care) and the ends valued by powerful sections of society (control) which were connected through the means at the disposal of the professions (skills and knowledge). For example, both social work and nursing have their basis in the control of the disorderly poor in the nineteenth century, in society generally and within institutions (Jones, 1979; Dingwall *et al.*, 1988; Hawker, 1989), and with the remedial therapies they participated in the maintenance of the industrial/military labour force. It is in the resolution of possible conflict with the more powerful sections of society that the origin of ideological subordination is to be found, in a trade-off against technical autonomy, in which the profession abandons claims to set the goals of its work autonomously in order to achieve control over the means by which the work is undertaken.

Organisational factors also play a part in these professional subdivisions. The greater status of acute nursing over psychiatric nursing, for example, is related to the custodial emphasis of the latter which derives from the organisational culture of many large psychiatric hospitals, and to the early gender and class segregations, in which middle-class women predominated in general nursing and working-class men in the psychiatric context (Dingwall *et al*, 1988). This division has its origins in the relationships between nursing and medical and administrative practices. It is reflected in the different expressions of professionalism, such as the patterns of membership of professional associations and trade unions, with the former more dominant in acute nursing (especially at senior level) and the latter more dominant in psychiatric nursing (Bellaby and Oribabor, 1980).

So the internal structures of the caring professions are divided by the issues of skill and knowledge which are central to those occupations' claims to professional status. The exercise of power in occupying and defending particular practices as the basis of the professions also involves the development of power structures within those professions. Struggles for enhanced status, autonomy and so on are affected by the extent to which the nature of other parts of the profession, by its levels of training, its forms of knowledge and skills or by the service users with whom it works, may weaken one's own claims. The company by which you are judged includes colleagues as well as clients.

Lateral closure: competing for space

In this discussion I have emphasised the similarities between the different caring professions. However, a consequence of similarities may be that these occupations are pursuing the same areas of expertise and clientele, and as a result are competing for space (Jones, 1979, p. 78; Malinski, 1988, p. 65). To what extent is this the case?

The boundaries between the caring professions are constructed around concepts of health and social problems. To the extent that these are clear and unambiguous then such disputes may be more easy to resolve, or may not arise. Dingwall (1980) points to the fact that clarity is often lacking, and that this has had an impact on the relationship between health visitors and social workers, for example. Dingwall argues that the creation of unified social services and social departments in the UK effectively blocked the development of health visiting in the child-care field (1980, p. 126). This example also demonstrates how an organisational base can be part of professionalisation, a strategy which was discussed in the previous chapter.

In the late twentieth century the phenomenon of dispersal is giving new form to such boundary disputes. The community is becoming the site of all types of professional intervention, including cure, care and control (Scull, 1984). This process, variously referred to as deinstitutionalisation or decarceration, involves the diffusion of the professional practices which were previously located in institutions into the wider society. The process is most marked in those areas which have been defined as caring or controlling. Acute health care, the apogee of curing practices, continues to be located in hospitals to the extent that complex technology is required. (Indeed, technology has strengthened the institutional base of acute medicine.) However, even in this area there is a degree of deinstitutionalisation, with shorter stays in hospital and greater use of outpatient and general medical care (Davidson, 1987), supported by community (or district or home) nursing.

The growth of the community as the location of professional intervention has again emphasised the extent to which the caring professions lay claim to the same practices. Assessment of risk, counselling, the management of resources and rehabilitation are all aspects of work which, to varying degrees, nursing, the remedial therapies and social work have sought to include within their spheres of competence and control. Although some of this work clearly relates to the high-status categories which have been outlined above (such as child protection work, in which social workers, health visitors, community nurses and hospital nurses may be involved, as well as members of other professions, especially law and medicine), it is also beginning to include previously low-status groups, such as people with learning difficulties or elderly people. The reason why this may be so is that with the expansion of the community base there is a greater need for professionals to work without surveillance, so there are opportunities for greater autonomy. In addition, there is more opportunity to stress complex skills. This can be seen in child protection work, where health visitors, district nurses and social workers may have overlapping roles (and in which general medical practitioners, paediatricians and teachers may also be involved) (Robinson, 1989). Work with elderly people, previously seen as routine administration of services, may now be regarded as an area of practice which requires assessment and counselling skills, with rehabilitation or the longer-term management of care as the goal. Work with people who have a severe learning difficulty may involve responsibility for resources or it may involve taking on the role of advocate. Both nursing and social work make claims to these areas of responsibility (Malinski, 1988; Robinson, 1989) and remedial therapists, especially in occupational therapy, also identify some of those listed here as within their areas of competence.

One apparent means of resolving disputes about contested areas of work has been the growth of multidisciplinary teams and case conferences. In recent decades the structuring of interprofessional relationships through teams or meetings has become something of a new orthodoxy, although a study of the actual composition of such teams in the USA showed 162 different combinations of professional membership (Kane, 1980, p. 140). Community care was noted as a predominant purpose amongst the teams surveyed. The *ad hoc* nature of such arrangements stems from the rationale behind them, that boundary maintenance is best achieved through informal negotiation around specific cases which transcends the problem of not having a single source of legitimacy for competing claims. However: 'For this work . . . there must be a degree of social equality between the parties such that *ad hoc* agreements on the division of tasks are not read as merely shuffling dirty work around' (Dingwall, 1980, p. 116). Dingwall continues by noting from the UK context that if one of the parties who form a multidisciplinary group is medical then the group becomes embroiled in status issues, as inequalities of power are introduced. This is supported by the evidence from the USA, that medical leadership of multidisciplinary groups 'was associated with a particular style of teamwork since those teams led by doctors were more likely to utilise non-consensual decision-making and adhere to distinct rather than blurred roles' (Kane, 1980, p. 143). That is to say, the doctors dominated them. However, the range of roles allocated did vary widely, with considerable overlap, and it was noted that in these teams psychiatrists, psychologists, social workers and nurses 'tend to share a frame of reference, have access to the same books and ideas, and simultaneously to discover the same subjects' (Kane, 1980,

p. 144). Yet this seems to have been observed in a minority of instances, and controlling relationships appear to have been more common.

Usurpation: continuing struggles

One of the principal reasons why the trait theorists (Etzioni, 1969; Toren, 1972) identified nursing, social work and the remedial professions (along with teaching) as 'semi-professions' is that they do not appear to have developed dominance in discrete areas of knowledge (Jolley, 1989). Despite the considerable growth of the caring professions, substantially based on claims to knowledge and skills, they still would not satisfy this criterion. The alternative view, which has underpinned my discussion, is that 'professional attributes are the symptom and not the cause of an occupation's standing' (Howe, 1986a, p. 96). Professionalism is limited by the success in gaining power over such factors as an area of knowledge and associated autonomy, rather than limited by the intrinsic nature of those factors.

Philp (1979) identifies the reason for this limitation, in a study of the forms of knowledge in social work, as the greater dominance of more established professions, especially law and medicine. This dominance has been achieved partly through the successful attribution of many aspects of social life as 'legal' or 'medical', and partly through the role which the established professions play in the maintenance of respectability (Philp, 1979, p. 96). The space occupied by the caring professions is the 'dirty work' of the older professions. The exclusionary closure of the caring professions, which has been discussed above, mirrors the usurpationary closure exercised in relation to those occupations which are more powerful.

Where social work is engaged in usurpationary closure relating to law and medicine, nursing and the remedial therapies are dominated almost exclusively by medicine. This is reflected in the concerns of academic writing from nursing, exemplified by the 'new' nursing histories being developed in the UK, the USA and Australia (Davies,

1980; Maggs, 1987). Bellaby and Oribabor (1980) point out that the reason why this is of such concern is that history is, in effect, the story of the present. Understanding nursing as the product of struggles with medicine is important because it has shaped, and continues to shape, contemporary issues in nursing. The relationship with medicine is important because it is the main obstacle perceived by most nurses to occupational autonomy.

A contemporary development which exemplifies this process is the growth of the nurse practitioner (Pitcairn and Flauhault, 1974; Johnson, 1978), a term which combines the ideas of nurse and medical practitioner. This is a development in which nurses have begun to exert claims to a capacity to practise independently. However, as Bullough (1975) notes, it is an expansion of the nursing role into territory over which medicine has established dominance. The capacity of nurses to diagnose and prescribe treatment has only recently become an issue formally recognised for discussion because of the success of medicine in keeping it off the public agenda. Medical dominance is strong not only because it relies on commonly accepted views of the relative statuses of medicine and nursing but also because it is buttressed by the state in the form of laws. These laws act as a form of medical power precisely because they are a restraint on nursing. The capacity of nurses to diagnose and prescribe is a product not of essential traits of nursing, but of the historic power of medicine expressed as common sense and enforced in law. It is that power against which nursing is struggling. This struggle is continuing, but it remains to be seen whether the establishment of clinical nurse practitioners will gain a place for nursing in medical practice, or if it will be used by a small group of nurses to become doctors (Johnson, 1978, p. 110). This latter course might be conceded by medicine as a means of maintaining its boundaries, but only if small numbers are involved (Watkins, 1987).

The remedial therapies also have their capacities defined in the interests of medicine, legally and in common sense. Indeed, as I have noted above, in the UK they form part of the group of occupations which are statutorily defined as the 'professions ancillary to medicine', a group which is also referred to on occasions as 'paramedical', and which includes dieticians, opticians, pharmacists and radiographers (Watkins, 1987, p. 213). The words 'ancillary' and 'paramedical' are reflections of the medical viewpoint: as an alternative these occupations could be thought of as professions without which medicine (especially in high technology hospitals) could not function. As with nursing, medical power has been exercised to control the use by these professions of any advantage which this dependency could create. In recent years remedial therapists have begun to challenge medical dominance, although this has been a diffuse and muted development (Watkins, 1987, p. 218). They too have made claims to the capacity to diagnose and prescribe within their own spheres of competence. The equivalent of the nurse practitioner may be a more realistic possibility for a larger proportion of remedial therapists, but such a change will only be supported by medicine to the extent that it is in the latter's interests. This can be seen in the report of a Canadian experiment to evaluate training in diagnostic skills for remedial therapists (Helewa *et al.*, 1987) in which they were measured against *junior* doctors in a way which implicitly reinforces their subordinate status within the treatment 'team'.

In the UK the relationship between social work and domiciliary care provides an example of usurpationary closure, in which an occupation which has struggled against control by others itself comes to dominate another. A similar tendency has been noted in social work in the USA (Wilensky and Lebeaux, 1965, pp. 303ff.). The unified social services and social work departments were the organisational means through which social work achieved a high degree of occupational autonomy. Although the primary goal of that unification was the establishment of a single social work structure (Hall, 1974), the process brought other services into the same corporate fold. The largest of these groups was the domiciliary services, then more commonly called the home help service. As the senior positions were almost unanimously taken by field social workers, domiciliary services workers were often added to the organisations in a marginal way (Harbert and Dexter, 1983; Harbert, 1988). In the intervening period home help (predominantly seen as a cleaning and laundry service) had developed into domiciliary care (parallel to residential care, provided in the service user's own home). The organisers of this service have changed from being administrators to a role which is very similar to that of the social worker, in addition to the management of teams of direct care workers (which social workers do not usually undertake). Domiciliary care organisers assess needs, gatekeep resources such as day care and advise service users about material and financial benefits (Hugman, 1984). However, social workers' views of domiciliary care organisers vary from a tendency to underplay the latter's skills and knowledge, to a more proprietorial defensiveness about areas of common interest (such as assessment and gatekeeping with regard to day and residential provision) (Harbert, 1988).

Hey (1980a) argues that domiciliary care organisers are a group which is possibly in the process of professionalising, and gaining a more autonomous standing. Organisers already had a professional body, now the Institute of Domiciliary Care Organisers, and a recognised qualification in the Diploma of that institute. However, their position was even more fragmented than that of social workers, with the Certificate in Social Service (CSS) also being recognised by some employers, and many organisers having no training at all. More recently, the state body validating social work training, the Central Council for Education and Training in Social Work (CCETSW), which also validated the CSS, has begun to implement an amalgamation of that with the Certificate of Qualification in Social Work (CQSW) to form a new Diploma in Social Work (Dip.SW). This will be implemented by 1993. In this move CCETSW, which is dominated by social work, has made a claim to define domiciliary care as a branch of social work, and the unsurpationary pressure has resulted in a shifting (not yet complete) of the occupational boundaries.

The common feature between the relationships of nursing and the remedial professions to medicine and social work to domiciliary care is the way they are centred on possible ambiguities of occupational definition. Medicine has achieved a more powerful position, ideologically and in statute, and has been able to maintain clearer boundaries despite the claims of nursing and the remedial professions. The ambiguities are not conceded. Social work, whose organisational power is strong relative to domiciliary care, but which lacks a supporting ideological dominance, has weaker boundaries. The ambiguities are less easy to control, and the result in Britain is a broadening of the professional boundaries in the merging of CQSW and CSS into the Dip.SW. The incorporation of nurses or remedial therapists as clinical practitioners in an intermediate form of medicine would be a similar strategy. In both cases these would be examples of competition being dealt with by the absorption of the competitor group or at least its most professionalised part.

Dirty linen in public: professional images

Caring professions, like all professions, are conscious of their public images. To an extent such images are beyond the control of any profession, but because nursing, the remedial therapies and social work lack the established power of law and medicine, for example, their sensitivity to public images as a barometer of general credibility is possibly more acute.

Positive images, which stress the socially desirable attributes of helpfulness, warmth, empathy and even self-sacrifice are valued in these occupations. These are characteristics which could be associated with widespread views of caring and with widespread views of women and femininity. As Oakley (1984) notes, being a good nurse may have an equivalence with being a good woman, and the same value is evident in the history of physiotherapy (CSP, 1980, p. 163). This may be a strength and a weakness. It is a strength because it provides a basis for women professionals to be positive about being women. It is negative because within a patriarchal society it creates constraints and may serve to limit women's power.

The widespread view is at odds with the professional self-image which is more likely to stress the skills and knowledge (Vousden, 1989). Despite the high profile which nursing has, the images of nursing held by other professions and the general public have not kept pace with the reality (Robinson, 1989). The contradiction between caring people (mostly women) and highly skilled professionals remain locked together in public opinion. This can be reduced to crude stereotypes. When nurses are criticised for taking industrial action they are more likely to be seen as soiling their high moral standing than to be engaged in a struggle over recognition of their skills (Robinson, 1989). Only fallen angels go on strike. Nurses' responses to this are to question their commitment to the profession (Mackay, 1989). The attacks on the image connect with attacks on the material base of their occupation (for example, health funding and organisational changes which include reduced staffing levels), and the rate of nurses leaving the profession has grown in recent years (Malinski, 1988; Hockey, 1987; Mackay, 1989).

Social workers consider their public image to be much more ambiguous (Pithouse, 1987). For the most part social workers in the UK have become used to media criticism over many aspects of their work, both in their individual accomplishment of specific tasks and also in the underlying purposes of their work:

> . . . periodic eruptions in the national press have suggested that social services have encouraged scroungers, sapped personal initiative, allowed children to be battered to death, overlooked hypothermia among the elderly, negotiated immoral 'contracts' with teenagers, broken up families, dragged children away from loving parents into care, and illegally cajoled people into psychiatric hospital against their will. Worst of all, in the view of the media, some social workers have gone on strike to get better wages. (Glastonbury *et al.*, 1982, pp. 53–4)

Becoming used to this onslaught and accepting it are not the same response, and as with nursing there has been a loss of professionals for whom the low public standing of the occupation has combined with the impact of public spending to create low morale. A parallel situation exists in the USA, from which context Cohen and Wagner comment that the lack of alternative employment may keep many more disaffected people in the profession than would otherwise choose to remain (1982, p. 154).

The remedial therapies have not appeared to share this problem. They have been less concerned with public awareness of their work, largely it would seem because their professionalisation has become structured around medical domination of access (Lankin, 1983; Wallis, 1987b). So the extent to which the public are aware of the remedial therapies is of less importance than their image amongst the more dominant medical profession. It may be also that the much smaller numbers within their ranks (compared to nursing), and the less contentious groups of service users with whom the remedial therapies work (compared to social work), combine to reduce their visibility in the media and to the public generally. The lack of attention to these professions in academic writing has already been noted. However, remedial therapists like other professionals are concerned about their occupational image, and this is reflected in the continuing debates over arts-and-crafts in occupational therapy, for example, where it may be regarded as reducing professional credibility in the eyes of other professions (Williams *et al.*, 1987).

What is at stake in the issue of public image is the capacity that an occupation has to ground its claims for professionalism in the public acceptance of its knowledge and skills. The relatively weak forms of knowledge, combined with the aura of women's work which gives high moral but low material status to these occupations have served to define and maintain an ambiguous place for these professions with the general public. Public images remain important, though, for two reasons. First they may be used by occupations and more powerful social groups (such as politicians) as counters in debates about autonomy, funding, training and so on. Second, they are interwoven with the self-images of professionals. The public contain the clientele, and as I will explore in the next chapter the clientele provides a mirror for the maintenance of occupational identity. So the public portrayal of the negative aspects of a profession is a matter of concern (for example, Bromley, 1988), and some parts of the caring professions seek to influence such portrayals in order to control the boundaries between the occupation and the wider society.

Occupation and power

Nursing, the remedial therapies and social work have achieved degrees of occupational closure, with differences between them and variations within each occupation between their successes in excluding other groups, competing laterally and usurping spaces claimed by more established groups. In each respect their contemporary forms are the product of these processes; they represent the types of professionalisation which these occupations have achieved. Not only are there differences between nursing, the remedial therapies and social work taken as wholes, but there are variations to be seem within each occupation as distinct parts have been more or less successful in this process.

Just as caring professions are occupational power structures, in which control and influence are exercised hierarchically, so too relationships between professions may be a form of hierarchy. The extent to which an occupation can be said to have been successful in the struggle for professionalisation must be based on the relationship within which it stands against the other occupations which make the claim to professionalism. These may be occupations with whom there is a close organisational relationship, or it may be that there is organisational separation. In each case the forms of professionalism, the ways of exercising power over an occupation, have been achieved in particular historical circumstances.

The growth of the caring professions has also been affected by aspects of social structure and relationships to which reference has been made, but which have not been analysed in any detail so far in this discussion. Gender

relations, and race and ethnicity have been important factors in the ways in which the caring professions have
developed, as have the ways in which the construction of
client groups helped to forge professional self-images and
practices. So in the following chapters these aspects of the
hierarchical and occupational structures and actions of the
caring professions will be examined.

5

Our Clients, Our Selves

Clients

It is part of the professional ideology, usually expressed as an ethic of service (McKinlay, 1973), that the professions exist for the benefit of any member of society who has need of their expertise. However, there has been a long crescendo of critical opinion which argues that such claims meet the needs of the professions rather than (or at least more than) they do those of service users (Illich, 1976; Wilding, 1982). Instead of an open association between the expert and the needy, the critical perspective suggests that professionals seek to control the client/patient, not only in the form of power exercised over individuals, but also to the extent of the capacity to define who and what a client/patient is and should be. The processes of becoming and being clients/patients serve as part of the definition and maintenance of professional boundaries with the rest of society.

This power has become a focal point in the latter part of the twentieth century for an opposition to professionalism. The ascription of client or patient status is rejected consciously by groups of people who recognise the impact it has had on their lives, and is resented by many others who lack the basis for the collective power of resistance (see, for example: Elder, 1977; Mittler, 1979; MIND Manchester Group, 1988). The use of the terms 'client' and 'patient' in this discussion is deliberate, intended to convey these roles as the socially constructed objects of professional power. Recent developments of alternative constructions will be discussed in the final section of the chapter.

Power to define the client/patient

The process of becoming a client/patient is one of negotiation. This may take place between the professional and the would-be client/patient, or it may involve other people and organisations. Friends, neighbours and relatives may play a part in a person becoming a client/patient, or other professions and agencies may refer or direct the person. The power of a caring profession to define the client/patient is located within this network of relationships and interactions.

A crucial component of the process is the status of the person making the referral (Smith and Harris, 1972; Smith, 1980). Other professions are likely to be regarded as having the knowledge and the expertise to make referrals which accord with the caring profession's view of its role and responsibilities. However, struggles for closure, both exclusionary and usurpationary, affect this interaction. Where a profession has uncertain status in relation to a referring profession then the possibilities of disagreement or dispute are increased. This can be seen, for example, in Dingwall's study of health visitor training (1977) in which the health visitors built up a range of perceptions of social workers, predominantly negative, based around the capacity of the social workers to accept or reject the health visitors' judgement about potential and actual clients. Dingwall explains this in terms of direct and indirect competition between social work and health visiting to define clients and their needs, when little difference could be observed between their roles: 'it is very hard for the observer to identify any significant difference in the form or content of the two occupations' work. Both are attempting to give social counsel, or exert social control in contexts defined by state legislation' (1977, p. 148). Yet because of the organisational arrangements of the welfare state in the

UK the two professions are obliged to work together, as each has access to and control over resources which the other may need to accomplish its work.

Similar boundary disputes in the definition of clients/patients can be seen in the relationships between caring professions and medicine. In this respect there is a sharp disjuncture between nurses and remedial therapists on the one hand and social workers on the other. The historical developments and contemporary organisation of the various professions create differences in control over the definition of clients/patients.

Nurses and remedial therapists have their patients defined for them by doctors. Both tradition and legal statute give the doctor the power of diagnosis and prescription. Prescription includes assigning specific tasks to nurses or remedial therapists. In this way defining the patient and the patient's needs also defines the caring profession which undertakes the direct treatment. In broad terms both the doctor and the nurse or remedial therapist will act on the basis of expectations established through training and previous negotiations. What doctors, nurses and remedial therapists expect of each other has developed historically (Keddy *et al.*, 1986). Yet there is not a single uniform set of expectations, and this area of interprofessional action is also disputed territory.

There is evidence from the USA, Canada and the UK that while nurses frequently have the knowledge and skills to undertake diagnosis this is circumscribed by the power of doctors to defend their own control over this area of work (Johnson, 1978; Keddy *et al.*, 1986; Schutzenhofer, 1988). Consequently, nurses have developed strategies for influencing doctors' decision-making. In a self-reporting study of nurses in the United States claims were made that direct rational argument was overwhelmingly the way in which such influence is exercised (Damrosch *et al.*, 1987). However, as the researchers themselves recognise, observation of actions in context were not made. Other commentators have noted that nurses who openly speak their minds or act against medical instruction are unpopular with doctors, and so often act on their ideas furtively (Keddy *et al.*, 1986, p. 751). The reporting of open rational action would appear to be related to claims for autonomy, which is part of the continuing professionalisation of nursing. Autonomy is centred on the power to define the patient and the patient's needs.

Remedial therapists, in recent years, have begun to work towards a greater degree of autonomy in defining their patients. While they are still constrained within the power of the medical profession, in its monopolisation of diagnosis and prescription, there has been a gradual emphasis on separate assessments by therapists (Mocellin, 1988). The move to separate assessment can be interpreted by the medical profession as a threat, and attempts are made to define remedial therapists back into the paramedical role through the use of concepts about the practicality and helpfulness of remedial therapists in a subordinate position to medicine (Wallis, 1987). The power to define patients is a key aspect to autonomy in practice, and as I discussed in the previous chapter can be influential in multidisciplinary work.

In contrast, social workers make their own assessments and plan their own work much more routinely. This is not related to levels or types of skill and knowledge, but derives from the establishment of a separate organisational and legal status distinct from medicine. The power of other professions tends to be that of influence. However, in this relationship also there are disputes and disagreements. As Wilding (1982, p. 30) notes, the medical profession tends to define all needs in terms of medical services. As a consequence doctors sometimes expect to direct social workers in situations where social workers do not share this expectation (Satyamurti, 1981, p. 104). In such situations the conflict is centred on competing definitions of the client, the client's needs, and the rights of the different occupations to define each of these. In other situations social workers may rely on the knowledge and skills of other professions and give a high status to information they supply in making assessments (Smith and Harris, 1972; Smith, 1980). This is usually understood by social workers as acceptance of the other's definition, implying that social work has the power not to accept. This view is sustained and supported within the professional culture, and may be encouraged by senior colleagues and managers who also have an interest in controlling such definitions (Hugman, 1984 pp. 362–4).

Another context in which social work clients are defined is that of the courts. In a formal sense social workers (in the guise of probation officers or court welfare officers) do not have the power to determine outcomes for their potential clients. Sentences are passed by magistrates and judges. However, there are clearly-established procedures of reporting and the provision of assessments, in which the social work role includes making recommendations in which outcomes can be strongly influenced (Parsloe, 1978). In this role the social worker is acting as the agent of the court as the legal element of the state, and it is through this role that social work can exercise power in the courts to define some people as clients.

In each of these contexts caring professions attempt to exercise power through control and influence over the work which they receive from other professions and agencies. However, not all their clients/patients are created in this way. Some engage in direct negotiations with the caring profession in a bid to become a client/patient.

Rees (1978) has shown, in a study of social work offices in Scotland, how potential clients effectively audition for the role. Their success or failure in the audition is dependent on the extent of the prior knowledge which they have about social work. It is also dependent on the criteria employed by the social worker to judge whether the person fits into appropriate categories of need (Whittington, 1977). Smith (1980), in a study of the assessment process, argues that this is the administrative creation of meaning: a system established to enable organisational records to be kept has the unintended consequence of assigning people to a client status. Although I agree that in this context meaning is created through administrative acts (it must be possible for the social worker to allocate the person to a category of need in both professional and organisational terms) the process I am describing is the exercise of the power to create meaning. The system is designed and run by professionals as part of the structure and method of work. Although, as I argued above, not all professionals have equal control over the system, all professional have considerable power over the potential clients, through knowledge of the criteria and the rules by which they are applied. A similar pattern has been demonstrated in the interactions between doctors and patients (for example, Rickman and Goldthorpe, 1977).

Members of the caring professions use a variety of classificatory terms about the people who use their services. Becker (1970) suggests that such classifications are based around the problems which service users pose for the professionals in achieving occupational goals. Those whom a profession accepts as clients/patients will, therefore, tend to reflect the professional image of the appropriate tasks to which it should direct its attention. In short, they will reflect the professional self-image: clients are the profession written into the wider society. As a consequence each profession seeks control over its clientele as a means of gaining control over its own occupational territory.

The strategies adopted by social work, nursing and the remedial therapies have been to create the hierarchies of desirable work which were discussed in Chapter 4. Cutting across those more objectively discernible distinctions are the simpler, more implicit ideas of the 'good' and the 'bad' client/patient. Not only are the more desirable areas of work those which allow the professional scope to practise the virtuoso skills, but the good client/patient is the person whose problems permit the professional to practise these skills in a way which is valued professionally. The good client/patient accepts the professional's methods of working, including the definition of needs and goals. The bad client/patient is one who attempts to assert his or her own demands, to subvert or to exploit the professional's intervention (Pithouse, 1987, p. 86). Such a person may be seen as 'manipulative', 'non-compliant' or 'difficult', presenting a situation which has to be managed by the profession.

Possibilities that a service user could exert any control in the process of defining the client/patient point to the replication of the duality of control and resistance in relationships between caring professionals and their clientele. It appears that the forms of power in the interactions between (clinical) practitioners and their senior colleagues are seen also in the provision of services. To what extent is this the case? It is to this question that I now wish to turn.

The power to control clients/patients

The ways in which caring professions control clients/patients can be either direct or indirect. In the earlier discussion of power it was argued that the most indirect forms are the most effective, and this is seen clearly at the point where neither professional nor client/patient identify such control as power.

Direct forms of control are those in which the professional can coerce, constrain or direct the client/patient. In the context of caring services this can include all aspects of life. Where someone lives, with whom they live, the work, education or leisure pursuits which they undertake, the food which they eat, whether and where they smoke, the clothes which they wear and their access to and use of money may all be under professional control, to varying degrees of subtlety. The most extreme form of this structuring of life was identified by Goffman (1968) as the *total institution*. The key features of the total institution derive from the location of all aspects of daily life within the one setting. Goffman developed this concept through an analysis of life in large mental hospitals. Although they had the objective goals of caring and treating, he argued that they became the means for professionals to shape the very identity of patients through control over daily life. That these institutions are being closed in Western Europe and North America reflects, in part, the extent to which this expression of professional control has weakened because it is losing its legitimacy.

Yet it is possible for such control to exist outside the bounds of large institutions. Residential homes providing care for children or adults do not, necessarily, encompass all aspects of life within the one setting. Children and young people go out to school or college and have friendships with others living elsewhere, and adults likewise may go out to work, for education or for leisure and have relationships outside a home. However, the professionals who staff homes, as well as those who make referrals or set policies, may continue to exert control through the informal rules which order daily life. Even the lack of encouragement and support may be as great a constraint for a person with a disability (whether physical or mental) as direct restraining action. In the movement into community-based services it is possible that the institution is dispersed rather than dismantled (Foucault, 1973; Scull, 1984). In such contexts the controlling power of caring professions may again become concealed, and an essential part of the radical critique of services has been to expose and challenge such power (see, for example, Wolfensberger, 1972; Giannichedda, 1988).

Outside institutions, controlling power is exercised in tasks which caring professions are given by the state. In probation work, and social work with juvenile offenders, the use of social work-trained staff enables social control to work through the guise of social care (Rodger, 1988, p. 577). The caring ideology of the service, to help and to treat, is grounded in the system of legally sanctioned punishment. In the UK a probation officer can ask a court to review a probation order if the client is in breach of its terms, and can use this explicitly or implicitly in relationships with individual clients to exercise influence (Day, 1981). The compliance of the client can be sought through the threat of a more coercive outcome. In the mental health services in the UK social workers and nurses play a major role in compelling clients/patients to enter or remain in hospital, and receive assessment or treatment. Although dependent on the diagnostic power of psychiatrists to define mental ill health, social workers in particular have a key role in compelling a person to enter a hospital (Olsen, 1984). In the mid-1980s the legislation was revised, but although more scope for appeal against detention was introduced, most of the checks on the power of the professionals involved were achieved by spreading accountability amongst other professions. While it may be that diffusion of this sort can provide the beginning of power-sharing with service users, it does not appear to have been achieved in this case, nor do the specific circumstances point to such a development. Wilding argues that a system of checks and balances must to some extent depend on the review of one professional's actions by another, but he notes that professionals may influence each other so that collusion remains a risk, and his observations seem pertinent to this example (Wilding, 1982, pp. 44–9).

A major reason why it may be difficult within professions and within the wider society to contemplate the sharing of power with service users is that by definition the need for caring suggests an incapacity to exercise a full adult social role. Parsons' classic formulation of the 'sick role' sought to explain the relationship between professionals (especially physicians) and people who are ill in precisely these terms (Parsons, 1952). His formulation has four main themes:

(1) the sick role legitimates exemption from normal social responsibilities;
(2) the sick person needs help and cannot be expected to become well through unaided action – it is the condition which must be changed and not an attitude;
(3) there is an obligation on the sick person to get well;
(4) so there is an obligation to seek *technically competent* help and to *cooperate* with that help in trying to get well. (Parsons, 1952, pp. 436–7)

Points (1) and (2) are conditional on points (3) and (4), so that the privileges of the sick role are balanced by obligations and the role is both temporary and dependent on the sanction of the wider society (Parsons, 1952, pp. 437–8).

So, for example, when a person is sick it is acceptable for her or him not to go to work, not to look after children or other dependents, not to attend to the obligations of friendship and so on. (Whether or not it is practicable is another issue). However, in accepting the sick role power is given to others; in particular doctors exercise considerable power in defining who is and who is not 'really' sick and therefore eligible for this restricted social role. In Parsons' analysis this is seen as socially desirable because it sets limits on the role, provides an incentive for people to 'get better' and at the same time limits ordinary social pressures which may be harmful to those who are ill (Parsons, 1952, pp. 312–13). Therefore, in these terms, the sick role contributes to the equilibrium and stability of society through the regulation of 'opting-out' and the protection of those who need to 'opt out' temporarily without being seen as deviant.

Despite its central place in thinking about health and illness, Parsons' concept has been criticised on several grounds (Wolinsky and Wolinsky, 1981, p. 229). The arguments against Parsons can be summarised in three points:

(1) his concept apples to acute physiological health, but has less validity in relations to chronic or psychiatric problems;
(2) Parsons does not acknowledge cultural differences or racism, and gives only scant attention to other questions of possible social inequalities (for example gender);
(3) Subsequent changes in the status of professionals turn his conclusions into further questions for investigation. (Wolinsky and Wolinsky, 1981, p. 231)

So, first, those who are sick long-term, people with disabilities, people with mental health problems, people who are frail or infirm because of old age and those who cannot cope with the demands of everyday life are all outside the Parsonian sick role (Osmond and Siegler, 1971). The type and extent of their needs and their perceived lack of capacity to 'get better', and sometimes a socially ascribed lack of will in getting better, reduce the protection afforded by the sick role to the point at which these people may become defined as deviant. The lack of power on the part of people in these groups (and by implication the exercise of power by others in relations to them) therefore should not be surprising, as in industrial societies deviance is contained and even punished rather than supported.

Not only is access to the sick role affected by the type of problems faced by individuals, but also by wider issues of social inequality. Factors of race and culture, of gender, of income and so on all play a part in the way the sick role is sought and in professional responses (Wolinsky and Wolinsky, 1981, p. 239). Wolinsky and Wolinsky suggest that less powerful groups may use the sick role to cope with apparent social 'failure', but in so doing are required to accept the power of those who exercise the authority to make such distinctions (and who, in these terms, are more likely to be white, male and middle-class). Wolinsky and Wolinsky argue that the power derived from these inequalities is only evident in a strong form in relation to the poorest sections of society because the growth of consumerism has meant that choice between and criticism of professionals is becoming more possible (1981, pp. 239–40). However, I would suggest it should be noted that these people are more likely to be black and/or female, to have long-term illness or disability or to be old, and I will return to these issues below in this and the following chapters.

Both the sick role and the ascriptions of deviance to more dependent groups provide the basis of power exercised by caring professionals at the individual level. The right of nurses, remedial therapists and social workers to expect answers to their questions and compliance to their directions is based upon a particular understanding of these roles. As I have noted previously such assumptions are likely to be shared, and service users are as likely as professionals to expect that professional instructions will be followed if the aim is to 'get better'. A refusal to comply seems more likely when the service user is defined as deviant rather than sick. Social workers may be more used to such challenge by their clients, because their service users are more likely to be seen as deviant both by other members of society and to recognise such a categorisation of themselves by others. This experience is shared with nurses in the fields of mental health and learning difficulties. It may even be that the deviant role is being rejected in challenges to professionals.

Yet the rights of caring professions to exercise power over service users are themselves ambiguous, reflecting both the disputed terrain of the definition of clientele and the types of service which they provide. The implications of the sickness and deviance roles for the power of caring professions must be understood in the context of the forms of professionalisation which these occupations have followed. In previous chapters I have identified the tendency for the caring professions to be concerned with those groups of people who are more likely to be located on the ambiguous boundary between the roles of sickness and deviance. Moreover, the sickness and deviance roles which provide the basis of power for caring professions provide greater power for the more established professions such as law and medicine. For example, the ultimate reward or sanction in a professional and client/patient relationship may be the ending of the client/patient role. Yet in most contexts nurses and remedial therapists have to refer the person back to the doctor for a final examination, and social workers also may have to refer the person back to a court or allow a court order to expire. When asked, 'why do I have to stay here?' (for example, in bed, or in a residential home), the answer may well be, 'because the doctor says so', or 'because the judge says so'. If 'because I say so' is used as a response it is more open to challenge, and the appeal to another profession or institution remains possible as a further source of legitimation for the instruction. The more a caring profession's work is open to such scrutiny and control by other professions the more circumscribed is its own power. In this way the power of caring professions based on roles of sickness and deviance is bounded by and grounded in the legal and institutional structures of society, operating through other occupations as well as in a direct form. Indirect forms of power also derive from these bases (for instance, the power to interpret rules in specific situations), but are mediated through the organisational roles which caring professional play (as employees

of a health authority or a social work agency, for example).
So their power can be limited by the resources over which
they have control or control of access, and by the public
recognition of the extent of their knowledge and expertise.

Control over resources may be obvious as a form of
power when the resources concerned are material, such as
aids for daily living to help a person with a physical disability or a place in a day centre. What may be less apparent, even to the professionals, is the power they exercise
through their command over the considerable resource of
their own time, from being available to help someone get
to the toilet or use a bed pan through to the time needed
to counsel or provide advice. At the point of contact with
the service user decisions about the amount time spent
with any one person and how it is used lies in the immediate grasp of the professional. This may be marginally less
the case for nurses and some remedial therapists in hospitals, but in the community the invisibility of work to
superiors (which was discussed in previous chapters) means
that practitioners have a lot of discretion.

Four effects of the professional control over resources
have been identified by Wilding (1982, pp. 39–41):

(1) irrespective of the intentions of policy-makers, pro-
    fessionals can determine the ways in which service
    actually operate;
(2) services can be deployed to meet the interests of the
    professionals rather than to meet client/patient need;
(3) planning and management can be undermined;
(4) the political nature of policy-making is usurped, and
    obscured.

These effects form a series, in that each establishes the
conditions of the next. The professional determination of
the delivery of services creates the opportunity to deploy
services in the professionals' interests, undermining planning and management, which in turn usurps and obscures
the political dimension of resource allocation. The conclusion is that what should be identified as a political process becomes regarded as a matter of technical judgement.

The biases which are introduced through professional control reflect distortions of race and gender in the structures of the professions themselves, and these will be examined in the following chapters.

Reducing the political dimension of resource allocation to an issue of technical judgement shores up the power of professionals over service users at all levels, including the practice level where individual decisions are made. However, for the caring professions the depoliticisation of resources is not without contradictions, because in the fiscal crises of the welfare state the demand for resources has continued to grow while the resources available in the public sector have reduced, and the cost of resources in the private sector has increased (Offe, 1984). This has led to campaigns in the UK by professional associations and trades unions against the reduction of government spending on health and welfare, and recommendations to their members to make the political dimension of resource allocation and planning explicit to service users (for example, see Glastonbury *et al.*, 1982, p. 163).

Nevertheless, in the public view, a decision to administer a treatment in a particular way or to allocate a material resource is the responsibility of the professional. This is not to say that it will be always uncontested. The acquiescence of service users will depend on their attitude to the role of client/patient and the legitimacy of the caring professional's exercise of power. These in turn will be affected by the gender, race, class, disability, age and sexuality of both parties. Legitimacy in this context derives from two sources: knowledge and organisational position.

Both control of knowledge by caring professionals and their organisational relationship to clients are connected with the class position of large sections of the latter; indeed, the large majority of social work clients in particular are working-class (Jones, 1983). This is not surprising, given the origins of caring professions in the wider social concern with the literal and metaphorical hygiene of industrial capitalist society based on productive labour. Although parts of nursing, the remedial therapies and social work also were originally recruited from the working classes, the development of training, career patterns and work autonomy (as far as that has been achieved) all serve to separate these occupations from the working class as it is popularly perceived and to locate them (notwithstanding the continued selling of their labour power to earn their living) in the middle classes. In terms of education, level of income and working conditions they are distinct from manual and clerical workers. The proletarianisation debate and the theory of the labour process draw attention to the ambiguities of the class differences between caring professions and their clients/patients, but do not resolve them.

Education creates a divide both in the knowledge and skills which are gained and in the values which are promoted as well as in the possession of credentials. Dingwall's (1977) study of health visitor training provides an example of how patterns of speech, dress and behaviour are related to professionalism, and to the relationships with clients. In his example this was exemplified in a discussion about the use of vernacular (1977, pp. 131–2). Studies of social work clients have shown that variations of speech patterns are understood by clients as a reflection of class differences with professionals (Mayer and Timms, 1970; Sainsbury, 1975). Bernstein (1973) argues that language use communicates class, and reinforces social divisions. The education of caring professionals reinforces this, as students learn both forms of knowledge and also the forms of language within which the knowledge is embedded. Thinking, doing and speaking the profession cannot be separated. While detailed aspects of knowledge will not be shared with other professions, ways of talking about and organising the world are shared (as they are with other parts of the middle classes). So despite their collective or personal origins, and despite the objectivity of their paid employment, working-class clients/patients perceive caring professionals as middle-class. This class difference is bound up with the exclusion of the working-class clientele from both professional knowledge and the way in which that knowledge is used to accomplish the everyday work of an occupation. The very claim to knowledge establishes an element of class position and adds to the legitimacy of professional power.

Where the form of knowledge claimed by the occupation is strongly demarcated the action of the professional will carry greater legitimacy with a service user than if the form of knowledge is weakly demarcated (Rodger, 1988). It is at this point that the struggles of the caring professions to establish areas of knowledge becomes crucially important in relationships with clients/patients. Where demarcation is strong, decisions and actions can rest on the legitimacy of 'you know best, you're the professional'. The issue of organisational position is obscured. Where the demarcation of an area of knowledge is weak then the organisational position is made more explicit. This may be legitimate, as in 'I know you've got to apply the rules'. At the same time it is more open to dispute in accusations of unfairness or misunderstanding. Fairness is a relative concept (Jordan, 1987), with clear cultural dimensions, and any people who are denied services for which they have asked may feel themselves by definition to have been misunderstood.

The organisational position, fragile in isolation as a legitimating criterion, is buttresed not only by the control of knowledge but also by the difficulty for a client/patient in exercising any choice about who provides nursing, remedial therapy or social work. A nurse, remedial therapist or social worker is assigned to the client/patient by the agency or the hospital, through ward rotas, attachment to clinics or caseload allocation by senior colleagues. In state and voluntary agencies there has been a reluctance to address the concept that the service user could have the right to ask for a change in practitioner, in all contexts and not only where there is an element of statutory authority on the part of the professional. The organisational basis of the employment of most caring professionals has served to limit the choices available to service users in a way which mirrors the restrictive cartels operating between other professionals. An example of this has been noted by Foster (1979), operating informally between doctors in Britain, with some implications also for nurses and remedial therapists. Even in private practice the primary fee-paying relationship is often with an institution or agency as a whole or with a professional such as a doctor, and this again places the caring professional in an indirect relationship with the service user. Either the institution/agency or the other professional is the employer of the caring professional, and in the last resort the service user exerts control through the channel.

A class division can be noted also between caring professions in that while the capitalist and middle classes may employ private nurses or physiotherapists they are unlikely to employ directly occupational therapists or social workers, at least by those names. The more physical the intervention or treatment the more it can be seen as acceptable in capitalist and middle-class terms. Occupational therapy and social work have failed to shake off the image of having developed specifically to restore the working class to productive labour. This has not prevented members of these occupations from selling their skills under other guises, as counsellors and psychotherapists for example. However, these are often the very skills which it is claimed are impossible (the orthodox critique) or irrelevant (the radical critique) to practise with the large working-class proportion of the clientele who use these services. To the extent that problems of health and welfare are suffered disproportionately by poor working-class people (Townsend and Davidson, 1982), then the largest number of service users will be from that class. The poor, it seems, will always be with the caring professions.

Boundary maintenance: us and them

Not only do caring professions exercise power over clients/patients through the structuring of welfare, that is material power, but they also dominate in the production of images and meanings concerning the status and roles of clients/patients. In short, they exercise ideological power. This has consequences both for the client/patient and for the caring professional. it is a process which serves to establish and sustain the identity of each.

In an earlier section of this chapter I discussed the creation of clients and patients by the action of professionals, in deciding who will or will not receive services. Definitional power goes beyond this, extending into the establishment of typifications about people who use welfare services, and the development of mental categories within which professional thinking takes place.

Mental constructs do not form a monolithic body; professional thinking is diverse and even contradictory. One example of this, prevalent in all the occupations under discussion, is seen in debates between an emphasis on the one hand on the objectivity of the problem, clinical or social, with which the service user is helped, and an emphasis on the other hand on the subjectivity of the person who is the service user. In nursing or remedial therapy the former is exemplified by a concentration on medical conditions (reflecting the dominance of medical knowledge), while in social work it is seen in the use of social science or administrative categories (Philp, 1979; Miller, 1989). The person becomes identified as 'a cardiac arrest', or 'a hemiplegia' or as part of 'a problem family'. Empirical research provides many examples of the conscious way in which these categories are used by professionals to structure their thinking and their communication (Smith, 1980; Satyamurti, 1981; Pithouse, 1987). They are a verbal shorthand, as well as forming a mental shorthand with which the nature of problems and appropriate responses can be summed up in a short phrase. (This shorthand can be used also to exclude outsiders, in which case it is often attacked as 'jargon'.) Because such categories are routinised they are rarely subjected to critical scrutiny, and their power rests on their taken-for-grantedness.

The alternative perspective, emphasising the subjectivity of the service user, is much less evident because it is more diffuse. It can be seen at the level of generalised appeals to values (Pearson, 1975). In social work this is represented *par excellence* by the writing of Biestek (1961), who codified seven principles of casework which centre on a notion of the historical individuality of the client. The service user, in this set of meanings, is a person primarily, whose situation has to be approached in its entirety prior to any intervention by the professional. This perspective in marking the boundaries of the nature of a client or patient moves more explicitly into the realm of moral definition, while the former, more objective approach to categorisation has the ·appearance of being value-free. The power of the subjective approach is twofold. It enables the professional to exercise control over the image of a service user according to circumstances (this person is deserving of help, while that person is not). Furthermore it provides a basis for appeals which a profession can make about itself through statements about the service user. The weakness of the approach stems from the contested nature of social values, and that as much as it creates the possibilities for the positive valuing of service users so it also opens up the potential for moral devaluation.

Pithouse (1987), in his study of social work, demonstrates how the movement from objective to subjective and from high to low moral value of the service user as an abstract concept is contextualised in relation to concrete situations. The same phenomenon has been noted in nursing (Walsh and Elling, 1977). Moreover, these are not perceived as clear and unambiguous choices by caring professionals. Objectivity and subjectivity, high and low moral value are contradictions which can be expressed about the same service users. As Pithouse expresses it, the service user is both a generalised worthy citizen and at the same time a type of person with substantial negative qualities marking them off from the rest of the public (1987, p. 85).

The negative qualities of the social work client may be easy to recognise, as social work serves people who cannot cope with their problems (England, 1986). Indeed, 'the problem family' or 'the delinquent youngster' may be the archetype for the public image of the clients of social work. Nursing and remedial therapies do not of themselves conjure up quite the same clear images, largely because people of quite different statuses will use their services in acute health crises. When the more chronic forms of health care are considered, including care provided for people with severe learning difficulties, long-term physical disabilities and mental health problems (especially if compounded by old age), then the need for nursing care or remedial therapy can bring with it stigma through the use of such services. In the USA acute health care in the public sector hospitals can also be stigmatising, because of their association with poverty. Large numbers of the clients/patients of these professions are stigmatised through the association they have with the receipt of the service.

As I noted in an earlier discussion, the stigma is attached to the service user, and the caring professions may try to avoid it through seeking to work with the higher-status groups or types of work. However, there is a circularity which develops from this, as the process to stigmatisation can become short-circuited so that the client/patient attracts a devalued status simply through seeking a service, irrespective of other criteria (including the individuality of her or his circumstances) (Gouldner, 1975). The more caring professions have avoided working with certain groups the more their general social status is reinforced and the more caring professions have avoided working with them.

Less apparent, but equally powerful, are professional concepts of culpability. The idea that the person may be responsible in some way for their condition or problems also affects professional images (although the reverse does not appear to work for highly devalued groups). The nurse may see the person with heart disease as careless in their diet and physical exercise, the physiotherapist may regard the young person with leg injuries from a motoring accident as having been reckless, the social worker may see the parent with rent arrears as feckless. In each instance the ascription of responsibility serves to undermine the standing of the service user as a capable person and the generalisation that people who need caring services are incompetent is reinforced.

Caring professionals maintain a social distance from their clients/patients. Satyamurti explains this as a response to a fear of being controlled by the service user (1981, p. 148). Strategies include the use of separate facilities (especially toilets), doors marked 'private' and formality of interaction. In hospital nursing the use of job title (for example 'nurse' or 'sister') instead of names is part of this process, where the anonymity of the professional and the personalisation of the patient expresses the relative possession and lack of knowledge of each about the other. In the community, or in remedial therapy or social work the use of surnames is the parallel. 'Thus when workers insist on the use of surnames in their meetings with clients this has more to do with issues of subtle control than a concern for a well mannered exchange' (Pithouse, 1987, p. 99). Control is even more evident when the service user is addressed by first name but is expected to address the professional by title and last name. This linguistic distinction, in the use of familiar and polite forms of expression, is a means through which power is communicated and reinforced (Day, 1981). Although this device is not used in all relationships with service users, it does enable the professional both to control the interaction and to use the interaction for control. To the extent that Satyamurti (1981) sees the stigmatising effect of welfare provision as a control mechanism then I agree with this analysis. However, I think that the relationship has wider implications. The distance maintained between caring professionals and their clients or patients is itself part of the stigmatising process.

Maintaining social distance not only provides the professional with power over images of the client/patient, it also serves to sustain the self-images of the professional. It reinforces the common-sense notions of nurses, remedial therapists and social workers as competent and caring (Dingwall, 1977; Satyamurti, 1981). To the extent that 'our' clients or patients are incompetent, then this reinforces 'our' competence – 'we' are capable when 'they' are not. Such a separation is based on the possibility that by failing to construct and defend clear boundaries the professional becomes too closely linked with the service user, a process which Goffman (1964) has called pollution.

This can be seen when professionals accuse one another of 'acting like a patient' or 'talking like a client', and use about colleagues terms which are normally reserved for those service users who exert any resistance to professional control, such as 'uncooperative' or 'manipulative', to discredit the colleagues' actions. It can be seen also when accusations are made by those outside the caring professions that they undermine social structures by giving impartial service (Siporin, 1982). Failing to make such distinctions threatens the way in which a separation of the deserving and the undeserving continues to permeate social thought about welfare provision (Jones, 1983), and may undermine the legitimacy of an occupation. The radical strands of the caring professions have been especially open to such attacks, because such occupations as a whole are part of these structures, and although they occupy particular positions within the social framework they cannot be entirely separated from the logic with which the framework is built. The contradictions which this engenders (service users are simultaneously worthy and unworthy) are coped with in the shifting sets of professional meanings and the ambiguities evident in everyday practice.

I have argued above that the nature of a profession is defined by the company it keeps (see Chapter 4). In the context of practice this can mean that the relationship between the provider and user of a service is structured in such a way as to maintain the image of the service provider. The caring professions often attract members because of their commitment to ideas of service and caring (see, for example, Dingwall, 1977, p. 73). Working with people who are seen to have considerable needs is the real work. However, at the same time there is an element of risk associated with such work, through the association with stigmatised social groups. The resulting objectification of subjective problems and the contradictions between the valued client/ patient and stigmatised people is a form of the strategy for coping with the conflicting demands of practice which was first noticed with respect to doctors by Becker *et al.* (1961). The forms it takes differs because of the variations between the professional groups involved, but the underlying dynamic is the same.

The client strikes back: challenging professional power

Who clients/patients are, the nature of their problems and the relationships which they have with nursing, remedial therapy or social work are created and sustained through organisational and occupational forces. In this way it may be said that service users are intimately bound up with the agencies and professions through which they receive services, while at the same time they are excluded from those agencies and professions. Clients/patients exist through the role which they play in health and welfare services (that of user), but their very inclusion in that role defines them as outsiders and so excludes them. This position clearly is contradictory, and while people seek the role of client/patient because they perceive a need for a service, they do so with the intention of ceasing to occupy the role at the earliest opportunity (health restored, welfare problems solved). For those people with long-term needs this presents a peculiar dilemma: to seek this role with all its contradictions, but without the possibility of resolving the situation. This, I think, reinforces the devaluation of long-term service users.

Responses to the contradictory position of service users vary from the acquiescent to the resistant. Despite the material and ideological power exercised by caring professionals, in which control over concrete services as well as the implications of stigma create circumstances in which it may make more sense for the client/patient to acquiesce, resistance is possible and even widespread.

Challenges to professional power at the individual level have been identified above in those actions which are labelled by professionals as uncooperative, manipulative, obstructive, ungrateful and so on. Each of these terms is the occupational response to a service user whose actions resist in some way the professional definition of the means, the scope, the goals or the values with which the service user is being expected to comply. The weakness of individual resistance lies in the potential of these ascriptions as a means of undermining the service user through moral devaluations. Yet there are limits to professional power at the individual level in so far as the contradiction between caring and controlling is not resolvable but remains in tension. The child who runs away from a residential home, the person who will not enter a mental hospital voluntarily, the person who will not take medication can force the professional into an overtly coercive role and so undermine the caring element of the work. In so doing the legitimacy of the role for the professional can be challenged. Although there have been attempts to theorise the necessity of control in caring (for example Day, 1981), studies of nursing in the UK and Australian social work, for example, have indicated that being faced with a stark reminder of the contradiction can confront the professional self-image, and may at times account for occupational wastage (O'Connor and Dalgleish, 1986; Hockey, 1987; Mackay, 1989).

Collective challenges to professional power are stronger, and have the potential for creating some change in relationships between caring professions and service users. This can be seen in the development of diverse groups which, in various ways, bring together service users with the aim of furthering their interests. These groups may be distinguished between self-help groups and pressure groups, although there are some which combine the two elements.

Self-help groups are usually organised around a specific theme, issue or problem. They are based on the assumption that, at best, the professionals lack the experience of a problem which would enable them to understand from a service user's viewpoint, or that at worst professionals are damaging and at best to be avoided (Wilson, 1987). Such groups provide alternatives to help from professionals, both in the sense of providing a choice and also working in a very different way. The term self-help includes not only service provision, but also consciousness-raising and mutual support. Indeed, it is the mutuality of such groups which is their defining feature.

As Collins and Stein note, the diversity of such groups makes providing a comprehensive list very difficult (1989, p. 98). However, such a list would include groups for people with alcohol problems, ex-prisoners, people addicted to tranquillisers, people who have been bereaved, parents of children with severe learning difficulties and the carers of elderly people. It includes also people who come together because of a common experience of their wider structural position, such as women's groups, gay and lesbian groups or groups for people of a specific ethnic or racial background (Sondhi, 1982; Dominelli and McLeod, 1989). (Groups organised around opposition to these oppressions exist also within caring professions.) Because of the diversity, generalisation about structures is also difficult, as some groups have only a few members while others form a national network between local groups (Collins and Stein, 1989). One key characteristic may be identified, that all such groups have a local focus, and where there is a national dimension it serves to bring together the local groups.

In contrast pressure groups tend to have a national focus. Again examples include groups about young people in care, mental health, people with physical disabilities and older people. Because of their campaigning nature many of these groups do not attempt to provide any direct services, but seek rather to influence policy and practice at all levels. This may be directed quite specifically at government agencies, as with the campaigns of the National Association of Young People in Care (NAYPIC) in the UK (Stein, 1983), or the patients' councils in psychiatric hospitals in Britain, the Netherlands, Italy and the USA (Rose and Black, 1985). Their actions have been focused on the rights of the service users, challenging administrative and professional practices and seeking an extension of the opportunities for service users to take responsibility for themselves. These are very focused groups, and as Stein notes in relation to NAYPIC any role which outsiders might have is restricted and controlled by the members (1983, p. 9). The Grey Panther movement in the USA differs from this in that its membership is wide; although it is concerned with issues of age and ageism membership is not restricted by age or any other criteria, and it confronts a diversity of issues (Phillipson, 1982). Outsiders to this movement are people who do not identify themselves with it; eligibility for membership is based on interest and concern.

A different type of service user group is that which brings together indirect service users. These are the informal carers, usually relatives and usually women, to whom caring professions are likely to be an alternative (rather than the other way round) (Bayley, 1973; Hicks, 1988). Because of the vast amount of care provided informally carers also have an interest in the relationship between direct service users and the professionals. Indeed, the interests of direct and indirect users may conflict (Ramon, 1988), and this can be exemplified in the opposite stances sometimes taken by patients' and relatives' groups over the closure of large institutions. Carers' groups have provided the opportunity for the indirect users of services to recognise and express their common interests, and they have achieved some influence amongst politicians and professionals as well as providing a means for individual carers to gain access to caring professionals (Ungerson, 1987).

Collective action provides an opportunity for the empowerment of service users who as individuals are powerless through dependence on professionals for services and through the stimagtising nature of their problems, but who can exert pressure on professionals when working together. Some groups exclude professionals, as I have noted, while some incorporate professionals, assigning them supporting roles under the direction of the service users themselves. The common factor is that all these groups have in some way the goal of enabling service users to assert their own perspective through the creation of a collective voice.

It should not be thought that the professionals against whom service users struggle are an undifferentiated mass. In part the circumstances which enable service users to exercise power relate to divisions within and between professions and the alignment if some professionals with service users, although this may be a minority (Ramon, 1988). The caring professions have been criticised from within as well as without, and members of these occupations have been included amongst the critics as well as those criticised.

Within this complex set of relationships there are some nurses, remedial therapists and social workers who have defined their role as sharing their power with service users (as have some members of other professions, such as medicine and law). Sharing power may take the form of supporting and encouraging service users to exercise control and influence, an example of which would be the use of professional skills to enable service users to participate in group meetings. Or sharing power may mean making professional power available on behalf of service users, by supporting demands for access to contexts which may have been closed previously (such as the right to be heard by policy-makers, managers, professional associations and trade unions as well as by individual decision-makers). Speaking on behalf of service users is a weaker version of this, as the right to speak concentrates power in the hands of the speaker, and there may be a conflict of interest. Countering this, the concept and practice of advocacy has developed, especially in Canada. Advocacy is based on the struggle for the voice of the service user to be heard, either in person (self-advocacy) or through another person acting on behalf of the service user (citizen advocacy), and seeks the establishment of the right of the service user to be heard by professionals and other decision-makers (Wolfensberger and Zauka, 1973; Williams and Shoultz, 1982).

A further development from advocacy, also in Canada, has been the practice of 'brokerage', in which the service user takes charge of planning and managing the use of services (Brandon, 1989). This approach has been developed in services for people with long-term care needs as a means of empowering them through the control of services. It makes financial resources available to be spent by the person on services, rather than having them planned by professionals or administrators. This may include employment of a broker (someone with knowledge of services and skills in advocacy) to act for the service user as an agent. At all times the professionals in the services purchased and the broker are 'employed' by the service user in the sense that the funding is under her or his control, and they may in some circumstances literally be employed. The principles underlying brokerage are based on a restructuring of the power between service providers and service users, where influence, reward and even (financial) coercion may be exerted through material means, enabling the service user to make decisions.

While the UK has seen the gradual impact of brokerage towards the end of the 1980s, a more substantial development (which also originated in North America) has been the 'case manager' model of practice, in which a budget is given to a professional to manage with or on behalf of the service user (Challis and Davies, 1986; Davies and Challis, 1986). Case management grew out of a criticism of the organisation of caring services and related professional practices, in which service users were fitted into available services rather than services being matched to needs. The 'case manager' and the service user negotiate services using a budget which may include public service provision, voluntary input and private services. This approach allows considerable flexibility, and the individual service user's choices to be considered, although unlike brokerage it does not assume the budget is actually given to the service user.

There are parallels between brokerage and case management on the one hand, and consumerism on the other. The client/patient (cast as a somewhat passive social role) becomes a consumer or customer (regarded in consumerist terms as a more active social role), in which the person using services exercises power through choices made in a welfare market-place. The basis for the service user to exercise power over services is that of the market force of demand. It is through this connection that such ideas became incorporated in UK policy in the late 1980s, and can be seen in the roles of professionals in public and private health and welfare agencies envisaged by Griffiths (1988) and those proposed by the Conservative government (DoH, 1989).

The circumstances in which these approaches have been developed are the growth of the 'New Right' and the subsequent restructuring of health and welfare based on a private sector model. The emergence of the 'New Right', and its impact on welfare provision exemplified by the policies of the Conservative administration in the UK and the Republican administration in the USA (Cousins, 1987), has the appearance of creating the necessary conditions for a rebalancing of power between professionals and their clientele. There is an emphasis on developing choice by breaking up large state agencies and the introduction of financial control strategies combined with low taxation and the promotion of market mechanisms in welfare. However, as Offe (1984) indicates, the social relationships which structure welfare are external to the market. In addition these changes are consequent on a strong state (Gamble, 1986). I have already noted that professions are dependent on the state for the legitimacy of their credentials, and the state needs professionals to undertake both care and control functions. While the challenge to professional power from the state has made use of consumerism to legitimate attacks on professions at the ideological level (Mishra, 1986), at the same time the extent of mutual dependency may strengthen the position of professions in so far as they seek technical autonomy, with the result that the material conditions for changing power relationships between professionals and their clientele are called into question.

There are two apparent contradictions in the development of these responses to issues of power over, and of, service users. The first is to be seen in North America, where the extension of welfare payments in health care in the USA, through Medicare and Medicaid, has resulted in an expansion of costs for the state and increased profits for commercial organisations (Cousins, 1987, pp. 153–4). (This includes not only profit-making hospitals and clinics, but also drug companies, equipment, suppliers and construction companies.) The net result has been a mushrooming of financial management techniques to reduce costs, which have in turn reinforced professional control over the services available. The outcome is that, although consumers can choose, they can only choose within a range of alternatives which are professionally determined. These do not include specialities which are unprofitable and this may lead to some communities being without basic health care facilities (Cousins, 1987, p. 155). The conclusion is the reduction of services for the most disadvantaged and devalued groups. Feminist critics have noted also that within this approach basic care can depend on the unpaid work of women relatives and neighbours (Finch and Groves, 1980; Finch, 1984; Dalley, 1988), and as such may improve services (in terms of choice and involvement) for some members of society at the expense of others.

The second contradiction is that consumerism may only partly change the basic relationship between service users and service providers, and does not change the underlying relationship between the state and unwaged service users. It is possible to argue that a different form of professionalism could emerge from consumerism. In the terms established by Johnson (1972) the free-market model of health and welfare appears to convert mediation professionalism into patronage. Would this not be to the benefit of caring professions, providing further opportunities for professionalisation along the lines of architecture, accountancy and so on, as well as to the advantage of service users? At the micro-level of everyday practice such a shift may well be possible, for example in the capacity of service users to make choices between the caring professionals by whom they are provided with services. However, at the wider level the majority of service users are likely to remain dependent on the state to some degree for the financial resources with which to exercise consumerist power. This maintains the political dimension of the relationship and the underlying structure continues to be mediative, with state control operating through the levels of funding which are provided. Without a right to a minimum income sufficient to meet an accepted average rather than a subsistence level of need (Jordan, 1987), the class position of the majority of service users will remain that of a claimant and not the property owner on whom the concept of patronage is based. State control may be maintained in the forms of reduced levels of financial support, stricter controls on eligibility or both.

Furthermore, as the forms of credentialism in caring professions are weaker than those of the 'established' professions there is greater pressure on the state to establish monitoring systems, which in turn are staffed by professionals. An example in the UK context is the inspectorial powers of state health and social services agencies in relation to the provision of private nursing homes and elderly people's homes. Although the power to act is exercised by the courts in the last instance, inspections and recommendations are made by nurses and social workers; so the professionals remain accountable ultimately to the state and not directly to the service users.

These patterns can be seen to have emerged in the UK during the 1980s through the Conservative government's use of public welfare payments to create a private market in staffed residential accommodation for elderly people (Henwood, 1986). This has precipitated a further potential crisis for service users. As costs have become almost uncontrolled, through a lack of viable alternatives to residential care combined with the owners and managers of such services seeking to maximise their income, the response of the state has been to introduce measures restricting the scope of such funds from 1991 onwards (Cohen, 1989). As a consequence private residential care may cease to be an option for service users who lack personal financial resources. In such circumstances the meaning of consumer choice increasingly becomes questionable. Community care (that is, care provided in the service user's own home) may become the only possibility irrespective of the desirability to the individual.

So, while brokerage and case management contain the seeds of possibility for reshaping the power relationships between professionals and service users, the ground in which they have been planted, as concepts and as practices, creates the conditions for them to grow in particular ways. In relations between service users and professionals providing general day-to-day care they may enable power to be shared. For their wider potential to be realised, outside the boundaries of specific instances, a greater commitment to meeting health and welfare needs socially and not through privatised individualism will be required. Without this wider perspective, which engages with the ideological determination of the *ends* of health and welfare, they are confined at the technical level of service provision in a restructuring of *means* to ends which are established elsewhere.

Moreover, brokerage and case management do not address directly the coercive aspects of caring professions (for example, in aspects of child care or of mental health) where service use is involuntary, although advocacy may do so in some circumstances (Collins and Stein, 1989). What of the service user who is compelled (for example, by a court) to receive a service, or where a caring intervention becomes coercive (for example, a child at a nursery with suspected non-accidental injury)? While service users may be excluded, by definition, from an exercise of power at an individual level in such circumstances, they remain citizens with basic rights which should be protected, it may be argued, within professional structures and practices. Democratic accountability of this type has been developed in relation to the police (Simey, 1989), suggesting a possible basis for the empowerment of people who are compelled to receive services in some way as well as those who may be regarded as voluntary users of services. Such developments have operated through the collective involvement of service user groups and members of the wider society in the establishment and monitoring of policies (Croft and Beresford, 1989). I will examine the practical implications of such approaches in the final chapter.

It is necessary also to consider an empowerment of service users which did not simultaneously disempower caring professionals through a commodification of welfare. In the context of the history of professionalisation in caring occupations disempowerment could occur through technical deskilling as the state exerted indirect control over the use of public funds. In turn this would compound inequalities, particularly of racism and of gender (which will be examined in detail in the following chapters). In the context of the privatisation of welfare, recasting the service user as consumer is likely to have this impact.

An alternative approach to the empowerment of service users must be one which recognises mutual collective interests between service users and members of caring professions. The alternative approach could be conceived of as a 'power *sharing*', going beyond the relationships between individual professionals and service users, necessary as that is in everyday practice. What would be required is a reframing of professional and organisational structures in which the interests of both service users and professionals are recognised and met. Such a development would 'not [be] asking for a change in individual attitudes but a reformation of the structure of professional service orientations' (Haug, 1973, p. 205). The uncertainty of changes in health and welfare have created the circumstances in which it is possible to envisage caring professions identifying commonality of interests with service users from the threats currently posed to health and welfare provisions. In the concluding chapter I will discuss the implications such prospects hold for the future of professionalisation in nursing, remedial therapies and social work. However, prior to that I want to examine two crucial areas in which relationships between caring professionals and service users, as well as those within caring professions, can be identified as forms and uses of power: racism and gender.

6

Racism in Caring Professions

The question of racism

Black people in the UK are more likely to be unemployed than white people, and where they are employed are more likely to have jobs which are lower-paid and of lower status in comparison with white people (Brown, 1984). This is so in health services and in personal social services. Not only are black people less likely than white people to be employed (relative to proportions of the population) but they are less likely than white people to be promoted into senior positions (Torkington, 1983; Rooney, 1987; Watkins, 1987; Dominelli, 1988; Grimsley and Bhat, 1988). With few exceptions (for example, Doeringer and Piore, 1985) sociologists of organisations and of the professions have tended to ignore racism. This has served to continue the invisibility of a major issue facing caring professions and has failed to provide the theoretical tools with which this problem can be grasped.

The UK pattern of racism in health and welfare employment is an institutional expression of the white racism which finds its origins in Western Europe and which has both 'exported' and buttressed at home through colonialism (Kovel, 1970; Asad, 1973; Wellman, 1977). Similar detailed patterns of employment, for example, are also to be seen in the USA, and there too there are clear links with the colonialist past (Brown, 1975). In the contemporary world South Africa probably represents the epitome of the fruits of post-colonial racism. Yet proper concern with the future

146

of that country should not obscure the relationship it has with the UK, the USA, the Netherlands and other white societies (historically and in the present), nor the fact that South Africa sits on a continuum with these countries rather than forming a sharply divided category of its own (Brittan and Maynard, 1984). The danger is that concern with the situation in another country can obscure the necessary understanding of one's own society. The critical analysis of racism must begin at home. For caring professions this must involve the understanding of racism within those occupations. So in this chapter I want to look at the way in which racism affects the organisation and employment of caring professions and then to go on to examine racism in practice as it affects both caring professionals and their service users.

Organisational racism

Racism in the employment of black people within health and welfare is demonstrated immediately statistical evidence is considered. For example, in 1982 one teaching hospital in the UK city of Liverpool had only three black nurses in training out of 306, no black staff nurses out of 146, three black sisters/charge nurses out of 92 and no black nurses above that level (Torkington, 1983, p. 14). There are a total of 471 black staff in the health authority (3 per cent of the total workforce) of whom 200 are nurses, 159 doctors and dentists and the other 112 are technical, clerical and ancillary workers (1983, p. 77). This is out of a total black population in the city of 40 000 (1983, p. 81). Even though measures have been taken through equal opportunities policies to end intentional bias, these figures show the long-term effects of discrimination in employment. This is not an issue only for the health services. In the same city the employment of black social workers shows a similar pattern (Rooney, 1987). What is important in highlighting Liverpool is that in the UK it has a very long-established black population (dating back to the nineteenth century), with an absence of large-scale migration in the 1950s and 1960s and an age structure which is comparable to that of the white population (Ben-Tovim *et al.*, 1986; Rooney, 1987).

There are similarities between the situation in Liverpool and that of social work in other parts of the UK (Stubbs, 1985). Where this picture differs from other analyses is in the area of health. Doyal *et al.* identify much larger proportions of black workers in the health service, with 17 per cent of trainee nurses born overseas, and in their own survey in a London hospital 81 per cent of- the trained nurses were born overseas (1981, p. 58). The difference between Liverpool and London can be accounted for by the migrant nature of the black workforce. Specific efforts had been made in London during the preceding decades to recruit overseas health workers, particularly from parts of the 'New Commonwealth'. Behind this plan, that black workers were to be used to solve a workforce crisis, lay a subtle racism. Black workers were recruited more to fill enrolled nurse or auxiliary posts than as registered nurses (large numbers of maintenance and ancillary workers and smaller numbers of doctors also are born overseas). Incorporated in this recruitment pattern is not only a sexism (women targeted for nursing recruitment) but also a post-colonialism in a search for black people from former colonies to undertake the lower-paid jobs. Carby (1982) criticises this as the reproduction of a 'black as slave' image which is comparable to, although distinct from, the 'woman as carer' image of sexism.

The comparison between Liverpool and London demonstrates that while planners, managers and politicians were working to attract black staff to the NHS from abroad there was a systematic exclusion of black British people from entry to caring professions. These factors demonstrate that the use of large-scale immigration and cultural stereotypes as explanations for the lack of black people in caring professions is in itself a failure to recognise the racism which is endemic in UK society.

In contemporary health and welfare organisations racism is evident in a number of ways: it may appear overtly in personal forms; it may be institutionalised in organisational structures and practices; and it may be seen in the framework of policies for the caring professions. In each case the effect is the same, to reproduce the power of white people over black people both as professionals and as service users through diverse biases in the provision of services.

Overt racism can prevent black people from obtaining entry to caring professions. There may be a selection of only those applicants with white-sounding names for interview, but for black people to get through this barrier so often is only to delay rejection. 'For many of us with English surnames we get as far as the interview room before the employer realises that you are black. It is the eyes that give them away. You can tell just by looking at the eyes that you have lost the job even before the interview starts' (quoted in Torkington, 1983, p. 13). Torkington reports that a study of postal applications for jobs showed that people with black foreign names were not invited for interview, though they lived in the same areas and had the same qualifications as their white counterparts. Torkington also provides an example from nursing, quoting evidence that up to ten years ago one group of hospitals in Liverpool actively discriminated on grounds of race and class (1983, p. 15).

Institutional racism differs from personal racism in that it arises not from conscious acts but from the failure of practitioners, managers and policy-makers to recognise the power structures of the everyday world, in which power is exercised by white people without their awareness. The consequence is seen in statements that 'this organisation is not racist' or that 'we treat everyone the same' which are not disingenuous, but which fail to take account of the differential distribution of social power (Brittan and Maynard, 1984; Dominelli, 1988). This analysis follows from the understanding of white racism not simply as a set of personal practices on the part of deviant individuals, but as part of the fabric of society. It is not something which white people can opt out of just be being well-intentioned. In the UK context this dilemma is revealed in attempts to redress the exclusion of access for black people to work in the caring professions, either through equal opportunities policies or through the use of special funding under Section 11 of the Local Government Act 1966 or under the Inner City Partnership and the Urban Aid grants (Waller, 1982; Rooney, 1987). Before examining the policy aspects of these practices, I want to look at their organisational impact.

The use of special funding has had the effect of creating a service which is marginal to the purposes and functioning of local authority social services departments (Rooney, 1987). While they have created opportunities for black people to gain access to employment in social work they have done so through the creation of distinct groups within departments. In an attempt to redress the inequalities in access to education different criteria for the selection of black staff have been used, so that living locally and involvement in the community rather than formal qualifications are seen as relevant attributes. However, when the relationship of specially funded posts to the rest of the organisation is examined, a boundary is visible, across which the specially funded workers cannot pass. As a result, a two-tier structure of employment has emerged which is constructed along racial lines. As Dominelli comments, when white people are employed under such finance they are more easily incorporated into the overall structure of the departments, while black people are more visible and are less likely to have had the opportunities to gain the credentials which would help them over the boundary (1988, p. 142).

Racism and the internal labour market

A major concern of Doeringer and Piore (1985) in their development of the 'internal labour market' concept was to explain the operation of racial discrimination in employment. The concept of the internal labour market is based on the distinction between a primary and a secondary sector, in which the primary sector is higher-paid, has access to careers, is stable and to which there is restricted

access from the secondary sector. The segmentations which
this produces are controlled through different points of
access to employment, in which workers within a labour
force have privileges over those in the general labour
market, and this internal control provides the basis for a
dual structure. Within these structures racism operates at
several levels. First, it can occur at the initial point of
entry, either deliberately as we have seen above or through
institutional factors (which may even run counter to overt
aims) (Doeringer and Piore, 1985, p. 137). Second, it operates in the movement between the two sectors through
mechanisms for transfer which are developed. Third,
racism operates inside each sector to the extent that they
may compromise a career based on a series of hierarchical
levels. Within sectors types of work, for example, can
be institutionalised and form the basis for discrimination
(whether intentional or unintentional) through decisions
about promotion and work allocation within that sector.
Doeringer and Piore refer to these latter two elements as
internal allocative rules (1985, p. 140).

The internal labour market, divided into two sectors,
can be represented diagrammatically (see Figure 6.1)
Within the diagram, the effects of employment practices
in caring professions are identified in racial terms. This
does not mean that no black people are employed in the
primary sector, or that no white people are employed in
the secondary sector (although it does assume that the
labour pool includes both black and white workers, and
this may not necessarily be the case). Doeringer and Piore
developed their theory originally in contexts in which deliberate and total segregation was operating. However, by
making the racial segregation explicit this draws our attention to the underlying structure. What is portrayed here is
the impact of factors such as education, housing, the wider
labour market and so on combined with the criteria used
for selection of staff which together created differential
opportunities for black and white people in obtaining
employment in caring professions. (Similarities with the
relative positions of men and women *vis-à-vis* primary and
secondary sectors will be explored in the next chapter.)

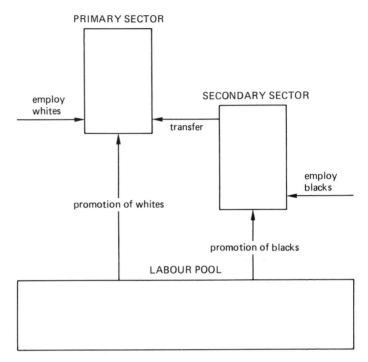

Figure 6.1 *Racial bias in employment patterns*

Source: adapted from Doeringer and Piore, 1985, p. 144:
'functionally unrelated promotion units with racial segregation'.

So although such a picture tends to produce a simplified explanation which requires further accounts of other factors such as gender and disability, it becomes possible in these terms to identify the attempts to create a body of black social work practitioners through the route of special funding as having led to the creation of a dual internal labour market in welfare. Figure 6.1 portrays the effective impact of specially funded projects on employment patterns in welfare organisations. The social workers who have been employed in specially funded posts have tended to be located at the lower practice levels, precisely because they have been recruited either from the existing workforce (in 'non-professional' areas of work) or externally on the basis of their membership of ethnic minority communities and not on the basis of the possession of recognised social work qualifications, while at the same time the latter is used as the sole criteria for access to the primary sector. Within the hierarchical career structures this has trapped a number of black workers who, without the provision of training opportunities, face a boundary between their secondary position and that of the qualified social worker to whom a career is potentially available (Rooney, 1987). Some of these forms of funding are time-limited; that is they are 'unstable' (Doeringer and Piore, 1985), and as a consequence they reinforce the secondary nature of this type of employment.

In the health service in the UK the division between primary and secondary employment has a different form. The major distinction in nursing has not been based as much on the possession of a qualification as on the type of qualification, divided between registered and enrolled nurses. This has parallels in the US system of registered and licensed nurses. Although enrolled nurses (and their licensed equivalents) are qualified nurses, the level of their qualification is regarded as lower, because the training period is shorter and is seen as having a more practical than academic base. So although enrolled nurses have been distinct from auxiliaries and assistants, they have shared with the latter group the features of the secondary labour market. The career paths which are open to registered nurses are not open to those with lower or no qualifications, pay scales are lower and jobs are less stable (with greater use of such nurses in part-time, contract and short-term working). This divide is one which has racial features, in that black nurses are more likely to be employed as enrolled and licensed nurses or assistants than as registered nurses, either in the UK or the USA (Doyal *et al.*, 1981; Brown, 1975). This has happened as a consequence of racism in other spheres (education, social security and so on) as well as from overt and institutional discrimination in selection. In this way health services also constitute internal labour markets divided between a primary and a secondary sector.

However, racism in the dual labour market is not defined solely by types of qualification. As we have already seen, the numbers of black nurses who progress to positions of seniority is extremely small. A possible explanation is that this is a result of early discrimination, and that the situation will change as more black nurses attain a sufficient level of experience to apply for such posts. However, such an argument is very weak because it assumes that racism is only a matter of isolated discriminations and that all other factors are equal. It ignores the continuation of institutional racism in selection procedures, and the continual training of staff towards promotion which is a major feature of the internal labour market (Torkington, 1983). Also it ignores the lack of evidence that would point in this direction. Rather, as Doyal *et al.* point out, the changes in immigration rules in the 1980s will have had the opposite impact, especially given the large proportion of black nurses who are migrant workers (1981, p. 66). That is, UK-born black people have not been recruited to the NHS, and the large majority of black workers have been migrant. Moreover, the changes in nurse training in the UK, *Project 2000*, indicate a move to a clearer two-tier distinction between registered and assistant nurses (Allan, 1989). It is intended formally that enrolled nurses will be able to take additional examinations and to progress to registration, but under present conditions there is little evidence that the structural disadvantage to black nurses have been considered.

In the remedial therapies the position of black professionals has not received more than a small amount of attention. For example, although figures are reported in research about the recruitment of occupational therapy students in the USA, showing that approximately 12 per cent are black (including Hispanic and native American) (Wyrick and Stern, 1987), the issues surrounding the figures are not discussed. The only conclusion drawn is the recommendation that 'high school conselors, occupational therapists and current students should target . . . minority students [sic] in high school' (Wyrick and Stern, 1987, p. 177). So although there is not a total 'colour blindness' in the consideration of who is entering occupational therapy, the reality of their lives both outside the profession and within it are not examined. That black potential occupational therapists are simply waiting to be encouraged to apply for training is a naive conclusion which fails to take account of the institutional, and sometimes overtly personal, racisms against which black applicants for professional training have to struggle. It assumes that the dominance of occupational therapy by white people is the result of the failure of black people to act rather than the reproduction of structural racism, and in so doing obscures the location of changes which are necessary in order to work against racism.

Equal opportunities: the solution or another problem?

Recognition of the racial biases in caring professions has produced a range of responses. In the USA the use of registration and government direction prohibiting discrimination, in the Federal Executive Orders and the Title VII of the Civil Rights Act 1964, applies to federal contractors, private employers and trades unions (Doeringer and Piore, 1985, pp. 134–5). Within this context the use of quotas and targets in the employment of black people has emerged as a possible means to provide objective measures of non-discrimination. In the UK the Race Relations Act 1976, Section 71, places a duty on local authorities to end discriminations, and to promote equal opportunities and good relations between racial groups (Wells, 1982, p. 43). This had led to the development of monitoring of 'ethnic origin', some attempts to examine practices (both professional and organisational) and to formulate 'equal opportunities policies'. However, in both the USA and the UK there have been unforeseen obstacles to the implementation of antidiscriminatory action, which reveal the necessity of understanding the central problem as racism and not simply an abstract issue of 'opportunity'.

A major weakness of attempts to address racism has been a failure to make connections between its various manifestations. This can be seen, for example, in the creation of separate groups of black professionals which are disconnected from the mainstream structures and which do not incorporate mechanisms for bridging the gap which I have already discussed (Rooney, 1987). It can be seen in a failure to recognise the ways in which issues of gender of class cross-out those of race, so that the position of enrolled nurses, for instance, is examined only from one dimension and not with respect to the multiple oppressions which may be experienced (Doyal *et al.*, 1981). Where such connections are not made the outcome can be the creation of further barriers for black people, who are used to provide a limited black presence, or simply used to provide labour, but who are denied open access on terms which it is possible to meet. (This is an entirely different issue from that of autonomous black groups, to which I will return below.)

The action of trades unions in relation to racism have been ambiguous. Although they provide a basis for groups of professionals to engage with their employing organisations, at the same time their attention to the interests of their members may fail to address the interests of black members either because they do not recognise their black membership or because they pursue policies which have the unintended consequence of perpetuating racist divisions of access to the labour market (Dominelli, 1988, p. 23, p. 39). Doeringer and Piore provide graphic evidence of overt racist practices on the part of manual craft unions in the USA, in which the maintenance of white domination was explicit (1985, pp. 148–9). In the UK trades unions also have engaged in racist practices (Miles, 1982). An example which affects caring professions has been when unions have responded to situations of reduced job opportunities by pressing for agreements in which inside applicants are given the first opportunity when vacancies arise, and the same implications are to be seen in the NHS from the operation of immigration controls (Doyal *et al.*, 1981). However, in conditions where a dual structure is operating this reproduces the exclusion of black people and so is institutionally racist. Although open recruitment has loop-holes and can be subverted (see Torkington, 1983, p. 16), internal recruitment in existing circumstances can only serve to protect white union members against possible external black applicants. Where this practice has existed it has undermined attempts to develop action for equal opportunities.

Credentialism, the primacy of formal qualifications, may also be an unintended source of inequality. Attention to particular forms of skill and knowledge may serve as exclusionary devices. Nursing, the remedial therapies and social work have been defined as occupations which have claims to specific types of skill and areas of knowledge. However, as I have noted above, these were established under particular historical circumstances which included the class and gender structures of the late nineteenth and early twentieth centuries as well as global colonialism. While the pattern of professionalism has developed and changed over the last century, it has proceeded in a series of develop-ments rather than through making a significant break with the past. Moreover, professionalism has taken place in conditions of continuing racism. As a consequence the types of skill and knowledge which have come to define caring professions are ethnocentric (Stubbs, 1985; Domi-nelli, 1988). While I would wish to avoid the opposite problem of 'racial essentialism' or 'ethnic absolutism' about which Gilroy warns (1987, pp. 64–8), nevertheless it can be seen that a concentration on over-generalised skills and knowledge obscures the importance of racism in the experi-ence of black people in white societies, at both personal and structural levels. The necessity of recognising these experiences and the capacity to relate to black communities is now argued for as a way of refocusing the issue of qualifications around anti-racism (Stubbs, 1985; Williams, 1987). This is more than multicultural knowledge, in which power effectively remains with white professionals (Man-ning and Ohri, 1982), but addresses the structures of pro-fessions as distinct occupations.

Not only is there the possibility for equal opportunities

policies to be undermined by the factors of organisation, unionism and professionalism, but also there has been an element of voluntary involvement in the UK on the part of service agencies, who are formally encouraged but not required to identify themselves as 'equal opportunity employers'. Surveys undertaken by the Equal Opportunities Review (EOR), the Commission for Racial Equality (CRE) and the Policy Studies Institute (PSI) (Owusu-Bempah, 1989; Ranger, 1989) have shown that although over half the public agencies declared themselves as equal opportunity employers there was not necessarily an explicit policy developed by the agency to guide practice, and Owusu-Bempah (1989, p. 23) records that in one study 88 per cent of the 144 policy statements examined were no more than a simple statement of intent. Ranger (1989, p. 16) notes from the CRE survey that some agencies relied on a general statement of intent, or the inclusion of a statement about equal opportunities in other documents. The provision of interpreters, translation of information into minority languages and training of staff appeared to be increasingly common, but Owusu-Bempah is more critical (1989, p. 25) and points to the way in which equal opportunity statements can be used as a smokescreen behind which institutional racism remains intact. It becomes, he argues, a form of image management which presents the 'acceptable face' of a new institutional racism.

The conclusion which can be drawn is that attempts to change the caring professions cannot be based solely on the idea of equal opportunities if they are to have any real impact. While the employment of more black professionals may in itself be an indicator of change, the potential for them to be marginalised or ill-used (for example in being treated as experts on 'ethnic issues' but not as equal professionals) remains (Stubbs, 1985). Stubbs refers to the concept of 'intermediate reforms' (1985, pp. 22–3) which are in themselves insufficient for effective change, but which may be necessary pre-conditions to more significant transformations. At the same time any reforms cannot be seen in a mechanistic or deterministic way as 'requirements', but as elements of strategies which must be related to concrete situations. The principles through which this can be achieved are identified by Stubbs (1985, p. 23) in three points made by Dominelli (1979) in relation to social work training, but which have general implications for nursing and remedial therapies also. These points may be summarised as follows:

(1)   anti-racist practice must be rooted in structural under-standings of racism;
(2)   equal opportunities policies must be framed and implemented in terms of a commitment to anti-racism, and;
(3)   black professionals can only be influential if they form 'leadership groups' to monitor policy and practice.

From a structural understanding of racism it becomes clear that equal opportunities must be based on anti-racism both as the means and as the goal. To enable this to take place the marginalisation of black professionals must be challenged, and this can only take place when structural positions to enable black people to exercise influence are created within professions and organisations.

As the concept behind attempts to address racism in caring professions the idea of equal opportunities is insufficient. In order for more effective changes to take place it must be seen as part of a wider strategy of anti-racism which would enable both individual actions and structural constraints to be challenged. Without this emphasis policies remain trapped at the level of ideal intentions because they can be subverted, opposed or can produce unintended consequences.

Racism and practice

Institutional and individual racism is to be seen not only in the structure of professions and organisations, but also in the services which they produce. In order to examine these in more detail three aspects will be focused on: physical health, mental health and child care. These areas of practice are not intended to represent the totality of issues around racism and practice, but they provide key examples which enable core themes to be explored. In doing so I do not intend to concentrate on detailed examples of individual racism, but to stress the institutional aspects. This is not because I intend to minimise the insult and distress caused to black people by individual racisms, whether intentional or unintentional. Graphic accounts are given by Torkington (1983) and Bryan *et al.* (1985), and certainly enable the impact of racism in concrete situations to be grasped. However, my concern here is to examine the more general implications for the caring professions and to place these in the wider context.

Physical health

There are two major ways in which racism affects the physical health of black people in white societies. There are the forms of knowledge utilised by health professionals, and the contribution of racism in all its forms to the creation of ill-health in black communities. The former is to be seen in the points of contact between black people and health services, while the latter reflects the structures of Western European and North American societies.

Torkington (1983) and Grimsley and Bhat (1988) have identified institutional racism in the lack of recognition given to diseases and physical conditions which specifically affect black people in the UK. These are the 'haemoglobinopathies' (Grimsley and Bhat, 1988, p. 191) which occur in the form of sickle cell disease, sickle cell trait, thalassaemia, glucose-6-phosphate dehydrogenase deficiency, mineralisation deficiencies which occur as rickets and osteomalacia and the vitamin deficiencies, especially of vitamins B_{12} and D. These health problems affect different groups in the UK, with haemoglobinopathies most prevalent amongst people of Afro-Caribbean or Mediterranean origin, and mineral and vitamin deficiencies most prevalent amongst people of Asian origin.

The impact of racism can be located in the general responses of the medical and nursing professions. Generally there has been a failure of institutional health knowledge to acknowledge the importance of these issues for black health service users. By this I mean that although such knowledge is available it appears to form a negligible part, if at all, of formalised state medicine. As the knowledge base of nursing, midwifery and health visiting is built partly on medicine the consequence is that ethnocentric concepts of health underpin their professional training. Although the reality of such conditions will be known to black nurses, this knowledge may be devalued as a result of ethnocentricity. Also, it is important to remember that black nurses themselves are members of different communities and do not share a single common stock of knowledge.

Debates have taken place around health measures in response to these conditions. However those debates have often been predicted on racist terms. For example, discussion of mineral and vitamin deficiencies amongst the Asian communities has tended to concentrate on cultural aspects which in their terms assume the normality and superiority of white British culture (Torkington, 1983, pp. 53–60). Not only have governmental bodies made significant mistakes in their comparisons of Asian and white cultures in the UK, but also they have neglected their own public health history. The most stark example of this is in the refusal of the (then) DHSS to agree to assist in the fortification of chapati flour and ghee despite the similar fortification of bread flour and margarine which is a standard part of the diet of white communities. At the individual level this may be compounded by 'well-meaning' advice from nurses and health visitors to persuade Asian families to change their diet in a way which individualises this dietary racism. Ironically this ignores the possibility that white people may have much to learn from black communities about healthy eating, including the use of fruit and pulses in Asian diets.

The lack of attention to haemoglobinopathies in medical research cannot be laid at the door of nurses as such, but it has a major impact on the work of nurses, midwives and health visitors with black patients. Pregnancy, childbirth

and child-rearing are all crucial aspects of life in which
nurses, midwives and health visitors are involved and in
which the identification of haemoglobinopathies and counselling about them can be crucial to the life chances and
well-being of black people. Torkington records the impact
this may have in individual cases (for example, 1983
pp. 70–1), and notes that other professionals, particularly
teachers, also should be given the necessary information
to discuss the problems with parents. Most importantly,
parents themselves should be given sufficient information
and support to cope. The institutional racism which underpins this situation can be identified in a comparison with
phenylketonuria (Torkington, 1983, p. 43), which almost
always only affects white babies, but for which all babies
born in the UK are now routinely screened.

There are other health issues which, while not specific
to black people, nevertheless carry implications of racism
because they are related to life conditions, and for black
people these are structured around racism. The relationship
between race and class is crucial in a social understanding
of health, but this does not imply an equation between
race and class (Miles, 1982; Brittan and Maynard, 1984).
The class position of many black people in the UK (and
other white societies) is a determinant factor in health, but
the impact of racism is more than a surface or mediating
element of black experience of health; it is fundamental.
The report of the working party on inequalities in health
demonstrates that not only are there class differences in
health, but that standardised mortality ratios are highest
for people born in the African Commonwealth, and for
women born in the Indian sub-continent and the Caribbean
Commonwealth (Townsend and Davidson, 1982). These
figures show the links between race, class and gender
(Grimsley and Bhat, 1988). Although the figures are based
on the country of birth, and therefore do not show black
people born in the UK (the majority), they indicate the
scale of health problems experienced by migrant black
people.

Social factors which are associated with the relationship
between class and health including housing, education,

transport, employment and income, are also factors within which racism impacts. Although there are connections between each of these aspects, such that employment and income may well establish the basis for the others, there is a degree of independence such that the allocation of unhealthy housing to black people may occur solely because they are black, for example (Bryan *et al.*, 1985). The importance of this for caring professionals is that they are working with service users whose lives are affected through the compounding or even causation of ill-health by racism.

Mental health

Some psychiatrists in their work with black people have recognised the cultural and ethnic dimensions to the diagnostic process (Littlewood and Lipsedge, 1989; Rack, 1982). However, widely different approaches are taken, and Mercer (1986) draws attention to the way in which attempts to deal with issues of race and racism may treat the issues as matters of cultural knowledge, in which it is assumed that the professional will necessarily be non-racist simply by virtue of such knowledge. Mercer argues that 'ethnic sensitivity' of this type obscures power behind a series of facts and displaces racism with a psychiatric anthropology as the main focus of mental health professionals. He suggests that, in fact, the major problem for black people is the use of cultural knowledge against them in psychiatric practice which continues to be racist in its underlying structures and to be located in a powerful position in a white racist society.

There are three explanations which are advanced for the high proportions of black people who are diagnosed as having mental ill-health, the high proportions who receive phenothiazines or electro-convulsive therapy and who are subject to compulsory hospital admission (Mercer, 1986; Littlewood and Lipsedge, 1989).

(1) the experience of migration to an alien society may be psychiatrically pathogenic;

(2) there are features of black people's life experience, notably racism, in white society which are psychiatrically pathogenic, and;

(3) psychiatric practices are racist because they are ethnocentric.

Each of these views is evident in psychiatry, and through that have impacted on nursing, occupational therapy and social work.

Migration may indeed be a life experience which exacts a psychological toll, as the individual adapts to new social circumstances. However, as an explanation it is insufficient because to the extent that it is an accurate statement it requires explanation itself. For those black people who were migrant and who have settled in the white society of the UK the experience cannot be taken out of context (Phizacklea and Miles, 1980). This is most likely to have included an expectation of a good job and better living standards (Foster-Carter, 1987, p. 54). Reality was poor housing, the jobs which white people did not want and daily encounters with personal racism. Littlewood and Lipsedge point to the destructive effects on personality of these experiences, and compare this with the mental health of black people moving north in the USA (1989, p. 241). Mental ill-health may be the price of attempted adaptation to a society which is accepting only on racist terms (and so effectively rejecting).

However, the majority of black people in the UK, and in the USA, are not im/migrant, and yet the incidence of mental ill-health appears to be high amongst black people whether migrant or not (Torkington, 1983, p. 50). This suggests that there are common features of their experience which may precipitate psychological crises. Institutional and personal racism in housing, education, employment and in encounters with white people are not confined to immigrants, but are part of the experience of being black in white society. Psychological evidence suggests that one outcome of this experience can be a poor self-identity arising from the association with the negative values portrayed in the surrounding white culture (in the media and through powerful institutions including professional services (Tajfel, 1978; Maximé, 1987). Yet, as Brittan and Maynard point out, this argument can be over-stated, so that the capacity for black people to resist is ignored (1982, p. 106). Such resistance will often take the form of the assertion of those aspects of black cultures which white society devalues, and this can lead to confrontations which are perceived by the more powerful (white) group in racial terms. In this respect the power of psychiatry is buttressed by its relationship with more overtly coercive state agencies, such as the police.

Mercer argues that it is this process which is behind the over-representation of young black men in diagnoses of schizophrenia (1986). At an individual level manifestations of resistance can be interpreted as bizarre, and because they are deviant to the dominant white culture result in diagnosis of mental illness. The racism of psychiatric diagnosis lies not only in the lack of awareness of black cultural forms, but in the power of white psychiatry to impose ethnocentric concepts onto the experience of black patients. A further example of this is in assumptions about depression in Asian women, in which this may be seen as 'culturally generated' in a way which ignores the possible connections between women's lives more generally compounded by racism (Brown and Harris, 1978; Bryan *et al.*, 1985). This is not to argue that black people do not experience mental distress of mental disorder, but that it is extremely difficult to disentangle the various dimensions, and that the mental health professions have often compounded the problem rather than seeking appropriate solutions. They have sought only to increase their own knowledge without questioning the power which they exercise (Mercer, 1986).

In summary, there is a debate between 'transcultural' and 'anti-racist' practice in mental health. On the one hand there are calls for the recognition of cultural diversity, and the inclusion of more black people in diagnostic and treatment teams, not only as psychiatrists and psychologists but also as nurses, occupational therapists and social workers (Ballard, 1979; Rack, 1982). On the other hand there is the charge that 'transcultural' approaches are more concerned with maintaining the power of white psychiatry, and that the presence of black professionals is in itself no guarantee of change without a thorough critique of the ethnocentricity of psychiatric concepts and the development of anti-racist psychiatry (Mercer, 1986). Torkington, for example, refers to evidence that black professionals trained in white theories may tend to share the same basis for their work (1983, p. 51). Some transcultural approaches have begun to address this issue (Littlewood and Lipsedge, 1989). The point remains one of whether changes in practices without changes in structures will do more than consolidate professional power. Yet, to the extent that practices cannot be understood separately from the structural context in which they are situated, change of one element in isolation is improbable and this suggests that transculturalism without anti-racism will at best improve individual sensitivity and at worst increase the power of professionals.

Nurses, occupational therapists and social workers are involved in every aspect of the mental health services, from diagnosis and assessment, through treatment to aftercare. Nurses and social workers, particularly the latter, have considerable statutory powers in the process of compulsory admission to hospital. So although they stand in a relatively less powerful position to psychiatry, they share broadly the same theoretical frameworks and may use these in the influence and control of black service users. The criticism of psychiatry is also the criticism of the caring professions which are involved in the mental health services.

Child care

Whereas the practices of caring professions in physical and mental health have developed largely within arenas controlled by medicine, the caring professions themselves have had much more direct control over the field of child care. Clearly these services do not exist in isolation, but have close connections with health and education. The effects of racism in education, in particularly, on the development of black children often will be the source as well as an integral part of the context of problems addressed by nurses, remedial therapists and social workers (Solomon, 1976; Maximé, 1987; Brah and Deem, 1986). With younger children and in residential schools the line between education and care is very fine, and at times may even be blurred. However, for the purposes of this analysis I will focus on those areas of professional intervention in child care which are dominated by the impact of the professions with which I am centrally concerned, that is which are defined around nursing (in the UK particularly in the form of health visitors) and social work. Within this discussion, to explore the effects of racism in professional practices, I want to highlight two elements: images of black families, and the relevance of existing services.

Black families have been pathologised within white welfare theory and practice. This has taken varying forms with different groups, but the underlying process has been one in which stereotypes are constructed and sustained. Afro-Caribbean families have been assumed to be disorganised, failing to provide basic socialisation for their children. In the USA this view has been strengthened by official reports, such as the Moynihan Report in 1965, which have lent a legitimacy to such stereotypes (Billingsley and Giovannoni, 1972; Dominelli, 1988), and these ideas have had an impact in the UK and other parts of Western Europe. Asian families, in contrast, may be stereotyped as over-strict or that (contradictorily) Asian mothers may be too passive and tied to the home, compounding sexism with racism (Carby, 1982; Bryan *et al.*, 1985; Williams, 1987; Dominelli, 1988). The consequence appears to be that proportionately more black children end up in care than white children, and whereas the white children may be from 'atypical' white homes, the black children may be from more 'representative' black homes (Lambeth Social Services Committee, quoted in Dominelli, 1988, p. 98). It is no small irony that at at the same time assumptions about family care of black elders may result in inadequate levels of service on the assumption that the family care is strong, although many black elders do not have family in the same country (Bhalla and Blakemore, 1981), and in any case having family living near may not be an appropriate criterion for the provision of service.

Such stereotypes are incorporated in the work of white nurses, health visitors and social workers in the approach they take to child-care issues, in the services in which they are involved in developing and running and in their encounters with black families. The ideas with which white professionals work and the decision-making systems within which they are operating combine to sustain the image of white families as normal and black families as deviant. Examples including having lower expectations for the achievement of black children, or conversely forming opinions about black children which make invidious comparisons with white children, and in both cases to ignore the views of black parents (Billingsley and Giovannoni, 1972). The outcome may be a failure to intervene at appropriate times, or it may be inappropriate interventions.

A major source of concern to black communities in the UK has been the reception of children into care and subsequent placement (ABSWAP, 1981; Small, 1987; Stubbs, 1987; Dominelli, 1988). This is paralleled by critiques of child-care practices in the USA (Billingsley and Giovannoni, 1972). There are two strands to this: the first is that the criteria and the systems have been established to meet the needs of white children and white families (Small, 1987); the second is that such services are predominantly staffed by white professionals who may or may not have any commitment to addressing issues of racism in their practice (Stubbs, 1985, 1987). The outcome is that black substitute families are not recruited, either because the criteria used preclude them or because white professionals lack the skills and knowledge to undertake such recruitment. A further factor is that the black communities can be suspicious of agencies, seeing them as 'child snatchers' (Dominelli, 1988, p. 98). So, in a professional climate in which the concept of permanence in child care has come to predominate, a tendency to place children with families wherever possible results in black children being placed with white families and so very rarely the other way round. Furthermore, the concepts of substitute families which underlie placements are ethnocentric (Fletchman-Smith, 1984, quoted in Ely and Denney, 1987). The stress on adoption in contemporary practice may be less appropriate than long-term fostering in many instances.

Not only in collective terms does this create a situation in which there is a one-way traffic of black children to white families, but it also has implications for the individual children and families involved. I have noted already the evidence from psychology that in racist society black people may have their self-image undermined, and Lords (1984) suggests that black people may even come to internalise negative values which pathologise themselves. The impact which this has on black children can undermine their sense of a positive black identity and render them less able to cope with racism (Gill and Jackson, 1983; Maximé, 1987).

Although these aspects of child care predominantly concern social workers, health visitors and other professionals are involved in various ways, most notably through multi-disciplinary case conferences. They too are part of the white structures within which these practices are situated. More immediately, health visitors, like social workers, are involved routinely in counselling and advice-giving to families with small children, especially mothers. In part this is connected to the paternalistic role of professions (Ehrenreich and English, 1979). However, it also plays an important role in the ways in which white agencies meet black service users. White family standards and values can be imposed on black families in the belief that white practices are, somehow, universal and superior in their relevance (Ahmed, 1987; Dominelli, 1988). Health visitors and social workers are also involved routinely in the assessment of small children and their families, physically and socially. These encounters in professional responses to behavioural problems and allegations of child abuse frequently are the site for racism based on stereotypes attributed to black cultures (Parton and Parton, 1988). Cultural racism can take a number of forms: a belief in the superiority of white culture; a refusal to acknowledge cultural differences ('colour blindness', which can often amount to an implicit belief in white superiority); patronising acceptance of black cultures as 'quaint' or 'exotic'; or the mishandling of knowledge about other cultures in which it is applied wholesale as if there is only one black culture (Ely and Denney, 1987; Dominelli, 1988). The outcome in situations of suspected or alleged child abuse can be either an over-reaction, evidenced by the figures for admission to care, or by an under-reaction which ignores child abuse in black families (Parton and Parton, 1988).

In opposition to the prevailing racism it is argued that the caring professions must develop a positive sense of the strengths of black families and child-care practices, and take full account of these in their work (ABSWAP, 1983). In other words, it requires changes within the caring professions themselves in terms of theories and concepts of practice. It necessitates also structural changes in the composition of policy-making in child care, in consultation with black communities and through the inclusion of black people in the policy formation process. The involvement of black professionals at all levels is part of this process, but, as I have already noted, without a commitment to anti-racism in professions and organisations there is a strong probability that black perspectives will be ignored or undermined.

Black action and white responses

In response to organisational and professional racism in caring services autonomous black groups have developed, both professional organisations and voluntary groups providing direct services, advice and campaigning about services. Direct service groups include nursery provision, fostering services, health projects, women's refuges, mental health centres and day care for older people (Bhalla and Blakemore, 1981; Torkington, 1983; Ahmed, 1987; Ely and Denney, 1987; Small, 1987; Dominelli, 1988; Littlewood and Lipsedge, 1989). In each case it is possible to identify the main factor in the formation of such groups as the racism of caring services and the wider society within which they are situated. Groups are established in response to the ignoring of needs, to 'enable black people to examine their position with their specific needs in mind' (Dominelli, 1988, p. 59) without being dominated by other interests and for mutual support in combating racism. Where there is an expectation that the caring services will resort too readily to compulsory admission to hospital or to the removal of children and at the same time will ignore health needs and the needs of elderly people, then avoidance of these services and the establishment of alternatives is the outcome.

White responses to black autonomy have often tended to be defensive or antagonistic. A consequence is that such groups are criticised as 'separatist', or even that they constitute a form of 'apartheid' or 'racism'. Phillips (1982) provides a framework for establishing the difference between autonomy and separatism, that autonomous groups have their origin in a concern with the needs of black people which are not met in white racist society and with the necessity of having such groups under black control. Several purposes can be identified in black organisations. First, there is the expression of a 'cultural and historical dynamic' in structures which are relevant to the past and present needs of their members (Phillips, 1982, p. 111). They are organisations to which their members can relate. Second, black organisations enable the meeting of needs which are not met by white structures. Then, third, black control enables organisations to be developed in directions which are appropriate to the views of their members. Continuing of identity and control is possible. To use the concept of 'separatism' about black organisation is to assume either that it destroys social homogeneity or that it is an illegitimate grouping of interest communities (Phillips, 1982, p. 114). The former is a fiction, while the latter is a freedom available to other communities of interest in society. The reason why objection is made to this form of interest grouping is that it challenges the power of white people (Dominelli, 1988).

Not all white resistance to black action takes the form of overt objection. For example, within a cultural pluralist response there may be a degree of acceptance of black services for service users, but this in itself may well depend on an assumption that they are marginal to the 'mainstream' services, and such acceptance can be difficult to disentangle from a patronising 'tolerance of exotica'. The same may be true of black professional projects within organisations which were discussed above (Rooney, 1987). When attempts are made to broaden the implications of such services or projects then resistances are encountered from the white power structures. At this juncture the intersection of racism with organisational and professional power is clearly delineated. Given the position of most black professionals in organisations, attempts to construct a black perspective can be reinterpreted as resistance in hierarchical terms; that is, as a subordinate–superordinate issue in a way which is decontextualising. Similarly, support for black services, where it exists, can be derived from a sense of relief that other services do not have to adapt, or else that black services can be separated within the larger organisation (Rooney, 1987, pp. 63–4). Despite the climate of increased awareness of empowering service users, whether or not the service user is black affects the reality of relationships with caring professions.

In addition to the development of black-controlled services there is also a continuing need for the opening-up of mainstream agencies to black professionals. I put it in these terms because it is clear that policies and practices which only regard the needs and problems of black people as 'extra' or 'special' perpetuate the professional ghetto (Ely and Denney, 1987, p. 102). However this does not suggest that black professionals should simply be expected to be integrated into agencies as they exist. I have noted how particular aspects of hierarchical organisation or professionalism reliant on certain approaches to qualifications are dominant, and these tend to exclude black people. As Rooney (1982) shows, integration fails as a goal because of the power exercised within these structures. The alternative is more fundamental change which provides equity in recruitment, training and promotion, for black and white professionals, and this will only be achieved through anti-racist policies and practices.

Yet Stubbs (1985) is cautious about the development of black professionalism alone as the vehicle for change. Although the involvement of black people at all levels is necessary, without a connection between this and the professional–service user relationship there is the possibility that black professionals will become marginalised from black communities. The real danger foreseen by Stubbs' analysis is that the appointment of a few strong and effective black managers will be grasped enthusiastically as the solution when the concrete impact will be the creation of a black middle class which leaves the position of much of the black communities unaltered (1985, p. 26). In other words, anti-racism must avoid boundary maintenance of the type I discussed in Chapter 4 which would absorb some black professionals while strengthening existing power relations.

The position of black professionals and service users cannot be considered in isolation from that of white professionals and service users. Challenging and changing white racism in white communities and organisations is a task for white people (Brah and Deem, 1986; Dominelli, 1988). This includes support for black organisations, and for black-led campaigns within unions, professional associations and other locations, but it requires also that anti-racism be developed in all aspects of policy and practice including direct work with white service users. Anti-racism therefore has implications in all aspects of organisation and occupation for white professionals in caring services. Unless it does so, ideas of empowerment are incomplete, because to the extent that they ignore racism they fail to take account of a key element of organisational and professional power.

7

Gender in Caring Professions

Gendered professions

In the previous chapter racial divisions and racism as forms
of power in nursing, remedial therapies and social work
were examined. Interwoven with racial stratification there
is also a gender dimension to the divisions of labour which
are to be found in all occupations. However, as Thompson
(1983) has warned, despite some similarities and significant
points of connection we should not regard the issues in
these debates as identical. There are discontinuities also
between race and gender as aspects of occupational structure and practice. So in this chapter I will examine the
gendered nature of caring professions, again looking in
turn at their organisation and at their practices.

In talking about gender I am not referring only to distinctions of sex (femaleness and maleness) but also to social
and cultural constructions (femininity and masculinity)
which are established on the basis of ascribed sex differences (Oakley, 1974; Game and Pringle, 1983). Oakley
makes the point in addition that sexuality is another issue
again, as not all relationships between the sexes are sexual
relations (and vice versa) (Oakley, 1974, p. 12). However,
underlying the occupational structures of industrial capitalist societies is the constant equation of sex and gender, in
which the two elements are conflated and form the basis
of distinctions in all aspects of work, including employment
patterns, career opportunities and earning levels (Hakim,
1979; Game and Pringle, 1983).

174

The distribution of women and men in the caring professions displays precisely this distinction between women and men. For example, in nursing, the proportions of women in the profession as a whole have been consistently gauged over the last two decades at between 90 and 97 per cent, and of men at between 3 and 10 per cent (LeRoy, 1986, p. 29; Jolley, 1989, p. 12; Mackay, 1989, p. 186). In contrast, the proportion of managerial posts occupied by women is only around 67 per cent while men occupy 33 per cent (Carpenter, 1977). Similarly, within the remedial therapies the proportion of women is around 95 per cent and of men around 5 per cent, while between 60 per cent and 85 per cent of senior posts are occupied by women with between 15 and 40 per cent occupied by men, varying according to location and sampling method of empirical studies (Gill, 1986, p. 386; Bailey, 1988, p. 310; Rider and Brashear, 1988, p. 233). The figures in social work are slightly different, although they show the same underlying structure. In the UK at the basic grade practitioner level the ratio of women to men is approximately 2:1, but at director level only around 10 per cent of posts are occupied by women (Popplestone, 1980; Davis and Brook, 1985; Foster, 1987). There are finer distinctions also to be seen between subdivisions of the broader practice/management divide, which will be explored in more detail below.

These ratios, which show that men occupy managerial positions out of all proportions to their numbers in the caring professions as a whole, pose several questions, about the reasons for the relative presence and absence of the sexes at different structural points, the ideological constructions which serve to legitimate these differences, and the implications of gender divisions for the exercise of power. Such questions are most usually framed in terms of the position of women, but alongside this is a less often stated problem: why are men absent from some areas of work and dominant in others? These questions will run through this chapter.

Caring professions as a gendered labour market

In the previous chapter the concept of the internal labour market was discussed in relation to race and recism. This concept has been extended by Barron and Norris (1976) who argue that there is also a dual labour market which is structured around differential access to employment between the sexes. They define the primary and secondary sectors in relation to sex and gender differences in job mobility (men are more likely to move for career reasons, while women are more likely to move for domestic reasons), social attitudes (constructions such as 'women are better at routine jobs'), training opportunities (different educational patterns), attitude to pecuniary reward (men are more likely than women to be regarded as primary wage earners) and attitude to collective identity (especially trades unions). In each case the primary sector is identified with men and the secondary sector with women. This dual labour market is the context within which the employment opportunities of women and men are structured. The phenomena of pronounced differences in pay, restricted mobility across the boundary, differential access to careers and the relative stability of jobs are all gender-related. Barron and Norris explain the maintenance of this duality through the relationship of work to the wider social positions of women and men in family structures, in patterns of education and so on.

The concept of the dual labour market applied to gender segregation has been criticised by Walby (1986, 1988), who suggests that it has a more restricted utility in considering manual work in manufacturing industry within which it was originally developed. In contrast, Hakim's (1979) concepts of vertical and horizontal segregation are seen as more flexible because they open up the possibility of considering not only segregation by hierarchy, but also a division between types of job (horizontal segregation) and the relationship between the two (also see Dex, 1985). However, although there are some features of health and welfare employment which require a multidimensional analysis, there are others in which a dual structure can be seen to be operating.

If the pay structures of caring professions in the UK are examined, it can be seen that they form bureaucratic continua. The gaps between each level are rarely very large, and in some cases there may well be an overlap, so that at the break between practice and management it is possible in some instances for a very experienced and long-serving practitioner to earn slightly more than a recently promoted first-line manager who is younger. In this sense there is not a pronounced cleavage between two sectors.

However, the distribution of the professions in specific grades results in large numbers occupying low-paid posts, and small numbers at high-pay levels (Hancock, 1989). Moreover, there are disproportionate numbers of men in these higher levels, and the further up the hierarchy one looks, the more the absence of women and the presence of men becomes noticeable. To take the example of social work in the UK, the numerical dominance of men forms a taper, gradually rising between hierarchical levels, from approximately one-third at basic grade practitioner level, to around 70 per cent in middle management, and to 90 per cent in the top posts (Davis and Brook, 1985, p. 4). Although the presence of men is not so great in the other caring professions, the same underlying pattern can be discerned. So it may be said that there is a segmentation rather than a clear bifurcation of sectors, and that this segmentation is gendered.

In each of the caring professions the development of aides, assistants and auxiliaries has drawn women into their lower echelons, while at the same time excluding them from hierarchical advancement through the creation and maintenance of boundaries to qualified practitioner and management grades. These posts are overwhelmingly occupied by women. Furthermore, ancillary grades have been seen as jobs in themselves and not as a precursor to first-level professional training; this has served to create a large group of women workers for whom mobility across boundaries is very restricted, and for whom as a consequence promotional opportunities do not exist (Hugman, 1984). In this sense an internal dual labour market is evident.

The stress on formal qualifications and often on geographical mobility for promotion in caring professions may also have restrictive implications for women because of family structures and educational patterns. Married women in particular may have limitations set on geographical mobility through their husband's employment (to the extent of not considering application for jobs which would or might require such mobility), and at the same time to have limited their further education for similar reasons (Finch, 1983). Because men's pay is usually higher, the logic of following his job rather than hers may be very strong. Child-rearing patterns also have an impact, through breaks between periods of employment, or part-time work, to accommodate the needs of children, which are almost always taken by women (Hall and Hall, 1980). Neither factor serves to enhance the perceived need for women to undertake further training or qualifications, which may be expensive. The anxillary positions of the caring professions provide just the type of employment which meets these criteria (Brown, 1975). In the lower levels of the qualified professional grades the more general social position of women has a similar impact, and this can be seen in the increased proportion of men in the higher levels.

In considering stability of employment Barron and Norris (1976) were concerned with the job itself rather than the occupant. In the caring professions there is a relatively high degree of job stability at all levels, but there is a high level of turnover of staff in the professional levels compared to the ancillary groups. My own research in social services departments showed that ancillary and clerical workers were the more likely to have long services in their jobs (Hugman, 1984). Figures from nursing research show registered nurses as most likely to leave (Mackay, 1989, p. 186). Yet this can be explained also in terms of a gender division. In the social services research, the women ancillary workers were all married to men whose earnings were much higher, and who demonstrated the type of job stability to which Barron and Norris (1976) refer. This was confirmed by the relative length of service between older qualified professional women who were married to higher-earning men, and who had had breaks in their working lives to rear children, and younger qualified women who were not married or whose husbands earned similar salaries and who did not have children. The former had longer periods of employment in the one location, while the latter were more mobile.

Horizontal segregation occurs within the caring professions in the tendency for specific types of work to be undertaken by women and others by men. In social work practice women are more likely than men to work with elderly people whereas men are more likely to work with mental health service users or in child care (especially child protection) (Howe, 1986b). This is a microcosm of the more general segregation of women into caring and nurturing work. It is replicated also quite sharply in the gender division between general nursing and psychiatric nursing, with men noticeably absent from the former and present in the latter. The relative absence of men from the remedial therapies also can be understood in these terms. The connection between horizontal and vertical segregation appears most clearly in social work, where promotional opportunities are defined around client group specialism. Such specialist areas of work are dominated by child care (an area in which men are present) and to a lesser extent by mental health, but in which work with elderly people usually is not accorded a high status and may often by undertaken by unqualified workers (mostly women).

Vertical and horizontal gender segregation in employment can be seen also at the boundaries of the caring professions. A pronounced division is evident in a comparison with other areas of professional work. Law, medicine, accountancy and architecture, for example, are occupational areas which, although opening up to women, continue to be dominated numerically (as well as in other senses) by men. In this respect the status and salary levels of the caring professions may be low relative to the opportunities available elsewhere for (white) men. In contrast, they can respect areas of work for (black and white) women (and black men) with relatively high status and pay compared with available alternatives (Brown, 1975, p. 175). Other boundaries, not only with aides and assistants, but with support workers such as clerks and domestic workers are also gendered (Crompton *et al.*, 1982; Davies and Rosser, 1986). With the exception of hospital porters, the army of semi-skilled and unskilled labour which sustains the organisation of health and welfare is female. As with aides and assistants their mobility into the professional ranks is restricted by credentials, but also the other features of the dual labour market are much more evident: different (and lower) pay structures, few promotional opportunities, and greater job instability.

Within the caring professions the labour market is divided. Although there are some features of a dual labour market it is not a straightforward duality. There are a series of divisions and segmentations within caring professions and between caring professions and other occupational groups each of which must be understood as gendered. This structure systematically disadvantages women and advantages men, and in so doing it replicates the gender relations of the wider society. Caring professions are embedded in the patriarchal social structures (Walby, 1986, 1988; Hearn, 1987), reproducing relationships in which the power of men over women is sustained. This power is expressed in assumptions about and the realities of differential employment of women and men, enabling men to pursue hierarchical careers and leading to the dominance of men disproportionate to their numbers in caring professions as a whole.

Caring professions as women's work

An early discussion of gender as an issue in nursing and social work is that of Simpson and Simpson (1969). However, they explain the forms of professionalism in these occupations through an uncritical acceptance of sex and gender differences as facts (Hearn, 1982). As a consequence their work provides diverse data about employment, opportunities and attitudes without recognising that these data themselves require explanation, and cannot simply be taken as read. That professions numerically dominated by women may be seen as inferior *because* women form the majority of their members is not considered (Phillips and Taylor, 1980, p. 79; Dex, 1985).

In contrast, Hearn (1982, 1987) has developed a conception of the caring professions as occupations which demonstrate power struggles between men and women. The forms of these occupations are produced through such struggles, and they share a history of feminist action incorporated into patriarchal structures and subsequently divided and controlled by men. As Hearn recognises, different aspects are more prominent in different cases, and in some cases processes have overlapped while in others they have been separate (1982, p. 191). However, caring professions share a common gender history.

As I have noted in previous chapters, the initial development of nursing, the remedial therapies and social work came from the work of women. Some were associated with early feminism and social reform movements (Walton, 1975; Dingwall, 1977), while others appear to have had a more ambiguous relationship with these forces (Baly, 1986, pp. 192–3). Patriarchal relationships restricted the space for the growth of women's professional roles, and the compromises which emerged show that the feminist action and initial incorporation identified by Hearn (1982) appear to be opposite sides of the same coin. The spaces which women claimed were those in which they could secure their position by reason of being women. In the context of colonialist society these spaces were those of white women, as for black women caring work was structured around slavery or imperialist servitude (Foster-Carter, 1987). These are the areas of emotionality, reproduction and child care, and service modelled on the domestic world, through which the position of women in the home or domestic service is replicated in health and welfare work. Within patriarchal society the nature of the work and the fact that it is performed by women combine as the basis for domination by men. As Hearn states, this may be in the form of service to individual men and/or service to professions where the internal domination by men is complete (1982, p. 192).

Nursing, especially in hospitals, represents a particularly clear example of the professionalisation of women's domestic roles. From the Victorian matron who had authority in the domestic sphere while subject to the overall male authority of doctors, nurses have been the 'housewives' of medicine (Gamarnikow, 1978). This is evident in early descriptions of nursing, which stressed a combination of domestic skills and obedience (Bullough, 1975; Williams, 1980), and the characteristics of a 'good nurse' and a 'good woman' may be widely regarded as identical still (Game and Pringle, 1983; Oakley, 1984). To the extent that an equation between women and caring (in both senses of the word) is part of patriarchal ideology the power of this perception is compelling for women as well as for men, and provides a frame of reference within which gendered occupational relationships are seen as natural.

Where the relationship may appear unnatural is when the nurse is a man. Game and Pringle compare the treatment of female and male nurses in which the equation of nurse and woman leads to problems of role identity. The problem is resolved by the solution that 'if they happen to be male and heterosexual, then they're not nurses' (1983, pp. 110–11). The corollary which might be anticipated, that homosexual male nurses are treated as equivalent to women, does not hold any they may be marginalised further because they pose a threat to patriarchal masculinity. Gender boundaries cross occupational boundaries, so that although heterosexual male nurses do not gain an equivalence with doctors, they have greater power both in relation to the doctors and to their female (and homosexual male) colleagues. It is *women's* sexuality around which caring as tending work is constructed (Parkin, 1989), so the presence of men creates ambiguities which are managed situationally to sustain patriarchal perceptions and relationships and to counter the threat of ambiguity.

An identification of remedial therapies as women's work in this way also can be made. Even when they are concerned with technical treatments, these have a domestic element to them. Indeed, the concept of daily living skills which is part of contemporary occupational therapy is grounded in the domestic world (Mocellin, 1988). In a previous era occupational therapists also provided diversionary activities, with the obvious parallel to play which in a patriarchal and industrial world is devalued. The arts-and-crafts image, with its associations of a quasi-mystic assumption of the value of creative activity (Levine, 1987) is one that occupational therapists have striven to abandon (Mocellin, 1988). The overt rationale for this development is in professionalising struggles (a search for a more 'scientific' practice), but was connected to the stereotypically feminine associations of many of the activities which historically were used in therapy, such as needlework and basket-weaving (although woodwork and metalwork might be used with male patients) (Reese, 1987). In comparison, the practices of physiotherapy are centred solely on the tending and rehabilitation of the patient's body, through exercise and massage, although the objective of improving the patient's capacities is broadly the same. The importance of tending as an ideological element in the history of physiotherapy can be seen in an early statement of the value of 'traditions of noble and devoted womanhood' in the profession (CSP, 1980, p. 163).

Both these groups have similarities with nursing and early social work in hospitals (which were influential, as I have noted above, in their development) in two ways. First, because they were created in the spaces which medicine controlled they have cultures of obedience to (male) doctors, who have the legally defined right to direct their work. Second, because of the content of the work they have been women's professions numerically. So despite the technical orientation of these professions the two factors combine to locate them as subordinate to the masculine instrumentality of medicine, that is in a 'feminine' role.

Men in remedial therapy also experience themselves as working in a woman's profession. As with nursing there is a tendency for men to regard certain types of tasks as more appropriately 'men's work', and this is shared by women colleagues (Rider and Brashear, 1988, p. 232). Such tasks include the provision of male role models for service users, to provide activities for male service users and to deal with physically 'hard to manage' service users. These assumptions are gendered in their sexual and social constructions of the differences between men and women. That is, where they talk of male roles they mean those which are stereotypically masculine, imply that there are distinctive masculine activities in therapy and assume increased physical strength on the part of men, reflecting the widespread equation of masculinity and strength in work ideologies (Mills, 1989). The necessity for the employment of men in remedial therapy is established around the assumption that there are some areas in which women are deficient. The evidence that this is not a form of marginality can be seen in the high proportion who are promoted into managerial levels (Mills, 1989, p. 233).

Social work shares gender origins with the other caring professions, and like them is concerned with the emotional, reproductive and domestic areas of life in its focus on the coping of families and individuals (with child care, with young people, with disabilities and with dependent elderly people) (Hearn, 1982; Davis and Brook, 1985; Hanmer and Statham, 1988; Dominelli and McLeod, 1989). Although there is an element of social policing in the social work role, especially in statutory contexts, it is largely the policing of the family and the home and this is locked in a contradiction with caring (Donzelot, 1980). In this sense social work is concerned with the scrutiny of women's domestic performance, controlling caring and caring through control (Wise, 1985; Hanmer and Statham, 1988). Historically these aims were achieved through the supervision and support of working-class women (as wives and mothers) and their children. Wilson (1977) points to the irony that, in the early days of social work, women professionals rarely shared their women clients' experience of being married, having children or undertaking their own domestic work. In the modern era the class divide often remains, but the situation of middle-class women has changed dramatically so that it is possible for feminist social work to be grounded on the recognition of the shared experience of professionals and clients as women, although issues for black feminists often are different from those of white feminists (Carby, 1982; Bryan *et al.*, 1985; Hanmer and Statham, 1988; Dominelli and McLeod, 1989). A cautionary note has to be attached to this analysis, however, as most social workers have not been clients (Hudson, 1985; Beresford and Croft, 1986).

The places which men have tended to occupy in social work practice have been associated more with control than care, and this in turn is explicable in terms of the construction of masculinity in ways which stresses instrumentality over emotion (Bowl, 1985; Seidler, 1985; Howe, 1986b). This can be seen in the male dominance in work with offenders (Parry and Parry, 1979; Hearn, 1982) which has parallels with the 'masculinity' of asylum work in nursing (Carpenter, 1980). There is a class dimension also to male involvement in direct practice, that men within social work were originally recruited from the more respectable sections of the working class (Parry and Parry, 1979). The greater degree of a control element combined with the development of organisational independence may account for the more rapid growth of the numbers of men in social work compared to nursing or the remedial therapies.

The social construction of caring professions as women's work has had the effect of legitimating their lower status, particularly in relation to the established professions. The very concept of the *semi*-profession serves as a disguise that the work in question concerns those areas of society which are regarded as the domain of women, as workers and consumers. The beneficiaries have been men, as husbands and fathers; but amongst men there are also divisions of class and race, in that the interests of men as a whole are defined in terms of the interests of employers, members of the established professions and so on, and the interests of white men dominate those of black men. As a consequence the caring professions have developed to service these interests, and so they replicate the patriarchal relationships of women servicing men (while at the same time reproducing racism). The relatively low salary levels (caring is done for love, not money) and the conditions in which managerial control is regarded as natural and necessary (which was discussed in Chapter 3) can be seen as the outcomes of the position of women within patriarchy, and not from the intrinsic nature of the tasks which they perform (Davis and Brook, 1985, p. 17; compare with the statements by male nurses quoted in Carpenter, 1980, pp. 141–2).

A carer or a career? Virtuosity revisited

A response to the ascription of lower or semi-professional status from within the caring professions has been a growing pressure towards a fuller form of professionalism (Glastonbury *et al.*, 1982; Jolley, 1989). This is the process of closure which was discussed in Chapter 4. As I noted there, appeals to virtuosity are important in the process of professionalisation. Claims to full professionalism are based around knowledge and skills which, it is argued, are uniquely possessed by a particular occupation. However, as Davies notes (1985, p. 33), virtuosity is associated with masculinity and general caring with femininity, and this point is made also by Bullough in her discussion of the care/cure divide between nursing and medicine (1975, p. 230). So to the extent that an occupation successfully makes claims to virtuosity as the key to full professional status it is creating the conditions in which men are more likely to enter and dominate that occupation. In Carpenter's telling phrase, 'feminine' positions are redefined in functional and managerial terms and so 'made ripe for male capture' (1977, p. 180). Hearn (1982, 1987) has argued that professionalisation is itself a patriarchal process, in which men have increasingly appropriated control over all areas of social and domestic life within industrial capitalism. Attempts to increase the independence of occupations like nursing, the remedial therapies and social work by strengthening their areas of expertise are grounded in claims to competence in controlling these aspects of social life. If this is the case, then the professionalisation of caring must be seen as the masculinisation of caring.

Men have entered the caring professions in increased numbers. The proportions differ between nursing, the remedial therapies and social work as we have seen because of the degree to which the content is regarded as women's work. However, as the figures stated above show, there is a substantial movement of men into managerial positions. As men have entered these occupations, which do not have full professional status, they have done so increasingly where the possibility of a masculine career has existed. Again the organisational developments of nursing and social work in the UK provide clear examples. Such developments were quite explicitly intended to attract men into these occupations as part of their professionalisation, and contained over sexisms in their views of women's capacities to manage (Carpenter, 1977, p. 180, on the Salmon Report in nursing; Davis and Brook, 1985, pp. 17–18, on the Younghusband Report in social work). (This bias was also incorporated uncritically into research on male nurses, such as Brown and Stones, 1973; and it appears in research on men in occupational therapy, such as Rider and Brashear, 1988.) Greater opportunities for management posts draw in men from middle-class backgrounds, for whom service to other professions would not be regarded as an appropriate aspiration, and men from working-class backgrounds for whom such opportunities create the possibility of mobility across class boundaries. Notwithstanding divisions of class and race between men, the gender relationships between management and practice also help to locate these developments within the patriarchal structures of the wider society.

Hearn argues that managerialism is the precursor to full professionalism rather than its antithesis precisely because it provides the basis for the entry of men to caring occupations (1982, p. 195). In contrast, many of the arguments for a new professionalism have assumed an opposition to managerialism, and one which is explicitly based on the valuing of direct work (Carpenter, 1977; Hey, 1980b); Glastonbury *et al.*, 1982). In the USA arguments have been made for the integration of the clinical specialist and management functions in nursing as a means of legitimising the role of clinical specialism. The outcome they seem is the combination of 'administrative with the professional authority' (Wallace and Corey, 1983, p. 14), or even that nursing should become the primary service, making referrals to medicine or remedial therapy within its own terms (Schutzenhofer, 1988, p. 103). Explicit reference is made in these arguments to the patriarchal structuring of women's experience. The growth of the senior clinician, it is argued, is tied to changing *women's* action within nursing in opposition to male domination (Wynd, 1985; Schutzenhofer, 1988), although there are dangers in this analysis of sliding into the blaming of women for their own oppression.

In the UK such debates have been somewhat more guarded. For example Jolley (1989), while recognising this critique of the position of nursing, finds the drive for full professionalism to be imbued with values that undermine the caring base of nursing practice. The (comparable) concept of the senior practitioner in UK social work is based on the separation of practice and management, and it has been suggested that such a move would provide a possibility for advancement for those who made a specific choice not to enter managerial positions (Hey, 1980b). In other words, 'clinical' seniority is constructed as an alternative to management. Nevertheless, the general trend in considering these changes has incorporated similar ideas about the need for caring professions to enhance the status of practice, and to create more career opportunities.

In these terms the major weakness of the move for senior clinicians/practitioners is that it is dependent on identifying and claiming skills and knowledge in the manner of the more established 'masculine' professions. Optimistically it is seen as providing a possibility of integrating caring and control in a way which equalises relations between the sexes. However, even to the extent that it provides the basis for women taking control of women's work, it appears probable that it could do so on the basis of masculinisation in that sense. Furthermore, the evidence from my own research in UK social services department is that the pressure for practitioner seniority may come from men who subscribe to the professionalistic values of practice but who see promotion into management as the only way of maximising their family income, replicating the experience of men in a diversity of work situations (Hugman, 1984, pp. 536–7; Dominelli and McLeod, 1989, p. 137). Indeed, were this to happen then Hearn's prognosis of full professionalisation as masculinisation would be realised (1982, pp. 195–6). At present women who do achieve a career may well be diverted towards specialist areas of work which are marginal to the professionals as a whole (Mackie and Pattullo, 1977). In other words, under present circumstances were seniority of practice and management to be combined we could expect to see the rapid occupation of such posts by men.

At present therefore the new professionalism which is evident in nursing, the remedial therapies and social work stands as a critique of masculine domination, but it is a critique which is unlikely to be realised without other developments. Moreover, the growth of general management in the welfare state which was discussed in Chapter 3 could accelerate the emergence of senior clinicians/practitioners not through the raising of the caring professions alone but only in association with the depression of medicine, law, and other established professions under overall management control, which is a pattern that has begun to be seen in the NHS in the UK (Cousins, 1987; Ralph, 1989). If this does happen it will give a twist to the future envisaged by Hearn, but it will be one which is still grounded in patriarchy.

A note on men, masculinity and caring

Much of the debate about gender in the professions has centred on the position and role of women. However, it is vital that if such debates are to be pursued (especially by men, including the present author), analysis does not only focus on women but on men, calling for an explanation of their positions and actions (Morgan, 1981, p. 86; Heath, 1987, pp. 8–9). How does the structuring of men's lives relate to this patriarchal domination in the caring professions?

Patriarchy is the exercise of power by men over women. It has developed in relation to capitalism, but as Walby (1986) has argued the relationship is neither deterministic or always harmonious. The separation of the public (employment) and private (domestic) spheres under capitalism creates tensions for patriarchy which are resolved through men's dominance of families at the individual level, and of the institution of the family through the state and the professions. This sustains general conditions for men to exercise power, irrespective of whether or not they are married (although that usually helps; see Finch, 1983) or of individual personality (even 'gentle' men benefit from gendered social relations; see Morgan, 1987, p. 192). Therein lies the issue for men. Patriarchy is to men's advantage, shared to some degree across class and racial boundaries (although it is internally divided by racism and class). Masculinity, socially constructed maleness, is structured around the exercise of this power. Following Hearn's assumption that patriarchy predates capitalism (1987), as capitalism separated men from the domestic sphere direct and indirect ways of sustaining male power became channelled into the professions. This can be seen in the male dominance of biological reproduction in obstetric control of midwifery and of social reproduction in the gradual male colonisation of other caring professions (Donnison, 1977).

The situational logic of masculinity and the family can undermine men attempting other forms of action. I have noted above the constraint which men in social work may experience on remaining in the practice positions which are nearer the caring core of their occupation. Ideologies of masculine roles within the family, such as the idea of being the primary financial provider, can be experienced at this level as limiting the range of options. This may be supported by the uncertainty of the relationship between masculinity and caring (Kadushin, 1976). To make a career decision counter to this logic may be costly for both public and private masculinity. Then, once having begun the career path there is an imperative to continue: masculinity is internally as well as externally competitive. Having made the break with practice there is a logic in making as much of the transition as possible. The career path is buttressed by other institutional sexisms. The effective restriction of part-time working in management levels and its proliferation at practice/clinical and support levels, is related to sexual divisions of domestic labour, especially child-rearing (Hall and Hall, 1980). I have noted also the absence of men from types of work (such as the more practical 'caring' tasks); men avoid them because they are 'women's work' and because they are 'women's work' they are not good steps in a hierarchical career. The constraint and the imperative combine to create a pressure for men which sustains a masculinity that denies the capacity men might have for an emotionality (including an involvement in the caring aspects of professional work) which is not subordinated to the exercise of power. The senior clinician/practitioner role might also benefit men in this way, were it to integrate caring and controlling in a more equal way, but within existing structures it is ambiguous for men as well as for women.

Gender in practice

Service users of the caring professions, whether direct or indirect, are predominantly women (Finch and Groves, 1980; Ungerson, 1987; Hanmer and Statham, 1988; Hicks, 1988; Dominelli and McLeod, 1989). Furthermore, the experience of being a service user, like that of being a professional, is structured patriarchally. This has implications for the provision of services, and for the relationships between service users and professionals, both at individual and collective levels. This takes the form both of the way in which services are allocated and delivered and in the extent and nature of services. To examine the implications of gender for direct work with clients/patients I want to take an overview of three major areas in which caring professionals have key roles: children and young people; mental health; and dependency in adults.

Children and young people

In the modern welfare state caring professionals are involved in most aspects of life concerned with children and young people. From contraception and abortion, through ante-natal clinics, giving birth, caring for pre-school children and school-age children to the care/control of adolescents, nurses, midwives, health visitors and social workers are concerned with providing direct services and administering welfare at the point of consumption. This point may be biological (a body, almost invariably a woman's or a child's) or it may be social (family relationships) or a combination of the two (caring practices). However, it is in the nature of patriarchal power that the way in which services are delivered obscures the gendered construction of sexuality and the family.

For example, Malinski describes how it was common practice in one US birth control clinic to remove the manufacturer's information and instructions from the packets of birth control pills and to tell the clients (often poor, black, unemployed and unmarried) that there were no problems associated with their use (1988, p. 68). Although this work was being done by women with women, the gendered power structures of the clinic created a situation where the interests of (white, middle-class) men were inbuilt into the clinic's procedures. Although I do not wish to deny that the women may have had an interest themselves in avoiding pregnancy, the possibility of their own involvement and control in contraception became lost in the medical power over women's fertility which appeared to be allied to the state's control of working-class and black families (for example, by keeping down the level of welfare benefit payments). The availability of abortion also is in male obstetric hands, and here again issues of race cross-cut those of gender, with black women often having to resist abortion being forced on them where white women may be fighting for access (Bryan *et al.*, 1985). This racism is highlighted when set against the view displayed by many nursing and medical staff that social and emotional attachment to a foetus is biologically based, and therefore natural (MacIntyre, 1976).

In the process of giving birth and becoming a mother the roles of caring professional frequently serve to confirm gender divisions between social roles (Calvert, 1985). The passivity required of a mother in medicalised childbirth is a microcosm of the passivity associated with femininity. For example, the advice and instruction given by midwives, nurses and health visitors can undermine the mother's status as an adult. In this context again the actions of women within patriarchal professionalism may mirror the role of male professionals giving advice and instruction to women (Ehrenreich and English, 1979). If there are problems in the care of small children, or parents are suspected of neglecting or harming the child then social workers and health visitors intervene, but their attention is frequently directed towards the mother. Even though it is almost always the father, or another significant male adult, who has abused the child the practices of social work and health visitors have been to concentrate on the mother, to the extent of placing responsibility on the mother for ensuring that further abuse does not happen (Hanmer and Statham, 1988, pp. 19–20). Such practices are based on theories of the collusion of women in male violence towards children, an intellectualisation which essentially blames women for the exercise of power by men (Parton and Parton, 1988).

From before birth and through the period when a child is growing up the practice of the caring professions is based on assumptions about the relative roles of women and men within the family. Services which might be expected to support mothers (and fathers) experiencing difficulties also contribute to the maintenance of these distinctions. In particular, the limited availability of nurseries and child-minders has consequences for women's employment, which might help mothers financially and socially, because employment presents child-care problems (Calvert, 1985). Moreover, child-minding takes place within the home and relies on the low-paid and isolated work of other women. Child-care provision is structured within the wider context of employment and social security policies which are themselves also grounded in a patriarchal framework. Such policies create an environment in which the assumption of gender divisions in employment and child-rearing become incorporated into professional practices. The result is that child-care, which might promote a better life for a mother and her children, is most likely to be available if she is assessed as 'unfit' in the mothering role (Hanmer and Statham, 1988). Despite the work of Rutter (1986) social work and health visiting theory is still predicated on the belief that young children cannot relate to more than one carer. So child-care is more easily available when it meets the needs of the caring professions to fulfil their state functions than for women to meet their family needs.

In adolescence people are treated variously according to their sex. For example the pattern of sentencing, influenced by the reports of social workers and probation officers, and the extent of resources provided for young men who offend differ from the state's response to delinquent young women (Gelsthorpe, 1987; Hudson, 1988). Not only do the stages of punishment for young men form a longer and more gradual series than those for young women, and the range of community-based alternatives to custody is more extensive, but the very types of action which will be regarded as delinquent are different. Most glaringly, professional intervention with a young man who is heterosexually active is very unlikely, whereas a young woman who is sexually active or a young man who is homosexually active will be regarded almost inevitably as in 'moral danger'. The former reinforces the ideology of masculinity ('boys will be boys') while the latter challenge patriarchy either through a resistance to male control of female sexuality or by confronting masculinity itself (Hudson, 1988).

In each aspect of the child's development the interventions of the caring professions are bounded by gender divisions. The practices of midwives, nurses, health visitors and social workers in the lives of children and their parents are formed and sustained within the same structural and ideological framework of the family and child-rearing as the occupations themselves. These practices enmesh with the experience of the caring professionals, and although theorised are based around taken-for-granted assumptions which integrate with the organisation of child and family health and welfare.

Mental health

The influences of psychiatry, psychoanalysis and psychology in the caring professions are long-standing and pervasive. Parry and Parry trace the origins of these influences to the Great European War, 1914–18, with an official concern about the disruptive impact on families, direct effects of war such as 'shell-shock' and the need in postwar reconstruction to improve industrial management and selection techniques for the armed forces (1979, p. 33). Social work in particular was influenced by psychoanalysis, first in the United States, and then in the UK through training undertaken in the USA. The strength of these developments was grounded in the claims of psychological theory: 'to penetrate beyond "superficial social characteristics", such as those of class or culture, to absolutely fundamental problems of personality. These aspects, hidden in the unconscious beyond the knowledge of the client, offered the chance of developing a specialised "mystery" and a warrant for professional authority rooted in science' (ibid., pp. 34–5). Similarly in psychiatric nursing attempts to create a more theoretical approach of this type were evident at an earlier stage in the USA than in the UK (compare Carpenter, 1980, with Church, 1989). The impact in occupational therapy has been even later, and has been more muted as the role of occupational therapists in mental health work expanded at a time when the debates of anti-professionalism and anti-psychiatry and a rediscovery of sociology began to change the intellectual bases of the caring professions generally.

Psychological theory is important for nursing, occupational therapy and social work because of the issues of gender differentiation which have been woven into its fabric (Mitchell, 1974). Psychological thinking failed to recognise this, to the extent that a study of clinical practice in the USA (Broverman *et al.*, 1970) showed that the concept of a 'mentally healthy adult' and a 'mentally healthy woman' were likely to differ (while the 'mentally healthy man' had equivalence to 'mentally healthy adult'). It has been argued subsequently that the explanation for the considerably higher incidence of women diagnosed/assessed as having mental health problems is a consequence of the social construction of women's lives, cross-cut by differences of class and race (Shepherd *et al.*, 1966; Chesler, 1974; Brown and Harris, 1978; Goldberg and Huxley, 1981; Bryan *et al.*, 1985). Marriage and motherhood figure prominently as restricting and devaluing for women, while at the same time bringing with them a multitude of practical difficulties.

Despite the forcefulness of this critique it has had only a partial impact on psychiatric nursing, occupational therapy and social work (Davis *et al.*, 1985). Attention to issues of gender and to feminism in the professional literature has grown slowly and patchily, and in practice has been in competition with the constraints of agency policies and the power of other professions, especially psychiatry (Goldie, 1977). Chesler (1974) argues that therapy in the United States is based on a relationship which parallels aspects of marriage, in that the passive woman, patient, comes to rely on the active man, therapist, for acceptance and approval. This is mirrored in the health service in the UK where control of therapy and treatment is in the hands of (mostly male) psychiatrists, and testing in the hands of (mostly male) clinical psychologists, supported by the mostly female professions of nursing, occupational therapy and social work. In rehabilitation and community care this has often had the consequence of sex stereotyping, with work training and work alternatives more open to men and women being prepared for a domestic routine (Davis, 1980). Women (and sympathetic men) in caring professions who have attempted to work against this may often have found themselves confronted by resources and ideas which are formed within the patriarchal *status quo*, and which may be accepted by service users themselves because of the constant experience of gender divisions in their own lives.

In Chapter 6 the roles of psychiatric nurses and social workers in situations of compulsion in mental health work entailing their involvement in the definition of mental ill-health at the individual level were discussed in the context of racism. Because psychiatric theories are imbued also with implicit gendered concepts nursing and social work are faced with a choice between complicity, confrontation or covert opposition in relation to sexism and racism at the same time. In each instance the solution which emerges is a product of the nurse's or social worker's own perceptions and that of the psychiatrist and other medical personnel involved. It would be wrong to portray psychiatry as monolithic in this respect (Goldie, 1977), and there would appear to be scope for caring professions to take more explicit account of gender in their practices.

Allen (1986) has argued that psychiatry should not be seen as an area which must be abandoned in order to end women's oppression. Rather, she asserts the possibility of practices which are built around the reality of women's lives against which the core of theory can be tested. Nursing, occupational therapy and social work each have a role to play in this, because they are interlocked with institutional psychiatry and psychological thinking, and at the same time are predominantly professions of women. However, their location within organisational structures and their relationships with the established professions create constraints which must be acknowledged in contemplating their potential for change in mental health.

Dependent adults

In their involvement with dependent adults the caring professions have two broad areas of work: to help people achieve and sustain greater degrees of independence; and to assist with the organisation, and sometimes the provision, of supportive care in those aspects of daily life which the service user cannot accomplish her/himself. This includes working with people who have dependency needs arising from ill health, physical disability, severe learning difficulties and old age. It is important to note with respect to old age that many problems are shared with younger groups of adults (physical disability for example), but are seen as different simply because of the person's age. Other problems may arise for older people from the way in which industrial capitalism has simultaneously provided the basis for longer life and constructed a devalued life role for older people (Phillipson, 1982). The sheer numbers of older people (taken here as over 65 years of age) in contemporary society (Wicks, 1982) contributes also to perceptions of this as a single group, rather than one which encompasses a range of strengths and potential as well as problems. In each of these areas of dependency there are two groups of service users. Not only is the person who has a physical disability, a severe learning difficulty or a long-term illness a focus for the caring professions but also there are a large number of relatives, friends and neighbours who provide the greatest part of the caring undertaken outside institutions (Finch and Groves, 1980, 1982; Ungerson, 1987; Hicks, 1988). As these studies show, the majority of dependent adults and the large majority of informal (that is, unpaid) carers are women.

There is a diversity of ways in which the caring professions reproduce gender divisions in their work with dependent adults and their carers. In geriatric hospital care it has been observed that nurses treat female and male patients differently (Evers, 1981). The dependence of men appears to be more acceptable because it is related to lower expectations of men's capacities for self-care, with a corresponding reluctance to accept dependence in women. In the provision of social care a similar bias can be seen to operate. Domiciliary and residential care services in the UK are provided disproportionately to men, or to the carers of men, or where men are the carers (Finch and Groves, 1985; Ungerson, 1987). The assumption behind this bias, put simply, is that men should be in paid employment and not in unpaid caring while women should be in unpaid caring and not in paid employment (Graham, 1983). Policies and practices in community care for older people have tended to reproduce this assumption implicitly, with the consequence that ideas about improving the life situations of direct service users are oppressive for informal carers (Finch, 1984).

Dependence in younger adults is bounded by similar bias on the part of caring services. Oliver (1983), writing about the problems of wives who care for disabled or chronically ill husbands, records a variety of ways in which the role of the wife *as a carer* is reinforced. In the UK, hospitals make assumptions that women will be able to receive their husbands home at short notice (or even no notice), often without community nursing support. Oliver notes that the presence of a wife itself can be a factor in early discharge from hospital (1983, p. 76). Social workers and community nurses tend to concentrate on the disabled or chronically ill person and either ignore the needs of the caring wife or ask in ways which prevent real exploration of problems (such as by asking in front of the cared-for husband) (1983, p. 87). The position of husbands is reversed according to the Equal Opportunities Commission report *Caring Services*, (quoted in Hicks, 1988, pp. 159–60). Not only caring services but also family and friends appear likely to offer greater support on the basis that it is more normative for men to go to work and/or have a social life. Caring professionals in this regard do not seem to differ much from the 'unqualified' majority in society. However, Hicks notes that when the male carer is older the difference in service provision is very small, and (with a few exceptions) older male carers in her sample did not appear to be much more forceful in dealing with professionals than women carers (1988, p. 162). It seems that the role of carer in itself is feminised in relation to the caring professions, in much the same way that they in turn are feminised in relation to medicine, law and other established professions.

Parents and siblings of adults with severe learning difficulties also face limited responses from the caring services (Bayley, 1973; Abbott and Sapsford, 1987). For most carers it is a situation which they have become used to over the entire life of the person with the learning difficulties. In the early stages the patriarchal arrangement of families means that most mothers will have undertaken all or much of the caring work, and this is supported through the

actions and inactions of professionals (Abbott and Sapsford, 1987). By the time the young person with severe
learning difficulties becomes adult the services may be
minimal and in many cases parents, which in turn usually
means the mother, can look forward to continuing the
care of the young adult. (The professional language can
infantilise adults with severe learning difficulties living with
their parents through the use of the term 'child', and this
serves to fix both at a particular stage in the life cycle in
a way which is devaluing.)

In each instance financial arrangements, which are not
under the control of caring professions, serve to buttress
the gender inequalities in service provision. There is a
rationale in the patriarchal family arrangement through the
general higher level of men's earnings, and the pressure
on men not to let caring 'interfere' with ordinary work
patterns. Men who take time off work, refuse overtime,
or who seek less demanding work in order to care will lose
out financially and perhaps forgo promotion (Hicks, 1988,
p. 128). So in a two-parent family there is a logic in a
gendered division of labour, one wage-earning and the
other caring, although it is an oppressive logic for women
and one which denies men the opportunities for caring.

Single parents and unmarried carers usually have a
straight choice between paid employment and caring. The
practices of professionals and the extent of services in combination with the dominant ideology of the caring role of
women makes this an unreal choice for many women.
Moreover, they are caught in a trap between professional
practices, the dominant ideology and the material structures of welfare. The social security and tax systems of the
UK assume that women generally are financially dependent
on men. For example, it is only in recent years that the
Invalid Care Allowance has been available for married or
cohabiting women, even where they had had to give up
work in order to care, and although the sum involved is
below income support level (Hicks, 1988, p. 343). This was
extended to include married or cohabiting women by a
reluctant government forced to do so in the European
Court. Their long-term response was to question the con-

tinued provision of this benefit, and an indication that it may be denied to all rather than paid to women living with a man. So the reality for most women carers continues to be poverty or total financial dependence on a male partner. The practices of the caring professions in the assessment and provision of services run parallel to this, and from both sides the patriarchal definition of women as carers is reinforced.

Sexist professions and change

This brief overview of some key elements of practice in the caring professions describes the ways in which at all stages of the life cycle services are gendered. Yet the sexism of professional practices is not self-contained, but is interconnected with the structures of social security, of the service organisations within which caring professions are employed and with the family structures of industrial capitalism. It is not that the patriarchal forms of organisation and professions which were discussed in the earlier part of the chapter are reproduced simply in daily practice, as if they originated from those institutions; rather what we see is a communication of gender divisions between the various institutions of society. Individual meetings of caring professionals and service users form interstices, the spaces between institutions in which patriarchy is reproduced interactionally. Similarly interactions *within* the institutions of the family, hospitals, health centres, social work offices and so on are also locations for the constant recreation of patriarchal relationships. Caring professions are sexist as they are part of sexist society.

The interactional dimension of gender division points to the possibility of criticism and change. Although we may not find ourselves acting in conditions of our own choosing, we are active in the production of our own history (Brittan and Maynard, 1984). At the same time it is necessary to recognise constraints which patriarchy imposes for women and men in caring professions who seek to develop anti-sexist practices. While it is over-simplistic only to see women as passive victims of a sexist society, at the same time it is important to recognise the all-pervasive nature of gender as a constraining social force: structures act as a limitation to individual action (Davis *et al.*, 1985, p. 90). As a consequence it has been a part of women's critique of patriarchy that challenges cannot be sustained individually and in isolation, but through collective responses (for example The Birmingham Women and Social Work Group (81), 1985). Women in caring professions may find it possible to challenge some aspects of gender divisions, for example through obtaining promotion, but the underlying framework of the relationships between women and men is not necessarily challenged by individual action alone (Popplestone, 1980; Foster, 1987).

As a man writing about caring professions, I want to highlight the role which men play in the possibility of change. Men in caring professions are in an ambiguous position. I have argued that commitment to caring does not sit easily with patriarchal masculinity, and as the figures quoted earlier show, the implications of psychological and social pressures often lead to a management job or work in the more controlling or 'knowledge-based' areas of the professions as a resolution. Such careers are not simply a consequence of socialisation into patriarchal thinking and action (although that is a component) but the common experience men share, despite the many differences of class, race, sexuality, disability or age, in the construction of masculine careers (Hearn, 1987). Bowl (1985), in a discussion of social work, has argued that men have to examine critically their own practices as caring professionals, and to make connections in their responses between the organisational context of practice and the work with service users, especially when the latter are men. This is not to 'protect' women from male service users, which would in itself be a patriarchal notion (The Birmingham Women and Social Work Group (81), 1985, pp. 139–40), but because changing masculinity in these contexts should be something which men in caring professions share with each other and with men service users: it is the responsibility of men generally and not of women. This requires more openness between men in caring professions about the reality of masculinity, the factors which impel and constrain men and attitudes and actions towards women colleagues and service users.

There is a parallel to be drawn between critiques of men's sexist practices in the social sciences and the actions of men in caring professions; the objective is to develop 'a critique of men's practices in the light of feminism' and not a critique or attempted cooption of feminism (Hearn, 1987, p. 182). Men can learn from women that such developments will not happen individually, but through sharing and dialogue (Tolson, 1977). This may be *ad hoc* in the workplace, or in a more organised way in trade unions and professional associations or through men's groups, but in all these situations the goal involves giving up the props of patriarchy, and the development of an anti-sexist masculinity within caring professions.

8

Power in Focus

Power: an overview

Nursing, the remedial therapies and social work are structured around several aspects of power. Power is to be seen not only in the formal hierarchies which have concerned orthodox analyses, but also in the way those hierarchies themselves are cross-cut by occupational and professional boundaries, relationships between professionals and service users and in structures of racism and of gender. These aspects of power do not simply overlap; they interlock, so that to grasp the full picture of the caring professions it is not possible to perceive any one aspect in isolation. The work which people undertake, whether or not they are professionally qualified, the hierarchical positions they occupy and so on are all linked, and all these factors are related to whether the person is black or white, female or male. The separate examination of each aspect in the preceding discussion has been a matter of emphasis and concentration and not an attempt to construct separate areas of analysis.

Examples of the interconnectedness of aspects of power in previous chapters have included the role of assistants and auxiliaries (in which a hierarchy is constructed in occupational terms, with clear race and gender components), special funding to address racism (which becomes locked into hierarchical and occupational relationships and so perpetuates the racism it is intended to end) and the exclusion of service users (whose lives are defined through aspects of hierarchy, occupation, racism and gender as they affect the structures, policies and practices of caring professions).

So consideration of one aspect leads to the necessary examination of other aspects and of the connections between them. Having made these connections it becomes more evident that the caring professions of nursing, the remedial therapies and social work have not fulfilled, and indeed in existing circumstances cannot fulfil, either the liberal reforming aspirations or the professionalising intentions of many of those who have struggled to create and develop them. In particular the idea of a service ethic, which is contained within both reforming and orthodox strands of professional history, must be reconsidered as a value which can only partly be realised within existing social relationships. This is not to argue that it should be abandoned, and I will return below to a consideration of how such a concept may serve as a critique of current structures and practices; what I am suggesting is that values have to be understood in context, and the extent to which they may disguise inequalities and oppressions firmly grasped.

The analysis of power suggests further questions about the ways in which caring professions are continuing to develop and the actions of caring professionals within such change. Having made aspects of power the central issue in my discussion, what are the implications for the various commitments which members of those professions may have towards the structures, policies and practices of their occupations?

Professionalisation *versus* proletarianisation

The debates about the structure and nature of caring professions which were reviewed in Chapters 3 and 4 have implications for the futures of nursing, the remedial therapies and social work. In broad terms these debates can be summarised as that between professionalisation and proletarianisation. There are common elements in the bases of each argument, but the analysis offered and the conclusions

drawn are quite markedly different and in this sense professionalisation and proletarianisation are mutually exclusive opposites.

Professionalisation can be seen as the 'orthodox' position
within the caring professions. Examples of this position
were noted in previous chapters in relation to nursing
(Jolley, 1989), occupational therapy (Wallis, 1987a) and
social work (Glastonbury *et al.*, 1982). The argument for
professionalisation assumes that the autonomous control of
an occupation, supported by reference to the 'traits' of
professionalism are necessarily beneficial for the members
of the occupation and therefore (by implication) for the
clientele. It is claimed that there is an essential core to
each professional group which can only be realised if the
occupation is under autonomous control, and the benefit
for service users is that once freed in this way they will be
able to receive the best possible service. The proposals
for the development of these professions arising from this
analysis are, therefore, that increased autonomy should
be sought, through the creation of appropriate structures,
through greater clarity in defining and claiming the areas
of skill and knowledge of each occupation, and through
action on the part of collective groups representing the
professions to secure and maintain both distinctions and
autonomy.

In contrast, the argument for proletarianisation has been
seen as the 'radical' position on professionalism. This argument has been most prominent in social work (Cohen and
Wagner, 1982; Simpkin, 1983), and is based on the proletarianisation of professional labour thesis which was discussed in Chapter 3. It assumes that occupations are
defined by the work that they are required to perform, that
professionalism is not beneficial for service users because it
serves to separate the members of occupations from the
clientele, and that the idea of autonomy for professionals
is unrealistic because managerial work controls have been
introduced systematically in all aspects of health and welfare. This argument can be said to have arisen as a critique
of professionalism. Instead it proposed that practitioners
in health and welfare work should recognise that they are

employed labour (skilled workers) and therefore seek through the trade union movement to defend themselves against deskilling and to develop their common interests with service users.

In Chapters 3 and 4 I examined the place of caring professions in organisational hierarchies and the form and structure of the professions as occupations. It was noted that both professionalisation and proletarianisation have some relevance to understanding the histories of nursing, the remedial therapies and social work, but that neither provides a complete analysis of these occupations. Both arguments have a degree of applicability, but both are limited. Nursing, the remedial therapies and social work have developed occupational self-images based around claims to autonomy and to skills and knowledge. However, at the same time such claims have been successful only to a limited degree, as nursing, remedial therapies and social work have developed within the context of state mediation, the greater power of more established professions (especially medicine and law) and with a growing tension between management and practice. In this sense they are in a contradictory position, in which both elements are evident but at the same time both elements conflict to the point where they appear to be mutually exclusive. It is this contradiction which has placed the caring professions in the ambiguous position which was grasped by trait analysis as 'semi-professional', an analysis which implicitly accepted the primacy of the professionalisation argument while seeking to deal with the empirical evidence which forms the basis of the proletarianisation thesis.

This leads the trait theorists to suggest that the 'semi-professions' should abandon their claims to 'full' professionalism and to concentrate on the skills which formed the basis of their occupational practices (see, for example, Etzioni, 1969). This I think is both partial and simplistic. It is partial because it selects certain features and uses them to explain the whole without making connections with wider issues. For example, as I have discussed above at some length, issues of racism and gender are central to understanding the caring professions. Although some trait theorists acknowledge gender as an issue (Simpson and Simpson, 1969) they do so in such a way as to ignore the centrality of patriarchal power, which shapes both organisation and practice through the definition of their work as caring. The implicit effect of the trait theorists' argument is for 'women's work' to 'stay in its place', and at the same time they gloss over the impact of racism within professionalism and caring work. The conclusions of trait analysis are simplistic because they ignore the way in which professionalisation is a process involving a struggle against the limitations of the wider social structure and against the actions of more powerful groups. A recognition of the issue of power provides a more fruitful basis to consider the contradiction between professionalisation and proletarianisation, and the exploration of alternatives.

Racism and gender: critiques and implications

Consideration of racism and gender has implications for understanding the organisation of caring professions and their practices. Critiques of racism and sexism in caring professions also carry with them implications for changes in the organisation and practices of those professions. As I have noted in previous chapters there are connections between questions of racism and gender although they are distinct issues and cannot be conflated.

It was noted that many attempts to deal with racism in the employment of caring professionals have contained severe inherent limitations. These can be seen in the forms of segregation which have occurred. The use of 'special projects' and the development of ancillary posts have created barriers for black professionals inside career structures in an attempt to remove barriers to the career structures overall, or have created professional ghettos in which the expertise of black professionals is confined to the needs of black service users. Similarly women have been confined routinely in hierarchically lower and occupationally marginal positions. It is often the idea of caring claimed by these occupations which has formed the basis for segregations of labour, in which all women and black men occupy the tending jobs while white men occupy the managerial jobs relative to their proportions in caring professions as a whole (and in absolute terms in social work management).

The implications are that change is required both in the structures within which caring professions work and in the ways in which those professions are perceived. In some respects these implications can be seen in demands for action on the part of those who are oppressed by racism and sexism. In this there is a marked divergence between the critique of racism and sexism. Where black professionals and service users recognise their oppression under racism and have developed approaches to survive and reject this oppression, so that the *recognition* of racism is defined as a problem for white people (Bryan *et al.*, 1985; Rooney, 1987) it is argued that women as well as men need to recognise the reality of sexist power and to develop strategies for exercising power against sexism individually and collectively (Wynd, 1985; Hanmer and Statham, 1988; Schutzenhofer, 1988; Dominelli and McLeod, 1989). It is argued also that the position of black women is different to that of white women because in a white society it is impossible to disentangle the two issues; white society may even force black women to prioritise racism over sexism (Carby, 1982; Bryan *et al.*, 1985). These connections can only be recognised through a consideration of the structural dimensions of racism and sexism as power, and so although individual action on the part of those who are oppressed by racism and sexism may be necessary it is not sufficient.

This is not to argue that the presence of black or white women or black men in itself is a guarantee of change. If they are isolated, or are not committed to anti-racism and anti-sexism then their presence would be little more than superficial. The first woman prime minister of the UK is a clear example of the way in which a single unsympathetic woman in an influential position can provide a legitimation for the retrenchment of the patriarchal *status quo*. Nevertheless, to say that individual action is necessary but not

sufficient is not to deny the importance of increasing numbers of black men and women and white women in positions of leadership and influence within caring professions.
Indeed, this may be necessary to achieve change, and as
an indicator that change is taking place. At the same time
a response to such changes from white men also is suggested which includes the recognition that the power and
advantage which they currently exercise (simply by virtue
of being white men) must be given up if racism and sexism
are to be opposed. It seems unlikely that this would happen
only through modifications of recruitment and promotion
practices, although these would be a part of such developments. To the extent that racism and sexism are sustained
through forms of organisation and professionalism then
challenges to existing practices would be integral to wider
structural change. Deliberate local recruitment, placing
more emphasis on community involvement as the basis of
knowledge and skill, working conditions which recognise
external factors (such as the provision of crèche facilities),
a genuine valuing of flexible working arrangements and so
on are examples of challenges to white patriarchal structures and practices in hierarchical organisations which posi-
tively affirm the social diversity which as yet is not reflected
in caring professions.

Anti-racism and anti-sexism raise questions about professionalisation as the agenda for the future, because the
very concept of 'profession' to which nursing, the remedial
therapies and social work have so persistently aspired is
based on white masculine assumptions about needs, skills,
knowledge, management and values. It is because this concept reinforces power inequalities that radicalism within
these occupations so often has been based around the total
rejection of professionalism. Clearly, to the extent that
nurses, remedial therapists and social workers recognise
the racist and sexist power within an orthodox approach
to professionalism they are faced with the choice of accepting or opposing those forces. This goes beyond proletarianisation, which gives primacy to a class analysis, and seeks
to acknowledge the ways in which class is interlocked with

racism and gender in the organisational and occupational structures of the caring professions.

The critiques of racism and gender also suggest that the individual practice relationships between professionals and their clientele should be different. Here too power is exercised oppressively, through the relationships between professionals and service users, in which both are also members of the wider society. As I have noted above, whether the nurse, remedial therapist or social worker is black or white, and the service user is black or white, will affect the outcomes of each professional/service user meeting. Although a professional practice which is insensitive to the individual service user culturally, in terms of sexuality, gender or any other aspect of their personhood will not be appropriate or effective, an 'ethnic sensitivity' or 'gender awareness' which simply reinforces the power of the professional over the service user through increased subtlety would not appear to be desirable. Greater awareness of these aspects of service users and their needs undoubtedly is necessary, but only in the context of challenging racism and sexism in all their aspects. As I noted in Chapter 6, intersubjective 'sensitivity' cannot be a replacement for anti-racism and anti-sexism in practice.

Service users and structures

A range of possible proposals to reconstruct the relationship between professionals and their clientele is considered by Wilding, who summarises them as: change in political accountability; the use of law; a reassertion of market principles; a redefinition of the professional/client relationship; and the deliberate construction of sources of countervailing power (1982, p. 143). These are, Wilding suggests, changes which could be made at the concrete organisation or practice levels. He considers also policy level changes which come close to the triangular model of mediation which I discussed in Chapter 1, in which professions and the state each meditate the other to the client/ citizen and so enable more democratic participation by members of society in establishing and modifying the aims and purposes of professions.

Wilding argues that the professions have to be persuaded that it is the existing relationships with their clientele which are the sources of unsatisfying work and inimical to the goals which those professions would claim rather than the forms of organisation or the degrees of professional autonomy taken in isolation. They have to be persuaded of the advantages of a partnership relationship both for themselves and for their clientele (Wilding, 1982, p. 144). However, the policies of the 'New Right' have utilised attacks on the legitimacy of the professions to assert market principles in health and welfare, in which changes in accountability and new professional/client relationships rely on the reconstruction of the service user as a consumer; but this is not partnership. Choice is created at the individual level, yet the wider issues of power are untouched because that is not part of the aims of these policies. Consumerism in the 'New Right' agenda appears to be a means to an end rather than an end in itself, and, as I discussed in Chapters 1 and 5, cannot be taken out of the context of the reduction of public expenditure.

So market forces can be seen as part of state policies to press the professions further into a mediative role in which the countervailing balance of power is exercised by service users as consumers rather than as citizens. (This is so whether or not the professionals are formally self-employed or agency-employed.) In addition politicians are cast in the role of state managers in a way which Wilding (1982) does not foresee. It means that the pluralist policy which he argues is necessary to open up professionalism to partnership is taken off the political agenda (1982, pp. 143–5). However, Wilding recognises that partnership would also be a means to an end, and that end is the reconstruction of professions so that they work for rather than over and against their clientele (1982, pp. 148–9). The question of the forms of professionalism is part of wider debates about the purposes of professionalism and ultimately about the type of society which we would wish to see develop.

If the policies considered by Wilding are undermined in

existing circumstances, are there more autonomous areas in which professionals can seek changes themselves which would enable more of a partnership with service users to develop? Hadley and Hatch (1981) refer to a range of ways in which the reorganisation of caring professions has been used to attempt precisely this type of change. They examine small-scale, local services in which both professionals and members of communities play a part which does not depend on the exercise of power by professionals. To make these examples the basis for a broader policy they argue it would be necessary to provide members of society with the right to initiate services, and the right to participate in service provision (Hadley and Hatch, 1981, pp. 161–5). This would necessarily include the right to form service users' associations and the right to information about the running of services. Such rights would also, by logical extension, be given to organisational employees. Their proposal assumes four points: plural provision; decentralisation and community orientation; contractual accountability; participative decision-making.

'New Right' policies also appear to have circumvented these proposals. Plurality of provision and contractual accountability are core aspects of the changes introduced in the UK in the latter part of the 1980s (DoH, 1989), in which the control of central government over caring professions has been strengthened at the expense of local representation. The idea of decentralisation and community orientation has been used as a rationale to support the strengthening of central control against the opposition of professionals and service users, especially when this is taken to be the 'community of interest' in the way Hadley and Hatch (1981) also use the concept. The critical element of Hadley and Hatch's proposals, that which is most clearly absent from 'New Right' policies, is participative decision-making. Although a number of Hadley and Hatch's detailed points would be helpful in greater partnership, this is the one point on which their proposals depend. In other words, it is not simply a matter of restructuring organisations which employ caring professionals, but of changing the basis on which professionals and service users relate.

A further weakness of Wilding and of Hadley and Hatch is that they do not address the issues of racism or gender. The proposals which are advanced do not indicate how the major power structures of racism and patriarchy are connected with the policies of creating partnership and/or participation. Without making such connections there is the very tangible risk that racist and sexist partnership and participation could emerge. The criticism that care in the community policies and practices are inherently sexist in the way in which they have been implemented because 'the community' is itself a gendered concept is one example of this (Finch and Groves, 1980; Finch, 1984; Croft, 1986; Dalley, 1988). Another example is the opposition to black control of services, discussed in Chapter 6, as forms of 'separatism' or even 'black racism' (Phillips, 1982). This is a reflection of white racism in caring professions and the wider society which obscures the needs of black service users and the contribution of black professionals. Without a conscious acceptance of the centrality of these aspects of power, partnership and participation may only serve to reproduce the inequalities and oppressions of the wider society within new organisational forms.

Reference was made in Chapter 5 to ways in which professional practices may be changed to enable service users to exercise choice at a service delivery level (in advocacy, brokerage and case management). The limitations of these approaches were also discussed, through their location in market mechanisms and the continuing control of the economic basis of the relationship between service users and professionals by the state. Nevertheless, such service developments do challenge the routine exercise of power by professionals over service users in the context of service delivery. Through the denial of responsibility, segregation, stigmatisation and lumping together of service users even the most minimal of rights which people might possess as citizens are taken away (Croft and Beresford, 1989). The alternative suggested is that people are involved in their own health and welfare, not as volunteers within a framework which is controlled by professionals but as active subjects exercising control in relation to their own needs and the services which are provided (Beresford and Croft, 1986; Croft and Beresford, 1989; Simey, 1989).

The major problem in achieving participation and partnership is identified by Taylor (1989) as the very partial concept of rights which has underpinned citizenship in western liberal democracies. In practice this ideal has been grounded in the social relations which have developed within industrial capitalism. The rights of citizens as they have been formulated in that context reproduce class, patriarchal and racist divisions precisely because the power to exercise rights is part of the form of social relations. Rights are not exercised equally because power is not exercised equally. Taylor seeks to replace the concept of rights with the power to achieve the meeting of need through access to resources. This power includes opposition to patriarchy and racism as well as changes in economic relations. As Dalley (1988) points out, such changes must mean change on the part of men and of white people of action in relation to others. I would add that it must mean also a change on the part of caring professionals in relation to service users, in the type of practices which have already been discussed and in the perception and structuring of themselves as distinct occupational groups.

It is under these circumstances that the ideas of a plurality of provision, the decentralisation and community-orientation of services and other organisational changes in service agencies would make sense. However, as Wilding (1982) and Taylor (1989) amongst others have recognised, the potential for achieving such ends within the regressive fiscal and social policies of the late twentieth century may be severely limited. Certainly it is impossible to conceive of egalitarian relationships growing and flourishing 'in a society whose pivot is inequality' (Wilding, 1982, p. 149). At the same time it is neither possible nor desirable to leave consideration of the content and structure of caring professions to some future context which is more favourable. It is necessary to examine those small-scale changes which are consistent with a critical analysis of caring professions while at the same time recognising the limitations of such changes.

Professionalism: a more democratic future?

The preceding analysis suggests that the future of caring professions cannot be based on orthodox approaches to professionalisation, and yet it is plausible to consider professionalism as a way of theorising nursing, the remedial therapies and social work which is not confined to the 'folk usage' of the term (Becker, 1970). Rather it points to the recognition of the exercise of power as an inherent if often covert element of the claims by such occupations to greater autonomy, and moves towards the ways in which those occupations can be changed to enable the more equal exercise of power between individuals and groups. The reason why members of caring professions might recognise an interest in pursuing such policies is that making the issue of power explicit challenges the concept of caring which is at the centre of these professions; it creates a dissonance which it is difficult to ignore and which cannot be explained by reference to a dichotomy between care and control. Power is central to both elements in professional work. The analysis presented in the preceding chapters has examined those aspects of power which are at the core of the caring professions. From this analysis the question may then be posed as to how professionalism would appear if the issue of power was made more explicit. So, in this concluding discussion, I want to explore the possible shape of a more democratic professionalism, and to consider the question of what elements might be necessary for its development.

First, the notion of autonomy would seem to be open to radical reformulation. As we have seen, the idea of autonomy plays an important role in the perceptions and actions of caring professionals. Yet at the same time as this idea has been used in opposition to the exercise of power by the state and by more established professions it has also provided a base for the exercise of power by caring professionals over other occupational groups (notably those defined as aides, assistants or auxiliaries) and over their clientele. If partnerships and participation are appropriate goals for professionalism then this approach to autonomy appears not to be tenable.

An alternative view of autonomy would be to define it as the possibility for caring professionals and service users to act together in formulating the ends and means of service provision. Such a view may challenge deeply-held assumptions. In a milieu which is both hierarchical and oppressive, caring professionals feel that service users make unrealistic demands on their services and so would not exercise such power responsibly. This perception would be challenged by the experience of partnership and participation, in which professionals and service users each learnt more about the limitations and possibilities with which the other is faced.

A major block to the sharing of autonomy by caring professionals (even to the small degree to which they currently exercise it) is the hierarchical organisation of society that contrasts autonomy with control by others. So it should be made clear also that I am not suggesting the replacement of one hierarchy with another. Indeed, more limited forms of existing hierarchies could form part of a democratic accountability. Not only must there be a general sense of what nursing, the remedial therapies and social work are (the potential for negotiation between professionals and services users is not unlimited), but also there must be a structure which establishes the basis for negotiation in individual situations. These could be developed from the collective organisations of professionals and service users which already exist, such as service user groups, professional associations and trade unions.

Models of participation and partnership which have been developed include service user groups and community councils (Croft and Beresford, 1989; Simey, 1989). Examples include patients' committees, members' groups at day centres, national bodies for people with severe learning difficulties or for young people in care, which were referred to in Chapter 5. Service users are empowered through working together, in recognising common issues and using their collectivity as a strength. There is a danger also in the possibility that such groups can be marginalised or coopted. The interests people have in taking more control in their own lives and the role of services within them can become obscured through involvement in organisational and operational detail (Croft and Beresford, 1989, pp. 15–16). This suggests that user involvement should also be directed to the policy level, in which the nature and scope of services and professional practices are defined. At the same time this is unlikely to happen, or to be more than an extension of existing hierarchies, while only the most senior managements of caring professions themselves are included in policy formation. Partnership and participation suggest that all levels of hierarchies (to the extent that these are necessary), members of communities and service users themselves should be included in the formation of policy.

The model of police accountability outlined by Simey (1989), from her experience in the UK city of Liverpool, provides one concrete example of the way in which the involvement of the community at a policy level is feasible, and one which recognises the practical difficulties involved. Regular open meetings between the police authority and members of the communities being policed, openness of all authority meetings to the public and a system of appointing lay visitors to police stations were the beginnings of greater collective accountability. These developments appear to utilise the division of ideological and technical autonomy, in a way which makes the ideological (policy) dimension accessible to public debate, although the divide between policy and practice was used by the chief police officer to attempt to limit wider participation, as was the power of the national state (Simey, 1989, p. 10). As Simey herself indicates, it is a model which does not require much adaptation to the caring professions, although it demonstrates that the commitment of professionals as well as service users is necessary and the continued separation of professionals from service users is possible (ibid., pp. 12–13).

The lessons from this model reinforce the desirability of extending service user involvement beyond specific operational issues and into the broader occupational groupings of caring professionals. Professional associations and trade unions provide collective contexts in which the nature of caring professions and their relationship to organisational structures are continually debated. To the extent that partnership and participation are pursued then such debates cannot continue without the voice of service users being heard. Their voice should be authentic and not translated by the professionals for their own purpose. To achieve this, collective action on the part of the caring professions would be necessary, to examine and change their own structures in order to enable service users to participate. Initially this might require a space being cleared so that the absence of the voice of service users become apparent, and because professional groups are not monolithic this is unlikely to happen without debate and conflict. However, the possible objection that professions cannot be understood or influenced appropriately from outside is implausible when the presence of more dominant professions on the governing committees of some caring professional associations is considered. This reinforces both the subordinate status of caring professions, and by inference devalues further the contribution which service users can and should make. A democratic profession would be one in which 'lay' representation on councils, committees and working-groups meant precisely that.

Similarly trade unions frequently assume that as part of the labour movement they are necessarily aware of and responsive to the needs and interests of ordinary people, including those who use the caring services. However, the membership of trade unions in the public services which employ caring professionals includes a range of occupational groups whose common interests are often formed around experiences of hierarchical employment and not of using services. Because they are placed in a contradictory position between state policies and the needs of citizens, trade unions can appear to act in the interests of their members against those of service users. As I have noted already trade unions can be both racist and sexist (Miles, 1982; Doeringer and Piore, 1985; The Birmingham Women and Social Work Group (81), 1985). The critique of trade unions is complex, because they have been a focus for the defence of state employees as workers; yet they too can institutionalise the divide between providers and users of services and ways must be found to create forms of partnership between those who produce and those who use caring services. An example of how this might be achieved, by professional associations as well as by trade unions, would be the development of systematic liaison and dialogue with groups which were service user-controlled, and not simply professionally run groups located outside statutory agencies ('voluntary' organisations).

Service users require both financial and social resources in order to be able to participate and to be partners. Financially, the resources to participate within service agencies as well as in political contexts lie within the control of elected politicians, and appointees to responsible bodies (such as UK health authorities, or management committees of voluntary associations), as well as senior managers. This means that professionals committed to such developments would have to be involved in seeking the provision of resources, and working with service user groups towards this end in the political arena locally and nationally. In this context partnership and participation ultimately depend on wider political change. In contrast, professional associations and trade unions are under the control of their membership. Although in this respect also it is possible for such developments to be undermined by internal opposition, to the extent that collective decisions can be made toward such participation then the resources exist with which this can be achieved. In the short term it may be possible for professionals to use their organisational position to utilise limited resources and to press for the acceptance of the necessity of user involvement in their employing agency.

Social resources which are essential for the participation of service users in defining the policies and practices of agencies and the caring professionals employed by them include the skills and knowledge which are necessary for effective involvement to take place. Hierarchical forms of professionalism undermine the existing skills and knowledge of service users, and changed practices should seek to address ways in which service users can be enabled to participate through the sharing of knowledge and skills (Dominelli and McLeod, 1989, pp. 39–40). This approach presents practitioners with a challenge to use their expertise with and for rather than over their clientele, and may at times present a paradox in which skills and knowledge are used for people at the same time as those people are helped to use and/or develop skills and knowledge for themselves (Hugman, 1989). For example, the nurse or social worker who is advising a person using long-term residential care can only enable that person to exercise choice by providing opportunities to make choices. Withholding information or suggestions on the grounds that it might 'influence' the service user would, I think, have the opposite effect and disempower her or him. It is *how* the information or suggestion is shared which is crucial, through the explanation of alternative options, through the disclosure of all available options, through advice which is clear about its own basis (that is, why courses of action might have particular outcomes), and so on.

Similarly, at the collective level, caring professions could enable the participation of service users by seeking their involvement on non-exploitative terms, for example through accepting the issues brought by service users as the basis for beginning a dialogue, and through helping service users to develop their skills in taking part in meetings. (This is, in any case, how professionals themselves learn such skills.) Advocates would also have a role in this approach.

In this respect also lessons may be learned from anti-racist and anti-sexist struggles in health and welfare and beyond. Not only do they show that the sharing of power is possible where a common basis for understanding the experience of service users exists, in that black-controlled services and services controlled by women can involve both professionals and service users, but also they provide concrete examples of how knowledge and skills can be shared (Dominelli, 1988; Dominelli and McLeod, 1989). This reiterates the importance of relating anti-racism and anti-sexism to caring professions as a whole, so that they form part of the central core of caring professionalism. The implications are that a more appropriate vision of what constitutes skills and knowledge is required, which would question the implicit claims of much orthodox professionalism to be competent to pass judgement on all aspects of life on the basis of limited experience and training.

Not only would a more democratic professionalism require different relationships between professionals and service users, but it should also provide the basis for a reconsideration of the boundaries between the caring professions. There is a logic to partnership across professional boundaries arising from the aspects of historical development shared by nursing, the remedial therapies and social work, and also in the common features of the contemporary issues and problems facing the caring professions. If interprofessional relationships are based on a mutual recognition of the skills and knowledge which each has developed then there is the possibility of an exchange of ideas and support in addressing the participation of service users, racism and sexism in the caring professions as a whole. An aspect of the divisiveness of hierarchical structures is that in areas such as the provision of services in the community caring professions are set in competition with each other, to the disadvantage both of themselves and of their clientele.

Where caring professions form links, either between professional associations and trade unions, or through common membership of such bodies, there may be a tendency to create new power structures which enhance the position of professionals at the expense of others. Such changes therefore, would only be fully positive if they occurred in the context of partnership and participation for service users, and anti-racist and anti-sexist policies and practices. Without changes in existing forms of power, the prospect of greater unity amongst caring professions could have negative implications.

It is only in the context of a more democratic professionalism that a concern with specific forms of organisational structures make sense. Decentralisation without changes in forms of power inside and outside the caring professions may simply serve to marginalise practice from the centre of management and policy-making, for example. The privatisation and commercialisation of services appears likely to have the same effect in the long term. In this respect the prospects for the democratisation of caring professions within the framework that has been discussed here may seem remote. Yet at the same time there appears to be some scope for change arising from the critiques of racism, sexism and power over service users, and a small but important beginning would be for caring professions to address these issues in their forms of organisation and their practices.

It is in this context also that the 'service ethic' claimed by professions stands as a critique of professionalism. To the extent that orthodox professionalism, integrated in current organisational patterns of service provision, excludes the service user from the active definition and structuring of ideas and practices and so creates the role of client/ patient as a passive object of its work, then the interests of the professionals have a primacy which contradicts the ethic of service. However, the 'service ethic' as an ideal points to the desirability of developing more open relationships between professionals and service users to make an ethic of professional service possible. In this sense the ethics of a profession are not abstract moral values, but are related to the social relationships within which professionals act. As we have seen, these are relationships of power.

A democratic professionalism would provide the basis for the pursuit of the service ethic which is contained in the historical ideals of nursing, the remedial therapies and social work. The choices concerning health and welfare in Western Europe and North America have so often been constructed around the alternatives of private markets with an associated fragmentary individualism on one hand and state corporatism with a related inflexible bureaucratism on the other. A democratic professionalism could be understood as key parts of a broader struggle for participatory politics and a more equal society (Wilding, 1982; Croft and Beresford, 1989). That the professional is the political has been recognised both by many of those who seek orthodox professionalism and by those who seek the dissolution of nursing, the remedial therapies and social work as professions. The third option, which begins from the contradictory situation in which we find ourselves, is to recognise explicitly the aspects of power in caring professions, and from the questions which are raised by the consideration of power to seek the development of caring professions which increasingly are directed towards empowering their members and those who use their services.

Bibliography

Abbott, P. and R. Sapsford (1987) *Community Care of Mentally Handi-capped Children*, Milton Keynes: Open University Press.

Abel-Smith, B. (1960) *A History of the Nursing Profession*, London: Heinemann.

Ahmed, S. (1987) 'Cultural racism in work with Asian women and girls', in S. Ahmed, J. Cheetham and J. Small (eds) *Social Work with Black Children and Their Families*, London: B. T. Batsford.

Allan, P. (1989) 'Nursing education: a luxury or necessity?', in M. Jolley, and P. Allan (eds) *Current Issues in Nursing*, London: Chapman & Hall.

Allen, H. (1986) 'Psychiatry and the construction of the feminine', in P. Miller and N. Rose (eds) *The Power of Pscyhiatry*, Cambridge: Polity Press.

Arendt, H. (1970) *On Violence*, London: Allen Lane.

Asad, T. (1973) 'Two European images of non-European rule', in T. Asad (ed.) *Anthropology and the Colonial Encounter*, London: Ithaca Press.

Association of Black Social Workers and Allied Professionals (ABSWAP) (1981) *Black Children in Care*, London: ABSWAP.

Atkinson, H. W. (1988) 'Head in the clouds, feet on the ground', *Physiotherapy*, vol. 74 no. 11, pp. 542–7.

Bachrach, P. and M. S. Baratz (1962) 'Two faces of power', *American Political Science Review*, vol. 56, pp. 947–52.

Bailey, D. (1988) 'Occupational therapy administrators and clinicians: differences in demographics and values', *The Occupational Therapy Journal of Research*, vol. 8, no. 5, pp. 299–315.

Bailey, R. and M. Brake (eds) (1975) *Radical Social Work*, London: Edward Arnold.

Ballard, R. (1979) 'Ethnic minorities and the social services: what type of service?', in V. S. Khan (ed) *Minority; Families in Britain: Stress and Support*, London: Macmillan.

Baly, M. E. (1986) *Florence Nightingale and the Nursing Legacy*, London: Croom Helm.

Baly, M. E. (1987) 'The Nightingale nurses: the myth and the reality', in C. Maggs (ed.) *Nursing History: The State of the Art*, London: Croom Helm.

Barr, H. (1989) 'Odd one out', *Community Care*, vol. 772, pp. 20–1.

Barron, R. D. and G. M. Norris (1976) 'Sexual divisions and the dual labour market', in D. L. Barker and S. Allen (eds) *Dependence and Exploitation in Work and Marriage*, London: Longman.

Bayley, M. (1973) *Mental Handicap and Community Care*, London: Routledge & Kegan Paul.

Becker, H. S. (1970) *Sociological Work*, London: Allen Lane.

Becker, H. S., B. Geer, E. C. Hughs and A Strauss (1961) *Boys in White: Student Culture in a Medical School*, Chicago: University of Chicago Press.

Bellaby, P. and P. Oribabor (1980) ' "The History of the Present" – contradiction and struggle in nursing', in C. Davies (ed.) *Rewriting Nursing History*, London: Croom Helm.

Benedict, R. (1942) *Race and Racism*, London: Routledge & Kegan Paul.

Ben-Tovim, G., J. Gabriel, I. Law and K. Stredder (1986) *The Local Politics of Race*, London: Macmillan.

Beresford, P. and S. Croft (1986) *Whose Welfare: Private Care or Public Services*, Brighton: Lewis Cohen Urban Studies Centre.

Berlant, J. L. (1975) *Profession and Monopoly*, Los Angeles: University of California Press.

Bernstein, B. (1973) *Class, Codes and Control*, London: Paladin.

Bhalla, A. and K. Blakemore (1981) *Elders of the Ethnic Minority Groups*, London: All Faiths for One Race.

Biestek, F. (1961) *The Casework Relationship*, London: George Allen & Unwin.

Billis, D., G. Bromley, A. Hey, and R. Rowbottom, (1980) *Organising Social Services Departments*, London: Heinemann.

Billingsley, A. and J. Giovannoni (1972) *Children of the Storm*, New York: Harcourt Brace Janovich.

Birmingham Women and Social Work Group (81) (1985) 'Women and social work in Birmingham', in E. Brook and A. Davis (eds) *Women, the Family and Social Work*, London: Tavistock.

Bowl, R. (1985) *Changing the Nature of Masculinity: A Task for Social Work*, Norwich: University of East Anglia Monograph.

Brah, A. and R. Deem (1986) 'Towards anti-sexist and anti-racist schooling', *Critical Social Policy*, vol. 16, pp. 66–79.

Brandon, D. (1989) 'The courage to look at the moon', *Social Work Today*, vol. 20, no. 50, pp. 16–17.

Braverman, H. (1974) *Labor and Monopoly Capital*, New York: Monthly Review Press.

Brewer, C. and J. Lait (1980) *Can Social Work Survive?*, London: Temple Smith.

Briggs, T. (1980) 'Research on intra-professional social-work teams in the United States of America', in S. Lonsdale, A. Webb and T.

Briggs (eds) *Teamwork in the Personal Social Services and Health Care*, London: Croom Helm.

British Association of Social Workers (BASW) (1977) *The Social Work Task*, Birmingham: BASW.

Brittan, A. and M. Maynard (1984) *Sexism, Racism and Oppression*, Oxford: Basil Blackwell.

Bromley, G. E. (1978) 'Grades and specialisation in social work practice', *Social Work Today*, vol. 10, no. 10.

Bromley, G. E. (1988) 'The nurse – the practitioner', in R. W. Clarke and R. P. Lawry (eds) *The Power of the Professional Person*, Lanham: University Press of America.

Broverman, I. K., D. M. Broverman, F. E. Clarkson, P. R. Rosencrantz and S. R. Vogt (1970) 'Sex role stereotypes and clinical judgements of mental health', *Journal of Consulting and Clinical Psychology*, vol. 34, pp. 1–7.

Brown, C. (1984) *Black and White Britain: Third PSI Survey*, London: Heinemann.

Brown, C. A. (1975) 'Women workers in the health service industry', *International Journal of Health Services*, vol. 5, no. 2, pp. 173–84.

Brown, G. and T. Harris (1978) *Social Origins of Depression*, London: Tavistock.

Brown, R. G. S. and R. W. H. Stones (1973) *The Male Nurse* (Occasional Papers in Social Administration, 52), London: G. Bell & Sons.

Brownmiller, S. (1976) *Against Our Will: Men, Women and Rape*, Harmondsworth: Penguin.

Bryan, D., S. Dadzie and S. Scafe (1985) *The Heart of the Race*, London: Virago.

Bullough, B. (1975) 'Barriers to the nurse practitioner movement: problems of women in a woman's field', *International Journal of Health Services*, vol. 5, no. 2, pp. 225–33.

Bulmer, M. (1987) *The Social Basis of Community Care*, London: George Allen & Unwin.

Calvert, J. (1985) 'Motherhood', in E. Brook and A. Davis (eds) *Women, the Family and Social Work*, London: Tavistock.

Carby, H. (1982) 'White woman listen! black feminism and the boundaries of sisterhood', in Centre for Contemporary Cultural Studies (eds) *The Empire Strikes Back*, London: Hutchinson.

Carpenter, M. (1977) 'The new managerialism and professionalism in nursing', in M. Stacey, M. Reid, C. Heath and R. Dingwall (eds) *Health and the Division of Labour*, London: Croom Helm.

Carpenter, M. (1980) 'Asylum nursing before 1914: a chapter in the history of labour', in C. Davies (ed) *Rewriting Nursing History*, London: Croom Helm.

Carr-Saunders, A. M. and P. A. Wilson (1962) *The Professions*, London: Oxford University Press.

Castle, J. (1987) 'The development of professional nursing in New South

Wales, Australia', in C. Maggs (ed) *Nursing History: The State of the Art*, London: Croom Helm.

Cawson, A. (1982) *Corporatism and Welfare*, London: Heinemann.

Challis, D. and B. Davies (1986) *The Case Management System*, Aldershot: Gower.

Chartered Society of Physiotherapy (CSP) (1980) 'Editorial', *Physiotherapy*, vol. 66, no. 5, pp. 162–4.

Chartered Society of Physiotherapy (CSP) (1984) 'NHS management inquiry', *Physiotherapy*, vol. 70, no. 2, pp. 67–74.

Chartered Society of Physiotherapy (CSP) (1988) 'Relationship between the physiotherapy and occupational therapy professions', *Physiotherapy*, vol. 74, no. 7, pp. 311–14.

Chartered Society of Physiotherapy (CSP) (1989) 'Physiotherapy helpers and community and other support workers', *Physiotherapy*, vol. 75, no. 5, pp. 289–91.

Cheetham, J. (ed) (1982) *Social Work and Ethnicity*, London: George Allen & Unwin.

Chesler, P. (1974) *Women and Madness*, London: Allen Lane.

Church, O. M. (1989) 'The emergence of training programmes for asylum nursing at the turn of the century', in C. Maggs (ed) *Nursing History: The State of the Art*, London: Croom Helm.

Cockburn, C. (1977) *The Local State*, London: Pluto Press.

Cohen, M. B. and D. Wagner (1982) 'Social work professionalism: reality and illusion', in C. Derber (ed.) *Professionals as workers: Mental Labor in Advanced Capitalism*, Boston: G. K. Hall.

Cohen, P. (1989) 'The Push Towards Privatisation', *Social Work Today*, vol. 21, no. 3, p. 10.

Collins, S. and M. Stein (1989) 'Users fight back: collectives in social work', in C. Rojek, G. Peacock and C. Collins (eds) *The Haunt of Misery*, London: Routledge.

Corrigan, P. and V. Corrigan (1979) 'State formation and social policy until 1871', in N. Parry, M. Rustin and C. Satyamurti (eds) *Social Work, Welfare and the State*, London: Edward Arnold.

Cousins, C. (1987) *Controlling Social Welfare*, Brighton: Wheatsheaf.

Croft, S. (1986) 'Women, caring and the recasting of need', *Critical Social Policy*, vol. 16, pp. 23–39.

Croft, S. and P. Beresford (1989) 'User involvement citizenship and social policy', *Critical Social Policy*, vol. 26, pp. 5–18.

Crompton, R., G. Jones and S. Reid (1982) 'Contemporary clerical work: a case study of local government', in J. West (ed.) *Work, Women and the Labour Market*, London: Routledge & Kegan Paul.

Dahl, R. A. (1957) 'The concept of power', *Behavioural Science*, vol. 2, pp. 201–5.

Dale, J. and P. Foster (1986) *Feminists and State Welfare*, London: Routledge & Kegan Paul.

Dalley, G. (1988) *Ideologies of Caring*, London: Macmillan.

Damrosch, S. P., P. A. Sullivan and L. L. Haldeman (1987) 'How nurses get their way: power strategies in nursing', *Journal of Professional Nursing*, vol. 3, no. 5, pp. 284–90.

Davidson, N. (1987) *A Question of Care*, London: Michael Joseph.

Davies, B. and D. Challis (1986) *Matching Resources to Needs in Community Care*, Aldershot: Gower.

Davies, C. (ed.) (1980) *Rewriting Nursing History*, London: Croom Helm.

Davies, C. and J. Rosser (1986) 'Gendered jobs in the health service: a problem for labour process analysis', in D. Knights and H. Willmott (eds) *Gender and the Labour Process*, Aldershot: Gower.

Davies, M. (1985) *The Essential Social Worker*, 2nd edn, Aldershot: Gower.

Davis, A. (1980) 'Personally speaking', *Community Care*, vol. 317, p. 12.

Davis, A. and E. Brook (1985) 'Women and social work', in E. Brook and A. Davis (eds) *Women, the Family and Social Work*, London: Tavistock.

Davis, A., S. Llewelyn and G. Parry (1985) 'Women and mental health: towards an understanding', in E. Brook and A. Davis (eds) *Women, the Family and Social Work*, London: Tavistock.

Day, A. T. (1985) '*We Can Manage*', Melbourne: Institute of Family Studies (Monograph 5).

Day, P. R. (1981) *Social Work and Social Control*, London: Tavistock.

Derber, C. (1982) 'Managing professionals: ideological proletarianization and mental labor', in C. Derber (ed.) *Professionals as Workers: Mental Labor in Advanced Capitalism*, Boston: G. K. Hall.

Derber, C. (1983) 'Managing Professionals: ideological proletarianization and post industrial labor', *Theory and Society*, vol. 12, no. 3, pp. 309–41.

Dex, S. (1985) *The Sexual Division of Work*, Brighton: Wheatsheaf.

Diasio-Serrett, K. (1985) 'Another look at occupational therapy's history: paradigm or pair-of-hands?', in K. Diasio-Serrett (ed.) *Philosophical and Historical Roots of Occupational Therapy*, New York: Haworth Press.

Dingwall, R. (1976) 'Accomplishing profession', *Sociological Review*, vol. 24, no. 2, pp. 331–50.

Dingwall, R. (1977) *The Social Organisation of Health Visitor Training*, London: Croom Helm.

Dingwall, R. (1980) 'Problems of teamwork in primary care', in S. Lonsdale, A. Webb and T. Briggs (eds) *Teamwork in the Personal Social Services and Health Care*, London: Croom Helm.

Dingwall, R., M. Rafferty and C. Webster (1988) *An Introduction to the Social History of Nursing*, London: Routledge.

Doeringer, P. B. and M. J. Piore (1985) *Internal Labor Markets and Manpower Analysis*, (2nd edn) New York: M. E. Sharpe.

Dominelli, L. (1979) 'The challenge for social work education', *Social Work Today*, Vol. 10, no. 5, pp. 27–9.

Dominelli, L. (1988) *Anti-Racist Social Work*, London: Macmillan.

Dominelli, L. and E. McLeod (1989) *Feminist Social Work*, London: Macmillan.

Donnison, J. (1977) *Midwives and Medical Men*, London: Heinemann.

Donzelot, J. (1979) *The Policing of Families*, London: Hutchinson.

Doorslaer, E. van and J. Guerts (1987) 'Supplier induced demand for physiotherapists in the Netherlands', *Social Science and Medicine*, vol. 24, no. 11, pp. 919–25.

Doyal, L., G. Hunt and J. Mellor (1981) 'Your life in their hands: migrant workers in the National Health Service', *Critical Social Policy*, vol. 1, no. 2, pp. 54–71.

Edwards, P. K. (1983) 'Control, compliance and conflict', paper presented to Aston/UMIST Conference on Organization and Control of the Labour Process.

Ehrenreich, B. and D. English (1979) *For Her Own Good*, London: Pluto Press.

Elder, G. (1977) *The Alienated: Growing Older Today*, London: Writers' and Readers' Publishing Co-operative.

Ely, P. and D. Denney (1987) *Social Work in a Multi-Racial Society*, Aldershot: Gower.

England, H. (1986) *Social Work as Art*, London: George Allen & Unwin.

Estes, C. (1986) 'The politics of ageing in America', in C. Phillipson, M. Bernard and P. Strang (eds) *Dependency and Interdependency in Old Age*, London: Croom Helm.

Etzioni, A. (ed.) (1969) *The Semi-Professions and their Organization*, New York: The Free Press.

Evers, H. (1981) 'Care or custody? The experiences of women patients in long-stay geriatric wards', in B. Hutter and U. William (eds) *Controlling Women: The Normal and the Deviant*, London: Croom Helm.

Fairclough, N. (1989) *Language and Power*, London: Longman.

Fanon, F. (1967) *Black Skin, White Masks*, New York: Grove Press.

Finch, J. (1983) *Married to the Job*, London: George Allen & Unwin.

Finch, J. (1984) 'Non-sexist alternatives to community care', *Critical Social Policy*, vol. 9, pp. 6–18.

Finch, J. (1989) *Family Obligations and Social Change*, Cambridge: Polity Press.

Finch, J. and D. Groves (1980) 'Community care and the family: a case for equal opportunities?', *Journal of Social Policy*, vol. 9, no. 4, pp. 487–511.

Finch, J. and D. Groves (1982) 'By women for women: caring for the frail elderly', *Women's Studies International Forum*, vol. 5, no. 5, pp. 427–38.

Finch, J. and D. Groves (1985) 'Old girl, old boy: gender divisions in social work with the elderly', in E. Brook and A. Davis (eds) *Women, the Family and Social Work*, London: Tavistock.

Fletchman-Smith, B. (1984) 'Effects of race on adoption and fostering', *International Journal of Social Psychiatry*, vol. 30, (1/2), pp. 121–8.

Foster, J. (1987) 'Women on the Wane', *Insight*, vol. 2, no. 50, pp. 14–15.

Foster, P. (1979) 'The informal rationing of primary medical care', *Journal of Social Policy*, vol. 8, no. 4, pp. 489–508.

Foster-Carter, O. (1987) 'Ethnicity: the fourth burden of black women', *Critical Social Policy*, vol. 20, pp. 46–56.

Foucault, M. (1973) *The Birth of the Clinic*, London: Tavistock.

French, J. R. P. and B. Raven (1959) 'The bases of social power', in D. Cartwright (ed.) *Studies in Social Power*, Ann Arbor: University of Michigan Press.

Friedman, A. (1987) 'Midwifery: legal or illegal?', in C. Maggs (ed.) *Nursing History: The State of the Art*, London: Croom Helm.

Friedson, E. (1970) *The Profession of Medicine*, New York: Dodd Mead.

Galper, J. (1975) *The Politics of Social Services*, Englewood Cliffs, NJ: Prentice-Hall.

Gamarnikow, E. (1978) 'Sexual divisions of labour: the case of nursing', in A. Kuhn and A.-M. Wolpe (eds) *Feminism and Materialism: Women and Modes of Production*, London: Routledge & Kegan Paul.

Gamble, A. (1986) 'The political economy of freedom', in R. Levitas (ed.) *The Ideology of the New Right*, Cambridge: Polity Press.

Game, A. and R. Pringle (1983) *Gender at Work*, Sydney: George Allen & Unwin Australia.

Gelsthorpe, L. (1987) 'The differential treatment of males and females in the criminal justice system', in G. Horobin (ed.) *Sex, Gender and Care Work*, Aberdeen: University of Aberdeen.

Gerth, H. and C. W. Mills (1948) *From Max Weber: Essays in Sociology*, London: Routledge & Kegan Paul.

Giannichedda, M. G. (1988) 'A future of social invisibility', in S. Ramon with M. G. Giannichedda (eds) *Psychiatry in Transition*, London: Pluto Press.

Gill, O. and B. Jackson (1983) *Adoption and Race*, London: B. T. Batsford.

Gill, T. (1986) 'Women as managers: implications for occupational therapy', *British Journal of Occupational Therapy*, vol. 49, no. 12, pp. 385–8.

Gilmore, D. (1988) 'Who's the consumer?', *British Journal of Occupational Therapy*, vol. 51, no. 2, pp. 48–50.

Gilroy, P. (1987) *There Ain't No Black in the Union Jack*, London: Hutchinson.

Glastonbury, B., D. Cooper and P. Hawkins (1982) *Social Work in Conflict – the Practitioner and the Bureaucrat*, Birmingham: BASW.

Goffman, E. (1964) *Stigma: Notes on the Management of Spoiled Identity*, Harmondsworth: Penguin.

Goffman, E. (1968) *Asylums*, Harmondsworth: Penguin.

Goldberg, D. and P. Huxley (1981) *Mental Illness in the Community*, London: Tavistock.

Goldie, N. (1977) 'The Division of labour amongst mental health professionals: a negotiated or imposed order?', in M. Stacey, M. Reid, C. Heath and R. Dingwall (eds) *Health and the Division of Labour*, London: Croom Helm.

Gordon, C. (ed.) (1980) *Michel Foucault: Power/Knowledge*, Brighton: Harvester Press.

Gospel, H. and C. R. Littler (1983) *Managerial Strategies and Industrial Relations*, London: Heinmann.

Gough, I. (1979) *The Political Economy of Welfare*, London: Macmillan.

Gouldner, A. (1975) *For Sociology*, Harmondsworth: Penguin.

Graham, H. (1983) 'Caring: a labour of love', in J. Finch and D. Groves (eds) *A Labour of Love: Women, Work and Caring*, London: Routledge & Kegan Paul.

Greenwood, E. (1957) 'Attributes of a Profession', *Social Work*, vol. 2, no. 3, pp. 44–55.

Griffiths, R. (1988) *Community Care: An Agenda for Action*, London: HMSO.

Grimsley, M. and A. Bhat (1988) 'Health', in A. Bhat, R. Carr-Hill and S. Ohri (eds) *Britain's Black Population*, (2nd edn), Aldershot: Gower.

Grove, E. (1988) 'Working together', *British Journal of Occupational Therapy*, vol. 51, no. 5, pp. 150–6.

Habermas, J. (1976) *Legitimation Crisis*, London: Heinemann.

Habermas, J. (1977) 'Hannah Arendt's communications concept of power', *Social Research*, vol. 44, no. 1, pp. 3–24.

Hadley, R. and S. Hatch (1981) *Social Welfare and the Failure of the State*, London: George Allen & Unwin.

Hall, P. (1974) *Reforming the Welfare*, London: Heinemann.

Hall, P. and T. Hall (1980) *Part-Time Social Work*, London: Heinemann.

Hakim, C. (1979) *Occupational Segregation* (Department of Employment Research Papers, 9), London: HMSO.

Hancock, C. (1989) 'The NHS: evolution or dissolution?', in M. Jolley and P. Allan (eds) *Current Issues in Nursing*, London: Chapman & Hall.

Hanmer, J. and S. Saunders (1984) *Well Founded Fear – A Community Study of Violence on Women*, London: Hutchinson.

Hanmer, J. and D. Statham (1988) *Women and Social Work*, London: Macmillan.

Harbert, W. G. (1988) *The Welfare Industry*, Hadleigh: Holhouse Publications.

Harbert, W. G. and M. Dexter (1983) *The Home Help Services*, London: Tavistock.

Haug, M. R. (1973) 'Deprofessionalization: an alternative hypothesis for the future', in P. Halmos (ed.) *Professionalization and Social Change*, Keele: University of Keele.

Hawker, M. and M. Stewart (1978) 'Auxiliaries as re-ablists: a multidisciplinary dimension', in M. Hardie and L. Hockey (eds) *Nursing Auxiliaries in Health Care*, London: Croom Helm.

Hawker, R. (1989) 'For the good of the patient?', in C. Maggs (ed.) *Nursing History: The State of the Art*, London: Croom Helm.

Hearn, J. (1982) 'Notes on Patriarchy, Professionalization and the Semi-Professions', *Sociology*, vol. 16, no. 2, pp. 184–202.

Hearn, J. (1987) *The Gender of Oppression: Men, Masculinity and the Critique of Marxism*, Brighton: Wheatsheaf.

Hearn, J. and W. Parkin (1987) *'Sex' at 'Work': The Power and Paradox of Organisation Sexuality*, Brighton: Wheatsheaf.

Heath, S. (1987) 'Male Feminism', in A. Jardine and P. Smith (eds) *Men in Feminism*, New York: Methuen.

Helewa, A., H. A. Smythe, C. H. Goldsmith, J. Groh, M. C. Thomas, B. A. Stokes and J. Sugerman (1987) 'The total assessment of rheumatoid polyarthritis – evaluation of a training program for physiotherapists and occupational therapists', *The Journal of Rheumatology*, vol. 14, no. 1, pp. 87–92.

Henwood, M. (1986) 'Community care: policy, practice and prognosis' in M. Brenton and C. Ungerson (eds) *The Yearbook of Social Policy in Britain 1985/6*, London: Routledge & Kegan Paul.

Hey, A. (1980a) 'Providing basic services at home', in D. Billis, G. Bromley, A. Hey and R. Rowbottom (eds) *Organising Social Services*, London: Heinemann.

Hey, A. (1980b) 'Social work – careers, practice and organisation in area teams', in D. Billis, G. Bromley, A. Hey and R. Rowbottom (eds) *Organising Social Services*, London: Heinemann.

Hicks, C. (1988) *Who Cares: Looking After People at Home*, London: Virago.

Hickson, D. J. and A. F. McCullough (1980) 'Power in organizations', in G. Salaman and K. Thompson (eds) *Control and Ideology in Organizations*, Milton Keynes: Open University Press.

Hockey, J. (1987) 'A Picture of Pressure', *Nursing Times*, vol. 83, no. 27, pp. 28–30.

Howe, D. (1986a) *Social Workers and their Practice in Welfare Bureaucracies*, Aldershot: Gower.

Howe, D. (1986b) 'The segregation of women and their work in the personal social services', *Critical Social Policy*, vol. 15, pp. 21–35.

Hudson, A. (1985) 'Feminism and social work: resistance or dialogue?', *British Journal of Social Work*, vol. 15, no. 6, pp. 635–55.

Hudson, A. (1988) 'Boys will be boys: masculinism and the juvenile justice system', *Critical Social Policy*, vol. 21, pp. 30–48.

Hughes, E. C. (1958) *Men and their Work*, New York: Free Press.

Hugman, R. (1984) *The Relationship between Organisational Structures and Occupational Ideologies in Social Services Departments*, Lancaster: unpublished Ph.D. thesis, University of Lancaster.

Hugman, R. (1986) 'Home care plus fieldworker equals social services officer?', *Social Work Today*, vol. 18, no. 14, pp. 14–15.

Hugman, R. (1989) 'Rehabilitation and community care in mental health (1): some implications for practice', *Practice*, vol. 3, no. 2, pp. 119–35.

Illich, I. (1976) *Limits to Medicine*, Harmondsworth: Penguin.

Johnson, M. (1978) 'Big fleas have little fleas – nurse professionalism and nursing auxiliaries', in M. Hardie and L. Hockey (eds) *Nursing Auxiliaries in Health Care*, London: Croom Helm.

Johnson, T. J. (1972) *Professions and Power*, London: Macmillan.

Jolley, M. (1989) 'The professionalisation of nursing: the uncertain path', in M. Jolley and P. Allan (eds) *Current Issues in Nursing*, London: Chapman & Hall.

Jones, C. (1979) 'Social work education, 1900–1977', in N. Parry, M. Rustin and C. Satyamurti (eds) *Social Work Welfare and the State*, London: Edward Arnold.

Jones, C. (1983) *State Social Work and the Working Class*, London: Macmillan.

Jordan, B. (1984) *Invitation to Social Work*, Oxford: Basil Blackwell.

Jordan, B. (1987) *Rethinking Welfare*, Oxford: Basil Blackwell.

Kadushin, A. (1976) 'Men in a Women's Profession', *Social Work*, vol. 21, no. 6, pp. 440–7.

Kane, R. A. (1980) 'Multi-disciplinary teamwork in the United States', in S. Lonsdale, A. Webb and T. Briggs (eds) *Teamwork in the Health and Personal Social Services*, London: Croom Helm.

Keddy, B., M. J. Gillis, P Jacobs, H. Burton and M. Rogers (1986) 'The doctor–nurse relationship: an historical perspective', *Journal of Advanced Nursing*, vol. 11, no. 6, pp. 745–53.

Klein, R. (1973) *Complaints Against Doctors*, London: Knight.

Kovel, J. (1970) *White Racism*, London: Allen Lane, Penguin Press.

Lait, J. (1980) 'Social work knowledge: a case of inflation', in D. Anderson (ed.) *The Ignorance of Social Intervention*, London: Croom Helm.

Lankin, G. (1983) *Occupational Monopoly and Modern Medicine*, London: Tavistock.

Larson, M. S. (1977) *The Rise of Professionalism: A Sociological Analysis*, Berkeley: University of California Press.

Larson, M. S. (1980) 'Proletarianization and educated labour', *Theory and Society*, vol. 9, no. 1, pp. 131–75.

Leonard, P. (1973) 'Professionalization, community action and growth in social services bureaucracies', in P. Halmos (ed.) *Professionalization and Social Change*, Keele: University of Keele.

LeRoy, L. (1986) 'Continuity in change: power and gender in nursing', *Journal of Professional Nursing*, vol. 2, no. 1, pp. 28–36.

Levine, R. E. (1987) 'The influence of the arts-and-crafts movement on the professional status of occupational therapy', *American Journal of Occupational Therapy*, vol. 41, no. 4, pp. 248–54.

Likert, R. (1961) *New Patterns of Management*, New York: McGraw-Hill.

Littler, C. R. (1982) *The Development of the Labour Process in Capitalist Societies*, London: Heinemann.

Littlewood, R. and Lipsedge, M. (1989) *Aliens and Alienists* (2nd edn) London: Unwin Hyman.

Lorde, A. (1984) *Sister Outsider*, New York: Crossing Press.

Lukes, S. (1974) *Power: A Radical View*, London: Macmillan.

Lukes, S. (ed.) (1987) *Power*, Oxford: Basil Blackwell.

MacIntyre, S. (1976) 'Who wants babies? The social construction of instincts', in D. L. Barker and S. Allen (eds) *Sexual Divisions and Society: Process and Change*, London: Tavistock.

Mackay, L. (1989) *Nursing a Problem*, Milton Keynes: Open University Press.

Mackie, L. and P. Pattullo (1977) *Women at Work*, London: Tavistock.

Maggs, C. (ed.) (1989) *Nursing History: The State of the Art*, London: Croom Helm.

Malinski, V. M. (1988) 'The nurse', in R. W. Clarke and R. P. Lawry (eds) *The Power of the Professional Person*, Lanham: University Press of America.

Manning, B. and A. Ohri (1982) 'Racism – the response of community work', in A. Ohri, B. Manning and P. Curno (eds) *Community Work and Racism*, London: Routledge & Kegan Paul.

Mauksch, H. O. (1966) 'The organizational context of nursing practice', in F. Davis (ed.) *The Nursing Profession: Five Sociological Essays*, New York: Wiley.

Maximé, J. E. (1987) 'Some psychological models of black self-concept', in S. Ahmed, J. Cheetham and J. Small (eds) *Social Work with Black Children and their Families*, London: B. T. Batsford.

Mayer, J. E. and N. Timms (1970) *The Client Speaks*, London: Routledge & Kegan Paul.

Mayeroff, M. (1972) *On Caring*, New York: Harper & Row.

McKinlay, J. B. (1973) 'On the professional regulation of change', in P. Halmos (ed.) *Professionalisation and Social Change*, Keele: Sociological Review Monograph 20, University of Keele.

Mercer, J. (1980) 'Physiotherapy as a profession', *Physiotherapy*, vol. 66, no. 6, pp. 180–4.

Mercer, K. (1986) 'Racism and transcultural psychiatry', in P. Miller and N. Rose (eds) *The Power of Psychiatry*, Cambridge: Polity Press.

Miles, R. (1982) *Racism and Migrant Labour*, London: Routledge & Kegan Paul.

Miller, A. (1989) 'Theory to practice: implementation in the clinical setting', in M. Jolley and P. Allan (eds) *Current Issues in Nursing*, London: Chapman & Hall.

Mills, A. J. (1989) 'Gender, sexuality and organization theory', in J. Hearn, D. L. Sheppard, P. Tancred-Sheriff and G. Burrell (eds) *The Sexuality of Organisation*, London: Sage Publications.

Mills, C. W. (1956) *White Collar*, New York: Oxford University Press, Galaxy.

MIND Manchester Group (1988) 'Developing an alternative community mental health service', in S. Ramon with M. G. Giannichedda (eds) *Psychiatry in Transition*, London: Pluto Press.

Mishra, R. (1984) *The Welfare State in Crisis*, Brighton: Wheatsheaf Books.

Mishra, R. (1986) 'The Left and the welfare state: a critical analysis', *Critical Social Policy*, vol. 15, pp. 4–19.

Mitchell, J. (1974) *Psychoanalysis and Feminism*, Harmondsworth: Penguin.

Mittler, P. (1979) *People Not Patients*, London: Methuen.

Mocellin, G. (1988) 'A perspective on the principles and practice of occupational therapy', *British Journal of Occupational Therapy*, vol. 51, no. 1, pp. 4–7.

Morgan, D. H. J. (1981) 'Men, masculinity and the process of sociological enquiry', in H. Roberts (ed.) *Doing Feminist Research*, London: Routledge & Kegan Paul.

Morgan, D. H. J. (1987) 'Masculinity and violence', in J. Hanmer and M. Maynard (eds) *Women, Violence and Social Control*, London: Macmillan.

Munroe, H. (1988) 'Modes of operation in clinical supervision', *British Journal of Occupational Therapy*, vol. 51, no. 10, pp. 338–43.

Nokes, P. (1967) *The Professional Task in Welfare Practice*, London: Routledge & Kegan Paul.

Oakley, A. (1974) *The Sociology of Housework*, London: Martin Robertson.

Oakley, A. (1984) 'What price professionalism? The importance of being a nurse', *Nursing Times*, vol. 80, no. 50, pp. 24–7.

O'Connor, I. and Dalgleish, L. (1986) 'Cautionary tales from beginning practitioners: the fate of personal models of social work in beginning practice', *British Journal of Social Work*, vol. 16, no. 4, pp. 431–47.

O'Connor, J. (1973) *The Fiscal Crisis of the State*, New York: St Martin's Press.

Offe, C. (1984) *Contradictions of the Welfare State* (ed. J. Keane), London: Hutchinson.

Oliver, J. (1983) 'The caring wife', in J. Finch and D. Groves (eds) *A Labour of Love: Women, Work and Caring*, London: Routledge & Kegan Paul.

Olsen, M. R. (1984) (ed.) *Social work and Mental Health*, London: Tavistock.

Osmond, H. and M. Siegler (1971) 'Goffman's model of mental illness', *British Journal of Psychiatry*, vol. 119, p. 419.

Owusu-Bempah, J. (1989) 'The new institutional racism', *Community Care*, vol. 780, pp. 23–5.

Parkin, F. (1979) *Marxism and Class Theory: A Bourgeois Critique*, London: Tavistock.

Parkin, W. (1989) 'Private experiences in the public domain: sexuality and residential care organizations', in J. Hearn, D. L. Sheppard, P. Trancred-Sheriff and G. Burrell (eds) *The Sexuality of Organizations*, London: Sage Publications.

Parry, N. and J. Parry (1979) 'Social work, professionalism and the state', in N. Parry, M. Rustin and C. Satyamurti (eds) *Social Work, Welfare and the State*, London: Edward Arnold.

Parry, N., M. Rustin and C. Satyamurti (eds) (1979) *Social Work, Welfare and the State*, London: Edward Arnold.

Parsloe, P. (1978) *Juvenile Justice in Britain and the United States*, London: Routledge & Kegan Paul.

Parsloe, P. and O. Stevenson (eds) (1978) *Social Service Teams: The Practitioners' View*, London: HMSO.

Parsons, T. (1952) *The Social System*, London: Tavistock.

Parton, C. and N. Parton (1988) 'Women the family and child protection', *Critical Social Policy*, vol. 24, pp. 38–49.

Payne, M. (1982) *Working in Teams*, London: Macmillan.

Pearson, G. (1975) *The Deviant Imagination*, London: Macmillan.

Phillips, A. and B. Taylor (1980) 'Sex and skill: notes towards a feminist economics', *Feminist Review*, vol. 6, pp. 79–88.

Phillips, M. (1982) 'Separatism or black control?', in A. Ohri, B. Manning and P. Curno (eds) *Community Work and Racism*, London: Routledge & Kegan Paul.

Phillipson, C. (1982) *Capitalism and the Construction of Old Age*, London: Macmillan.

Philp, M. (1979) 'Notes on the form of knowledge in social work', *Sociological Review*, vol. 27, no. 1, pp. 83–111.

Phizacklea, A. and R. Miles (1980) *Labour and Racism*, London: Routledge & Kegan Paul.

Pincus, A. and A. Minahan (1973) *Social Work Practice: Model and Method*, Hasca: Peacock Publishers Inc.

Pitcairn, D. M. and D. Flahault (eds) (1974) *The Medical Assistant: An Intermediate Level of Health Care Personnel*, Geneva: World Health Organization.

Pithouse, A. (1987) *Social Work: The Social Organisation of an Invisible Trade*, Aldershot: Avebury.

Popplestone, R. (1980) 'Top jobs for women: are the cards stacked against them?', *Social Work Today*, vol. 12, no. 4, pp. 12–14.

Qureshi, H. (1990) 'Boundaries between formal and informal care-giving work', in C. Ungerson (ed.) *Gender and Caring*, Brighton: Harvester Wheatsheaf.

Rack, P. (1982) *Race, Culture and Mental Disorder*, London: Tavistock.

Ralph, C. (1989) 'Nursing management and leadership – the challenge', in M. Jolley and P. Allan (eds) *Current Issues in Nursing*, London: Chapman & Hall.

Ramon, S. (1988) 'Towards normalisation: polarisation and change in Britain' in S. Ramon with M. G. Giannichedda (eds) *Psychiatry in Transition*, London: Pluto Press.

Ranger, C. (1989) 'Strategy needed for services to ethnic groups', *Social Work Today*, vol. 21, no. 6, pp. 16–17.

Read, J. (1989) 'To be ourselves: challenging the abuses of psychiatry', *Asylum*, vol. 3, no. 3, p. 9.

Rees, S. (1978) *Social Work Face to Face*, London: Edward Arnold.

Reese, C. C. (1987) 'Gender bias in an occupational therapy text', *American Journal of Occupational Therapy*, vol. 41 no. 6, pp. 393–6.

Reverby, S. M. (1987) *Ordered to Care: The Dilemmas of American Nursing*, Cambridge: Cambridge University Press.

Rickman, J. and W. O. Goldthorpe (1977) 'When was your last period?: temporal aspects of gynaeological diagnosis', in R. Dingwall, C. Heath, M. Reid and M. Stacey (eds) *Health Care and Health Knowledge*, London: Croom Helm.

Rider, B. A. and R. M. Brashear (1988) 'Men in occupational therapy', *American Journal of Occupational Therapy*, vol. 42, no. 4, pp. 231–7.

Robbins, J. W. (1972) 'Why management for physiotherapists?', *Physiotherapy*, vol. 58, no. 5, pp. 154–5.

Robinson, J. (1989) 'Nursing in the future: a cause for concern', in M. Jolley and P. Allan (eds) *Current Issues in Nursing*, London: Chapman & Hall.

Rodger, J. J. (1988) 'Social work as social control re-examined: beyond the dispersal of discipline thesis', *Sociology*, vol. 22, no. 4. pp. 563–81.

Rojek, C., G. Peacock and S. Collins (1988) *Social Work and Received Ideas*, London: Routledge.

Rooney, B. (1987) *Racism and Resistance to Change*, Liverpool: Merseyside Area Profile Group.

Rose, S. and B. Black (1985) *Advocacy and Empowerment: Mental Health Care in the Community*, London: Routledge & Kegan Paul.

Rowbottom, R., J. Balle, S. Cang, M. Dixon, E. Jaques, T. Packwood and H. Tolliday (1973) *Hospital Organisation*, London: Heinemann.

Rowbottom, R., A. Hey and D. Billis (1974) *Social Services Departments*, London: Heinemann.

Rutter, M. (1986) *Maternal Deprivation Reassessed* (2nd edn), Harmondsworth: Penguin.

Sainsbury, E. (1975) *Social Work with Families*, London: Routledge & Kegan Paul.

Salaman, G. (1979) *Work Organisations: Control and Resistance*, London: Longman.

Satyamurti, C. (1979) 'Care and control in local authority social work', in N. Parry, M. Rustin and C. Satyamurti (eds) *Social Work, Welfare and the State*, London: Edward Arnold.

Satyamurti, C. (1981) *Occupational Survival*, Oxford: Basil Blackwell.

Schutzenhofer, K. K. (1988) 'The problem of professional autonomy in nursing', *Health Care for Women International*, vol. 9, no. 2, pp. 93–106.

Scull, A. (1984) *Decarceration* (2nd edn), Cambridge: Polity Press.

Seidler, V. (1985) 'Fear and Intimacy', in A. Metcalf and M. Humphries (eds) *The Sexuality of Men*, London: Pluto Press.

Shepherd, M., B. Cooper, A. Brown and G. Kalton (1966) *Psychiatric Illness in General Practice*, London: Oxford University Press.

Silverman, D. (1970) *The Theory of Organisations*, London: Heinemann.

Sim, J. (1989) 'Methodology and morality in physiotherapy research', *Physiotherapy*, vol. 75, no. 4, pp. 237–43.

Simey, M. B. (1989) 'The poverty of politics', *Social Work and Social Sciences Review*, vol. 1, no. 1, pp. 6–14.

Simpkin, M. (1983) *Trapped Within Welfare* (2nd edn), London: Macmillan.

Simpson, R. L. and I. H. Simpson (1969) 'Women and bureaucracy in the semi-professions', in Etzioni, A. (ed.) *The Semi-Professions and their Organization*, New York: Free Press.

Siporin, M. (1982) 'Moral philosophy in social work today', *Social Services Review*, vol. 56, no. 4, pp. 516–38.

Small, J. (1987) 'Transracial placements: conflicts and contradictions', in S. Ahmed, J. Cheetham and J. Small (eds) *Social Work with Black Children and their Families*, London: B. T. Batsford.

Smith, G. (1980) *Social Need*, London: Routledge & Kegan Paul.

Smith, G. and R. Harris (1972) 'Ideologies of need and the organisation of social work departments', *British Journal of Social Work*, vol. 2, no. 1, pp. 27–45.

Solomon, B. B. (1976) *Black Empowerment: Social Work in Oppressed Communities*, New York: Columbia University Press.

Sondhi, R. (1982) 'The Asian Resources Centre', in J. Cheetham (ed.) *Social Work and Ethnicity*, London: George Allen & Unwin.

Specht, H. and A. Vickery (eds.) (1977) *Integrating Social Work Methods*, London: George Allen & Unwin.

Spender, D. (1980) *Man Made Language*, London: Routledge & Kegan Paul.

Stein, M. (1983) 'Protest in care', in B. Jordan and N. Parton (eds) *The Political Dimensions of Social Work*, Oxford: Basil Blackwell.

Stevenson, O. (1981) *Specialisation in Social Services Teams*, London: George Allen & Unwin.

Stewart, A. M. (1988) 'Future possibilities for a continuum of professional development', *British Journal of Ocupational Therapy*, vol. 51, no. 8, pp. 262–4.

Stubbs, P. (1985) 'The employment of black social workers: from ethnic sensitivity to anti-racism', *Critical Social Policy*, vol. 12, pp. 6–27.

Stubbs, P. (1987) 'Professionalism and the adoption of black children', *British Journal of Social Work*, vol. 17, no. 5, pp. 473–92.

Tajfel, H. (1978) *The Social Psychology of Minorities*, London: Minority Rights Group.

Taylor, D. (1989) 'Citizenship and social power', *Critical Social Policy*, vol. 26, pp. 19–31.

Taylor-Gooby, P. and J. Dale (1981) *Social Theory and Social Welfare*, London: Edward Arnold.

Thompson, P. (1983) *The Nature of Work*, London: Macmillan.

Titmuss, R. (1968) *Commitment to Welfare*, London: George Allen & Unwin.

Tolliday, H. (1972) 'The organisation of physiotherapists in the hospital service', *Physiotherapy*, vol. 58, no. 5, pp. 156–60.

Tolson, A. (1977) *The Limits of Masculinity*, London: Tavistock.

Toren, N. (1972) *Social Work: The Case of a Semi-Profession*, London: Sage.

Torkington, N. P. K. (1983) *The Racial Politics of Health*, Liverpool: Merseyside Area Profile Group.

Townsend, P. and N. Davidson (1982) *Inequalities in Health*, Harmondsworth: Penguin.

Ungerson, C. (1983) 'Why do women care?', in J. Finch and D. Groves (eds) *A Labour of Love: Women, Work and Caring*, London: Routledge & Kegan Paul.

Ungerson, C. (1987) *Policy is Personal*, London: Tavistock.

Ungerson, C. (1980) 'The language of care', in C. Ungerson (ed.) *Gender and Caring*, Brighton: Harvester Wheatsheaf.

United Kingdom Central Council for Nursing, Midwifery and Health Visiting (UKCC) (1986) *Project 2000 – A New Preparation for Practice*, London: UKCC.

Versluysen, M. C. (1980) 'Old wives' tales? Women healers in English history', in C. Davies (ed.) *Rewriting Nursing History*, London: Croom Helm.

Vousden, M. (1989) 'Selling nursing', *Nursing Times*, vol. 85, no. 34, pp. 25–9.

Wærness, K. (1984) 'Caring as women's work in the welfare state', in H. Holter (ed.) *Patriarchy in a Welfare Society*, Oslo: Universitetsforlaget.

Walby, S. (1986) *Patriarchy at Work*, Cambridge: Polity Press.

Walby, S. (1988) 'Segregation in employment in social and economic theory', in S. Walby (ed.) *Gender Segregation at Work*, Milton Keynes: Open University Press.

Wallace, H. A. and M. J. Corey (1983) 'The clinical specialist with manager: myth *versus* realities', *Journal of Nursing Administration*, vol. 13, no. 2, pp. 13–15.

Waller, B. (1982) 'Developing an appropriate service: a local authority's use of Section 11', in J. Cheetham (ed.) *Social Work and Ethnicity*, London: George Allen & Unwin.

Wallis, M. A. (1987a) ' "Profession" and "Professionalism" and the emerging profession of occupational therapy (Part 1)', *British Journal of Occupational Therapy*, vol. 50, no. 8, pp. 259–62.

Wallis, M. A. (1987b) ' "Pofession" and "Professionalism" and the emerging profession of occupational therapy (Part 2)', *British Journal of Occupational Therapy*, vol. 50, no. 9, pp. 300–2.

Walsh, J. L. and R. Elling (1977) 'Professionalism and the poor: structural effects and professional behaviour', in E. Freidson and J. Lorber (eds) *Medical Men and their Work*, Chicago: Aldine Publishing Co.

Walton, R. (1975) *Women in Social Work*, London: Routledge & Kegan Paul.

Wasserman, H. (1971) 'The professional social worker in a bureaucracy', *Social Work*, vol. 16, no. 1, pp. 89–95.

Watkins, S. (1987) *Medicine and Labour: The Politics of a Profession*, London: Lawrence & Wishart.

Weeks, D. R. (1980) 'Organizations and decision making', in G. Salaman and K. Thompson (eds) *Control and Ideology in Organizations*, Milton Keynes: Open University Press.

Wellman, D. (1977) *Portraits of White Racism*, Cambridge: Cambridge University Press.

Wells, M. (1982) 'Race relations policies in social services departments – the tasks and the problems' in J. Cheetham (ed.) *Social Work and Ethnicity*, London: George Allen & Unwin.

Whittington, C. (1977) 'Social workers orientations: an action perspective', *British Journal of Social Work*, vol. 7, no. 1, pp. 73–95.

Whittington, C. and P. Bellaby (1979) 'The reasons for hierarchy in social services departments: a critique of Elliott Jaques and his associates', *Sociological Review*, vol. 27, pp. 513–39.

Wicks, M. (1982) 'Community care and elderly people', in A. Walker (ed.) *Community Care: The Family, the State and Social Policy*, Oxford: Martin Robertson, Basil Blackwell.

Wilding, P. (1982) *Professional Power and Social Welfare*, London: Routledge & Kegan Paul.

Wilensky, H. L. and C. N. Lebeaux (1975) *Industrial Society and Social Welfare*, New York: The Free Press.

Williams, D., J. Harrison, C. Newell, J. Holt and C. Rees (1987) 'Crafts: a criminal offence?', *British Journal of Occupational Therapy*, vol. 50, no. 1, pp. 12–15.

Williams, F. (1987) 'Racism and the discipline of social policy: a critique of welfare theory', *Critical Social Policy*, vol. 20, pp. 4–29.

Williams, K. (1980) 'From Sarah Gamp to Florence Nightingale: a critical study of hospital nursing systems from 1840 to 1897', in C. Davies (ed.) *Rewriting Nursing History*, London: Croom Helm.

Williams, P. and B. Shoultz (1982) *We Can Speak for Ourselves*, London: Souvenir Press.

Wilson, E. (1977) *Women and the Welfare State*, London: Tavistock.

Wilson, J. (1987) 'Self-help and consumerism', in D. Clode, C. Parker and S. Etherington (eds) *Towards the Sensitive Bureaucracy*, Aldershot: Gower.

Wise, S. (1985) *Becoming a Feminist Social Worker*, Manchester: Studies in Sexual Politics, 6, University of Manchester.

Wise, S. (1988) *Doing Feminist Social Work*, Manchester: Studies in Sexual Politics, 21, University of Manchester.

Wolfensberger, W. (1972) *Normalization*, Toronto: National Institute of Mental Retardation.

Wolfensberger, W. and H. Zauka (1973) *Citizen Advocacy*, Toronto: National Institute of Mental Retardation.

Wolinsky, F. D. and S. R. Wolinsky (1981) 'Expecting sick role legitimation and getting it', *Journal of Health and Social Behaviour*, vol. 22, no. 3, pp. 229–42.

Woods, C. Q. (1987) 'From individual dedication to social activism: historical developments of nursing professionalism', in C. Maggs (ed.) *Nursing History: The State of the Art*, London: Croom Helm.

Wrong, D. (1979) *Power*, Oxford: Basil Blackwell.

Wynd, C. A. (1985) 'Packing a punch: female nurses and the effective use of power', *Nursing Success Today*, vol. 2, no. 9, pp. 14–20.

Wyrick, J. M. and E. B. Stern (1987) 'The recruitment of occupational therapy students: a national survey', *American Journal of Occupational Therapy*, vol. 41, no. 3, pp. 173–8.

Young, A. F. and E. W. Ashton (1956) *British Social Work in the Nineteenth Century*, London: Routledge & Kegan Paul.

UK official papers

Cumberledge, J. (chair) (1986) *Neighbourhood Nursing: A Focus for Care*, London: HMSO.

Department of Health (DoH) (1989) *Caring for People: Community Care in the Next Decade and Beyond*, London: HMSO.

Kilbrandon, C. (chair) (1964) *Children and Young People in Scotland*, Cmnd 2306, Edinburgh: HMSO.

Local Government Act 1966, London: HMSO.

Maud, J. (chair) (1967) *Report of the Committee on the Management of Local Government*, London: HMSO.

Race Relations Act 1976, London: HMSO.

Salmon, B. (chair) (1966) *Report of the Committee on Senior Nursing Staff Structure*, London: HMSO.

Seebohm, F. (chair) (1968) *Report of the Committee on Local Authority and Allied Personal Social Services*, Cmnd 3703, London: HMSO.

Younghusband, E. (chair) (1959) *Report of the Working Party on Social Workers in the Local Authority Health and Welfare Services*, London: HMSO.

USA official papers

The Civil Rights Act 1964, Washington, DC: House of Congress.

Index

243

246 *Index*